Mentoring in STEM Through a Female Identity Lens

Heroes Make a Difference for Women

Edited by

Cecilia (Ceal) D. Craig, Ph.D.

Fellow, Society of Women Engineers
Retired engineering director and education researcher

Women's Studies

VERNON PRESS

www.vernonpress.com

In the Americas:
Vernon Press
1000 N West Street, Suite 1200
Wilmington, Delaware, 19801
United States

In the rest of the world:
Vernon Press
C/Sancti Espiritu 17,
Malaga, 29006
Spain

Women's Studies

Library of Congress Control Number: 2024936938

ISBN: 979-8-8819-0120-2

Also available: 979-8-8819-0017-5 [Hardback]; 979-8-8819-0080-9 [PDF, E-Book]

Dedications

Rarely is a work of merit accomplished alone. As the editor, I dedicate my efforts for this book to my husband of 51 years, Tim Craig, an engineer who never let me give up and always supported me, from my first years studying mechanical engineering, then becoming a manager and then director, moving to three states, and even when I went back to school to earn a PhD at 61 and leave high tech to become a researcher. He died in May 2023.

Tim's last months and afterward were challenging for me to meet this book's schedule. Thus, I truly recognize and appreciate the patience of all the authors during this challenging time for me. Thank you and I sincerely hope all our readers will find your incredible work and results to be of benefit to increasing the number of women in STEM.

Thank you to all the peer reviewers: you know who you are! People from across the world helped this book's authors make their work even better for you, the reader.

Thank you to Dr. Deborah Harmon for helping me at the end with editing and checking. Very much appreciate your efforts!

Since I first studied engineering in the early 1970s, my goal has been to share with women that STEM careers can be for them and possibilities for young women are endless. Dear Readers: Thank you for being a part of that effort. Solving real-world problems to benefit the world is fulfilling and worthy of the journey.

Table of Contents

Jennifer Kouo
Johns Hopkins University, USA

Stacy Klein-Gardner
Vanderbilt University, USA

Zingiswa Jojo
Rhodes University, Eastern Cape, South Africa

Phyllis Okwan
Southern University and A&M College, Baton Rouge, USA

Joe Omojola
Southern University at New Orleans, USA

Murty Kambhampati
Southern University at New Orleans, USA

Jacqueline Genovesi
The Academy of Natural Sciences of Drexel University, USA

Ayana Allen-Handy
Drexel University, USA

Kimberly Sterin
Drexel University, USA

Kimberly Godfrey
The Academy of Natural Sciences of Drexel University, USA

Sheryl Kline
University of Delaware, USA

Darrin Collins
University of Illinois, USA

Erica Dixon
Relay Graduate School of Education, USA

Deborah A. Harmon
Eastern Michigan University, USA

Cheryl L. Price
University of Massachusetts (UMASS), USA

List of Figures

List of Tables

List of Acronyms

BEST	Become Excellent in Science and Mathematics by Training
CCW	Community Cultural Wealth
CoP	Community of Practice
CRF	Critical Race Feminism
CRT	Critical Race Theory
CSP	Culturally Sustaining Pedagogies
DUETS	Developing Urban Education Teachers
DREAMer	Referring to a- Development, Relief and Education for Alien Minors minor
EST	Ecological Systems Theory
FIRST®	For Inspiration and Recognition of Science and Technology
FRC®	FIRST Robotics Competition (high school program)
MARS	Minority, Achievement, Retention, and Success
MSKB	Mathematics and Science Kamp for Beginners
GEMS	Gateway for Excellence in Mathematics and Science
OST	Out-of-School Time
SD	Standard Deviations
SDP	School District of Philadelphia
STEM	Science, Technology, Engineering, and Math
WINS	Women in Natural Sciences

Introduction
Supportive Relationships: A Spectrum of Heroes for Women in STEM

Cecilia (Ceal) D. Craig

Editor, Druai Education Research, USA

Abstract: The continued low percentages of women in STEM degrees, in particular in engineering and computer science programs, is a problem considering the increasing need for people in those careers throughout the world. Supportive relationships at different stages help females aspire to and succeed in those careers. In this chapter that sets the stage for the ten chapters to follow, the problem is illustrated, using data from the United States. A framework of Supportive Relationships along three axes — Involvement, intent, and reach — is posited. With successful programs providing opportunities for supportive relationships, more women in STEM fields can be a result. Combating stereotype threat and nudging young women to non-traditional career choices, against circumscription and compromise. Developing interpersonal connections by helping students see STEM professions as being a place for women. This introduction concludes with an overview of the ten chapters.

Keywords: heroes, supportive relationships, circumscription and compromise, career theory, mentors, mentorship programs, women of color

***

Setting the stage for the book

What is the problem the authors in this book hope to solve or provide solution ideas for? The "so what?" question is often asked of researchers. It is the continued low numbers of women in STEM careers in most countries of the world. Moreover, even with growing societal acceptance of women in traditionally male-dominated careers, challenges for women in Science, Technology, Engineering, and Mathematics or STEM continue into this millennium. Focusing on technology and engineering in the STEM acronym, consider the status of bachelor's degree graduation rates for women in engineering and computer science fields from 1949-50 to 2020-21 (most recent published data; U.S. Department of Education, National Center for Education Statistics, 2022) explored in the next paragraphs and graphs.

Women earned a percent of engineering and engineering technologies bachelor's degrees in the 1950s through 1974, less than 2.0% (NCES, Table 325.45; see Figure 0.1). More and more women entered engineering programs between 1983 and 1993 until the rate stagnated at about 14%, rising again slowly until 2001-02 when it reached a peak of 19.0%, though dropping to a low for the new Millennium of 16.5% in 2008-09. Since then, the rate of women graduating in engineering rose slowing to 23.0% in 2020-21, a high for the entire period that data was captured by the Department of Education Statistics. While this is good news for gaining more women in engineering fields, after 70 years, with only 23% of baccalaureate engineering degrees being earned by women, that rate is not what I had hoped for when I graduated in mechanical engineering in 1974.

Figure 0.1. Engineering and engineering technologies bachelor's degrees, female as percent of total

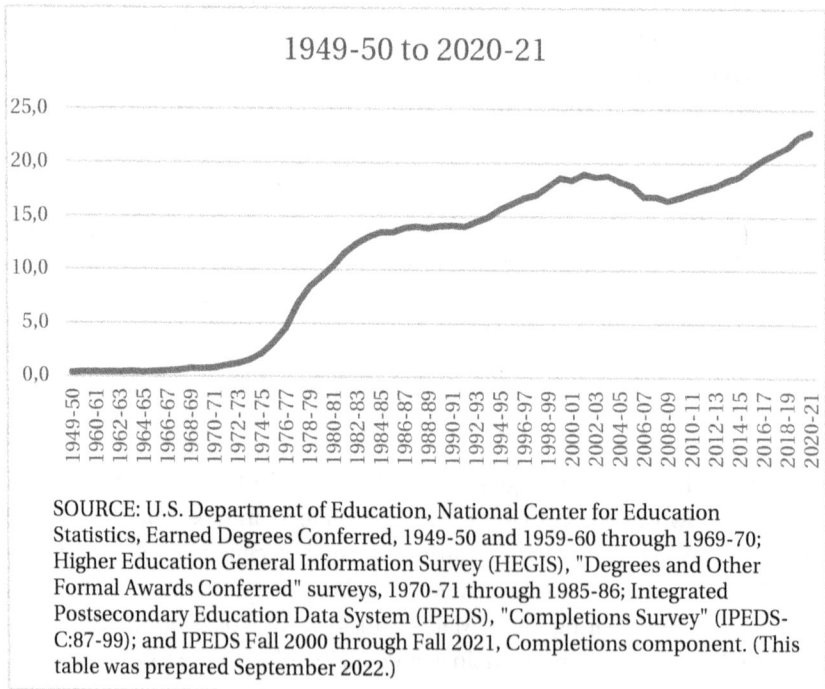

SOURCE: U.S. Department of Education, National Center for Education Statistics, Earned Degrees Conferred, 1949-50 and 1959-60 through 1969-70; Higher Education General Information Survey (HEGIS), "Degrees and Other Formal Awards Conferred" surveys, 1970-71 through 1985-86; Integrated Postsecondary Education Data System (IPEDS), "Completions Survey" (IPEDS-C:87-99); and IPEDS Fall 2000 through Fall 2021, Completions component. (This table was prepared September 2022.)

Computer degrees at the bachelor's level began to appear in the mid-1960s. The percent of women earning computer science bachelor's degrees rose quickly, peaking in 1983-1984 at 37.1%. But this positive picture changed after that peak, dropping slowly and then more rapidly around 2000, reaching lows of 17.6% twice: 2007-2008 and again 2010-2011, finally very slowly rising in the past ten years to 21.9%. (NCES, Table 325.35; see Figure 0.2).

Figure 0.2. Computer and information sciences bachelor's degrees, female as percent of total

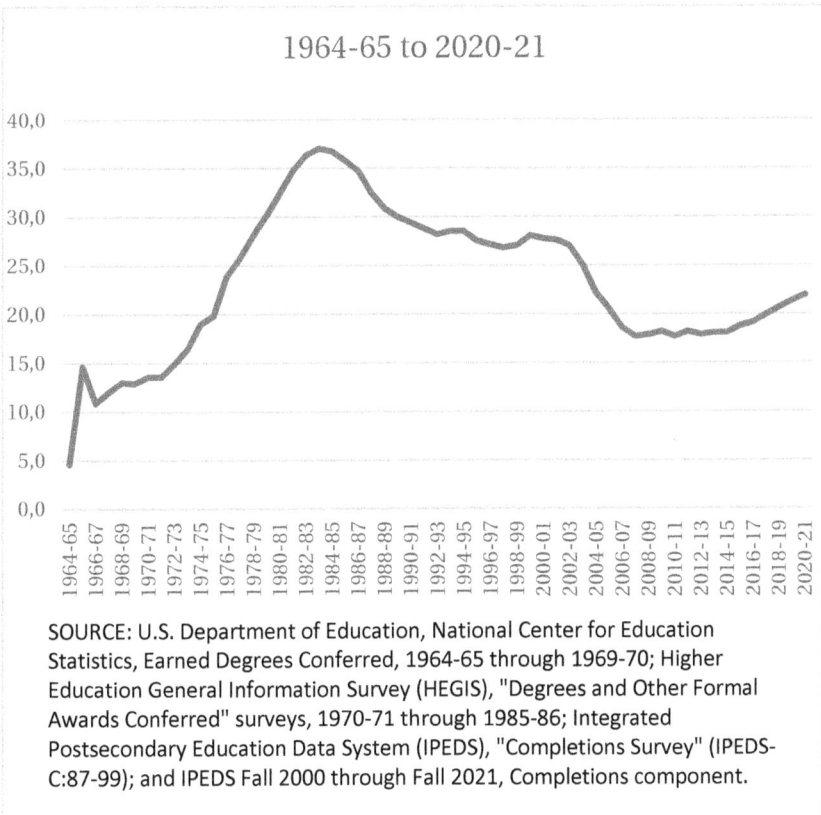

SOURCE: U.S. Department of Education, National Center for Education Statistics, Earned Degrees Conferred, 1964-65 through 1969-70; Higher Education General Information Survey (HEGIS), "Degrees and Other Formal Awards Conferred" surveys, 1970-71 through 1985-86; Integrated Postsecondary Education Data System (IPEDS), "Completions Survey" (IPEDS-C:87-99); and IPEDS Fall 2000 through Fall 2021, Completions component.

One commonly researched approach to changing these stagnant or slowing improving trends has been mentoring programs: beginning in elementary grades through graduate school, in professional spheres and academia. This book will provide recent research, including several longitudinal studies, where the value of mentoring has been shown to make a difference in the numbers of women in engineering and computer science (and other STEM) fields.

Supportive relationships: A spectrum of heroes for women in STEM

Throughout this volume, sharing mentoring and mentorship programs involving science, technology, engineering, and mathematics (STEM) for students and teachers, the reader will find examples of *heroes* for women in STEM that have inspired girls and women to pursue, persist, or nurture careers in STEM for those identifying as female[1]. One might ask, why use heroes versus heroines or sheroes? Using the word heroes to describe supportive relationships is a conscious act demonstrating STEM careers are available to all gender identities. These heroes can come in many forms.

The influence of these heroes on those who identify as female, specifically for those interested in or pursuing STEM careers, can be "transformative" (National Academies, 2019, p. 15). My own experience in high school, when I was exploring colleges and careers in the late 1960s, pivoted around two people: a mentor and a role model. The mentor, a white male high school chemistry teacher, had a long-term reach, someone I met most days, involved with my school learning experiences, and encouraged me to try out a National Science Foundation six-week summer program for aspiring seniors. The summer of 1969, the year the United States landed on the moon, taking classes exploring statics, calculus, and FORTRAN, ignited in me the desire to become an engineer. A role model was an adult family friend, a woman I thought was an engineer, who lived over 1500 miles from me. While we did not communicate frequently, she always encouraged me to pursue this nascent dream, sending me cards and letters. About eight years later, after I graduated with a bachelor's degree in mechanical engineering and began my career as an engineer, she shared with me that she was a nurse, not an engineer. Nonetheless, seeing someone *like* me, a female, in what I thought was an engineering career was enough for me to believe I could be one, too. These heroes had influence. Next, these types of supportive relationships are defined using two models.

---

[1] *Identifying as a female* is the phrase will be used periodically to emphasize that gender identity has many nuances. Most of the time in this book, *female* will be used. *Girls* is meant to include those are in pre-teen, *young women* for teens and early college students, and *women* for those in upper levels of undergraduate programs and older. All of these words and phrases are meant to include those who identify with that gender identity.

Defining supportive relationships or heroes

Supportive relationships are known by many names: mentor, coach, role model, parent, and teacher. Mertz (2004) proposed a two-variable model with *intent* and *involvement* as variables, using a triangle visually to show supportive relationship levels. This model had relationship names like a role model, teacher, counselor, sponsor, patron, or mentor. This model provided a classification and description for the study.

Am expansion of this two-variable model was proposed by Craig (2014), adding *reach* as a variable in a strengthening direction opposite to the involvement level (p. 32). For example, a mentor could have a larger influence on a mentee over a period of time and a single mentor might have several mentees, but not usually hundreds. Thus, the mentor's reach may be smaller when compared to a role model's reach. A role model speaking at a conference or flying in space can connect with much larger numbers of people. View Figure 0.3 to visualize this modified model.

Figure 0.3. Supportive relationships have three characterizing dimensions: Intent, Involvement, and Reach

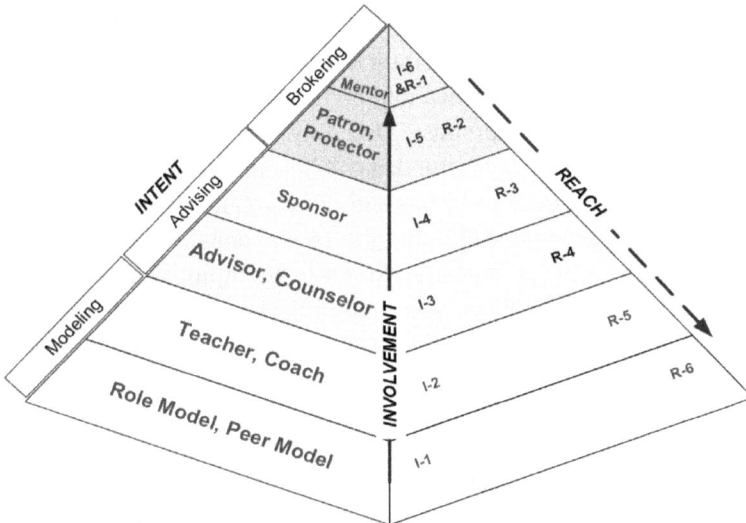

Note: Adapted from Mertz (2004, p. 551), with permission from Craig (2014)

Another orthogonal definition with similar concepts for STEM mentors was provided by the National Academies of Science, Engineering, and Medicine in

2019. After exploring historical mentoring perspectives, the authors shared how they had evolved to a relationship-centric definition, using the below definition in their study considering relationships ranging from long-term ones between a mentor and mentee to group and peer mentoring relationships.

> Mentorship is a professional, working alliance in which individuals work together over time to support the personal and professional growth, development, and success of the relational partners through the provision of career and psychosocial support (p .37).

Mentorship relationships can be dyads or groups, short- or long-term (e.g., short-term: days, hours, a few weeks; long-term: many weeks, months, years). Mentors and mentees can be separated by age and experience or be peers and colleagues. Interactions can occur face-to-face or virtually. Institutions provide opportunities for mentoring relationships to develop with formal programs; other relationships form from peer or near-peer groups found in colleague or student groups. Each chapter provides examples showing the range of these kinds of relationships, their impact, and, in many cases, the long-term outcomes.

Why are supportive relationships important?

Supportive relationships are important for young women to combat stereotype threats and nudge young women into non-traditional career choices, against circumscription and compromise. Over fifty years ago (1981), Gottfredson theorized gender as the first factor that children and young people use to filter, or circumscribe, future occupations and careers (Gottfredson & Lapan, 1997). People are familiar with the idea that girls receive dolls and boys receive trains as gifts. Young women and girls share stories about not seeing someone like them when they hear about, meet, or read about engineers or computer scientists. (Craig, 2014). Gottfredson's theory of circumscription and compromise (2004) posited

> four developmental processes are especially important in the matching process: age-related growth in cognitive ability (cognitive growth), increasingly self-directed development of self (self-creation), progressive elimination of least favored vocational alternatives (circumscription), and recognition of and accommodation to external constraints on vocational choice (compromise). (p. 4).

This theory provided a foundation to discuss and study career interest development. Gottfredson and Lapan (1997) suggested three developmental processes were used by girls and young women when thinking about careers: "(a) the development of *images* or perceptions..., (b) the progressive *circumscription* [of] career options children consider acceptable for themselves, and (c) *compromise*" (p. 420, emphasis present) as they face the real world of what they see.

To circumvent these limiting responses in girls and young women, mentors can help guide a young person to see a different image, to avoid eliminating or circumscribing a career option and thereby avoid compromising their initial career interest (Gottfredson, 2004). Reinforcing these concepts, Cassie and Chen (2012) found grade ten to be a critical time for young women, finding that any efforts to encourage consideration of non-traditional careers, that is, careers where women may be underrepresented, made a positive difference for those young women's career interest development. Every chapter in this book describes how mentors provided opportunities through various approaches, helping girls, young women, college-age women, and teachers to see new images for themselves and avoid circumscription and compromise.

Mentorship programs have been studied extensively, exploring various factors and investigating many variables. A mentoring program's longitudinal is one such factor. Beauchamp et al. (2022) found a "strong positive relationships with youths' sense of social connectedness" ("Discussion," para.2), though it did not strongly influence STEM career interest. While the National Academies (2019) did find "improved outcomes for mentees" (p. 87), though those programs were not associated with STEM specifically. Two chapters herein will share their results from long-term mentoring programs aimed at K-12 and undergraduate women to inform this research gap.

Developing interpersonal connections helps students and teachers see STEM professions as being a place for women. Mentors and role models, including all the types of supportive relationships in-between, help girls and women explore connections within themselves, more specifically, if the relationship is a positive one. (Beauchamp et al., 2022).

In a metareview of mentoring women in STEM (Beck et al., 2022), "50% of the 26 articles that identified challenges and barriers cited 'gender' as an obstacle for women and girls in STEM fields" (p. 174), noting "psychological effects" from grade school through college. (p. 174). Oppression/patriarchy, social institutions, or systemic were the other challenges and barriers categorized by the authors besides gender. The authors found in their metareview mentoring programs that worked to ameliorate negative stereotypes, provide emotional and psychosocial support, and create positive, self-supporting identities for women and girls.

Women of color often experience further or different challenges when pursuing a career in STEM. Mentor programs can positively influence Black STEM undergraduate women (Dickens, 2021). Mentor programs for people of color can sometimes be seen as ways to *fix problems* instead of being supportive of their uniqueness and helping them navigate a different world while retaining that important identity (McGee, 2020). At a recent American Educational Research Association, Research on Women and Education Special Interest Group conference (Zohery et al., October 2023), a group of college women in STEM programs shared how they explored their unique connection as Islamic women, pursuing STEM careers, born in the United States, and women of color. These young women are working to remove the mindset of colonization from STEM using participatory action research approaches. Unique or nuanced variables may need to be considered when developing and evaluating mentorship programs supporting women of color. Several chapters herein focus on STEM mentor programs for girls, young women, and academics of color from the United States and South Africa and can provide deep research in this area.

Why are more women in STEM fields needed?

As already shown earlier, the percentage of women graduating in STEM careers, in particular in engineering and computer science, has not measurably changed in over 20 years. Moreover, women in those fields leave them more frequently than their male counterparts (Hill, Corbett, & St. Rose, 2010). Additionally, while more STEM faculty are women, academia continues to have a paucity of women STEM faculty (Gray, 2023), in particular women of color STEM faculty (Wright, Gunther, & Bitar, 2023). In summary, consider a voice from one who has experienced these challenges:

> In my own path in science, hearing stories of people who studied geology in our solar system made me say, "that's what I want to do." But when I was an intern at NASA, *very few people looked like me.* [emphasis added]
>
> - Ellen Stofan, Ph.D., Under Secretary for science and research at the Smithsonian Institution. (Smithsonian, 2021)

How can we change the narrative? Carroll writes (2018):

The current narrative around the role and contribution of women in STEM has been framed around the existence of barriers, such as hiring and career progression biases, hostile environments, cultural and ethical dilemmas, and lack of role models. Designing solutions to dismantle these barriers often relays the message that women need to fit in.

We can change the conversation and focus on leading women towards STEM careers. (para. 9-10).

Summing up

Supportive relationships such as mentoring can have a profound influence on those who aspire to a STEM career and identify as female. These relationships can take on many names, viewed through the variables of intent, involvement, and reach. Or, as alliances providing those in them with psychosocial and career support.

These supportive relationships, these heroes, can positively influence career decisions and help sustain girls, young women and women who pursue STEM fields. Women of color may experience other challenges while sharing some of the same as white women. Mentoring programs for women of color may need to recognize any unique needs.

The authors in the next ten chapters will share their research about these important practices, many with long-term participation data and findings, others with proposals and questions. Some will share intimate and moving stories told in poetry and journals, shared experiences, and challenges along the way. With these ideas, changing the narrative for girls, young women, and women in STEM careers or hoping to pursue them. We hope you will enjoy the book. It takes a village to change the world, and we have become one over the past year developing this volume.

References

Beauchamp, A. L., Roberts, S.-J., Aloisio, J. M., Wasserman, D., Heimlich, J. E., Lewis, J. D., Munshi-South, J., Clark, J. A., & Tingley, K. (2022). Effects of research and mentoring on underrepresented youths' STEM persistence into college. *Journal of Experiential Education, 45*(3), 316-336. https://doi.org/10.1177/10538259211050098

Beck, M., Cadwell, J., Kern, A., Wu, K., Dickerson, M., & Howard, M. (2022). Critical feminist analysis of STEM mentoring programs: A meta-synthesis of the existing literature. *Gender, Work, and Organization, 29*(1), 3-370.

Carroll, K. (2018, October 15). Gender imbalances in STEM field. *GirlUp.* Retrieved October 14, 2023, from https://girlup.org/voices/gender-imbalances-in-stem-fields

Cassie, D. W., & Chen, C. P. (2012). The gender-mediated impact of a career development intervention. *Australian Journal of Career Development, 21*(1), 3-13.

Craig, C. D. (2014). *How robotics programs influence young women's career choices: A Grounded Theory Model* (Publication No. 3614057) [Doctoral dissertation, Walden University]. ProQuest Dissertations Publishing.

Dickens, D., Ellis, V., & Hall, N. (2021). Changing the face of STEM: Review of literature on the role of mentors in the success of undergraduate black women in STEM education. *Journal of Research Initiatives, 5*(3). Retrieved from https://par.nsf.gov/biblio/10355703

Gottfredson, L. S. (1981). Circumscription and compromise: A developmental theory of occupational aspirations. *Journal of Counseling Psychology, 28*(6), 545–579. https://doi.org/10.1037/0022-0167.28.6.545

Gottfredson, L. S. (2004). Using Gottfredson's theory of circumscription and compromise in career guidance and counseling. *Career development and counseling: Putting theory and research to work,* 71-100. Retrieved from http://www.udel.edu/educ/gottfredson/reprints/2004theory.pdf

Gottfredson, L. S. & Lapan, R. T. (1997, Fall). Assessing gender-based circumscription of occupational aspirations. *Journal of Career Assessment 5*(4), 419-441, doi:10.1177/106907279700500404

Hill, C., Corbett, C., & St. Rose, A. (2010). *Why so few? Women in science, technology, engineering, and mathematics.* Washington, DC: American Association of University Women. Available from http://www.aauw.org/learn/research/whysofew.cfm

McGee, E. O. (2020). Interrogating structural racism in STEM higher education. *Educational Researcher, 49*(9), 633-644. https://doi.org/10.3102/0013189X20972718

Mertz, N.T. (2004). What's a mentor, anyway? *Educational Administration Quarterly, 40*(4), 541-560. doi: 10.1177/0013161X04267110

National Academies of Sciences, Engineering, and Medicine. (2019). *The science of effective mentorship in STEMM.* (A. Byars-Winston & M. Lund Dahlberg, Eds.). The National Academies Press. https://doi.org/10.17226/25568

Smithsonian. (2021, April 15). Hearing the voices of women leaders, in science, technology, and innovation. *Smithsonian: American Women's History Museum.* Retrieved October 14, 2023, from https://womenshistory.si.edu/news/2021/04/hearing-voices-women-leaders-science-technology-and-innovation

Wright, B., Gunther, O., & Bitar, J. (2023, July 24). Why STEM equity must address the experiences of women of color. *The Education Trust.* Retrieved from https://edtrust.org/resource/why-stem-equity-must-address-the-experiences-of-women-of-color/

Zohery, V., Alam, S., Husain, Y., & Khan, M. (2023, October 13). *Sisters in STEM: Muslim women leading a participatory action research project for decolonizing STEM education.* AERA Research on Women and Education Fall Conference, Las Vegas, NV.

Section and Chapter Outline

Section: Mentor characteristics

Chapter 1: Ten essential characteristics of highly effective mentors

The first chapter proposes ten characteristics of an effective STEM mentor. This proposal was developed from longitudinal (2008 - 2022) research primarily with PreK - college participants' experience from a long-term mentoring program in the southern United States. Joe Omojola, Murty Kambhampati, and Phyllis Okwan from Southern University in New Orleans and Baton Rouge campuses focus in this chapter on describing those characteristics and explaining why they are important.

Section: Gender identity and stereotypes

This section has one chapter exploring gender identity and stereotypes that women in STEM face. These concepts are a good grounding for the remaining two book sections that will share specific programs and research about mentoring programs for women in STEM.

Chapter 2: Examining teacher perspectives of gender stereotyping in pre-college engineering education.

The authors explored here a perspective not commonly seen in research, that of the teacher's perspective. Most research on stereotype threats and gender identity has been from a student or person's point of view. In this chapter, Medha Dalal, Tara Nkurmah, Jennifer Kouo, and Stacy Klein-Gardner explored gender inequity in engineering education from a teacher's perspective of stereotypes, stereotype threat, and bias and offered culturally relevant teacher mentoring approaches to promote equitable pre-college engineering education. Their qualitative research explored issues of gender-inequities, stereotypes, stereotype threat, and biases from a teacher's perspective and examined STEM teacher characterizations of stereotypes, stereotype threat, and implicit biases. They sought to understand teachers' perceptions of their roles in mentoring young women in building their engineering identities.

Section: Mentoring young women in STEM

This section has four chapters, three on K-12 programs and one for undergraduate students. Chapter 3 brings new perspectives from a program in

South Africa; Chapter 4 shares longitudinal research on a mentoring program in the southern United States with K-12 students, while the program's impacts on undergraduate women in STEM is covered in Chapter 6. Chapter 5 describes longitudinal research through a lens of young Black women in STEM.

K-12 Research section

Chapter 3: Mentorship and support for young South African women advancement in mathematical-related careers

In this chapter, Zingiswa Jojo describes mentorship initiatives exploring the role of Mathematics Education in empowering young South African Women and girls to advance to mathematical-related careers. The study of young women, ages 17-18, uses humanistic learning theory as a framework for the perceptions and conceptions of girls, specifically with regard to their self-concept, self-realization, and self-identity (Wadjajanti, 2019). The chapter connects with ideas from the prior chapter on stereotypes and gender identity. Jojo provides ideas for overcoming these challenges with STEM role modeling and mentors in South Africa and ultimately strengthening young women's beliefs towards mathematics learning.

Chapter 4: Mentoring K-12 students in STEM

Phyllis Okwan, Joe Omojola, and Murty Kambhampati, at Southern University in New Orleans and in Baton Rouge, in this chapter, share the longitudinal STEM mentoring program for over 400 elementary-age students from 2008 to 2022. They will describe the programs, methods, and activities to achieve their desired goal of motivating young students to aspire to become a scientist.

Chapter 5: What we really need: Mentoring from the perspectives of Black women in STEM

This exciting 40-year longitudinal study of the Women in Natural Sciences (WINS) program involved extended engagement year-round in grades 9-12 for low-income young Black women in urban public high schools. Jacqueline Genovesi, Ph.D. and Ayana Allen-Handy, Ph.D. combined 40 years of iterative evaluation to create a finely-honed enrichment program. They used *culturally* sustaining pedagogies centered on minoritized women's distinct ways of knowing and being as their framework. Along with their co-authors, they bring a new perspective focused on young Black women in STEM with this substantiated long-term study.

Undergraduate programs research section

Chapter 6: The impact of effective mentoring on undergraduate STEM programs

Dr. Murty Kambhampati, Dr. Joe Omojola, and Dr. Phyllis Okwan from Southern University in New Orleans and in Baton Rouge authors from Chapter 4, share another aspect of their long-term mentoring program, specifically mentoring of early college students from a particular area needing remedial education in New Orleans, Louisiana. The authors from Southern University in New Orleans and in Baton Rouge will provide key learnings from their critical work.

Section: Mentoring professional women in STEM

The first two chapters in this next section move to mentor professional STEM women in academia, first with an informal peer mentoring group and then examining the differences between sponsoring and mentoring, bringing connections to the introductory model for the book with layers and axes of supportive relationships. The final two chapters share outcomes for pre-service STEM teachers both through an identity lens connecting to the second book section on gender identities and their nuances and importance.

Academia programs

Chapter 7: Found poetry – Highlighting reciprocal mentor relationships and role shifting within an informal peer mentoring group

Utilizing social STEM identity theory as a lens (Kim et al., 2019), the aim of this chapter's study was to examine reciprocal mentor relationships and role shifting as a peer mentoring group questioned academic needs, tensions, and desires. The informal peer mentoring group of three women academics spanned the *clogged pipeline.* Amber Simpson, Ph.D., Signe E. Kastberg, and Caro Williams-Pierce share a conceptual framework with two aspects – a psychological sense of belonging and social acceptance using a *social STEM identity theory.* The authors share this deeply personal qualitative study with thoughtful insights and learning for others.

Chapter 8: Leveraging mentoring and sponsoring relationships in academia

Academics often need both mentors and sponsors to gain tenure and achieve success in the academic world. This chapter explored the differences between mentoring relationships and sponsoring relationships and how they relate to career promotion within academia, along with differences between how men and women perceive these relationships. Carole Sox and Sheryl Kline advocate a call to action for equitable and proactive strategies to assist with career advancement, with a focus on employing formal mentorship and sponsorship relationship programs in higher learning institutions.

STEM Teacher professional education

Chapter 9: Cultivating expressions of Black womanhood in science education through culturally responsive mentorship

Darrin Collins, a high school science teacher and doctoral student at the University of Illinois, and Erica Dixon, a graduate student at Relay Graduate school of Education, explore the impact of culturally responsive mentorship (CRM) on the development and expression of a pre-service teacher's woman of science identity through a framework of culturally responsive mentorship. In their qualitative case study, they explore how culturally responsive mentorship promoted and fostered the expression of Black womanhood in science education.

Chapter 10: DUETS: Developing urban education teachers in STEM

The final chapter reports outcomes from a longitudinal (five-year) program called DUETS that is aimed at recruiting and retaining STEM preservice teachers and STEM teachers of color. This study used a framework of dual identity: the duality of being a woman and an African American preservice teacher. Deborah Harmon, Ph.D. and Cheryl Price, Ph.D., found that mentoring prepared and helped retain these teachers. They share learning and recommendations for readers.

SECTION.

Mentor Characteristics

This section has one chapter proposing ten characteristics for effective mentors. This is based on longitudinal research of females of all ages over 25 years.

Chapter 1: Ten essential characteristics of highly effective mentors

- Joe Omojola, Murty Kambhampati, and Phyllis Okwan

Chapter 1

Ten Essential Characteristics of Highly Effective Mentors

Joe Omojola

Southern University at New Orleans, USA

Murty Kambhampati

Southern University at New Orleans, USA

Phyllis Okwan

Southern University and A&M College, Baton Rouge, USA

Abstract: Mentoring is the process whereby an experienced individual uses her/his knowledge, experience, and skills to assist in speeding up the growth or development of another person. Mentoring is hard work that requires a lot of dedication, interpersonal understanding, professional relationships, work ethic, and persistence. In this chapter, we present what we consider to be the ten essential characteristics of highly effective mentors. The discussion is based on what we have learned, collectively, as mentors for over twenty-five years. During this mentoring period, over 75 percent of those we have mentored (K-12, undergraduate students, graduate students, and faculty) are female (White House News Release 07-172, November 19, 2007; National Archives, 2015). These ten essential characteristics are (1) the ability to work and collaborate across boundaries, (2) honesty, (3) the ability to evaluate talent and communicate potential, (4) willingness to sacrifice, (5) the ability to communicate, (6) willingness to give others a second chance, (7) ability to take the necessary time for human development, (8) commitment to mentee's welfare, (9) ability to listen, and (10) ability to manage multiple projects. We will explain each characteristic, explain why it is needed and give instances where it was applied. Finally, we explained some elements of our mentoring program.

Keywords: mentoring, characteristics of mentors, second chance, working across boundaries, effective mentors, communication, manage multiple projects, and ability to listen

***

Ten essential characteristics of highly effective mentors

Many articles and books have been written on mentoring techniques, benefits of mentoring, the role of mentors and mentees, etc. (Adam, 2023; Allen et al., 1997; Allen et al., 2004; Boyle & Boice, 1998; Chan, 2008; Cunningham & Eberle, 1993; Darling et al., 2006; Feldman et al., 1999; Healey & Welchert, 1990; Hollingsworth & Fassinger, 2002; Johnson, 2002 & 2003; Payne & Huffman, 2005). Ortiz-Walters and Gilson (2005) examined the mentoring experiences of African, Hispanic, and Native-American protégés in an academic setting. Paglis et al. (2006) concluded that mentoring adds value to productivity and self-efficacy. It has also been established that successful mentoring can lead to greater student achievement, retention, and knowledge-sharing (Vasquez & Pandya, 2020). As a background to our mentoring activities, Louisiana's Public Education ranks 45 - 50 out of 50 states in the United States of America (Public School Rankings by State, 2023). Within the state of Louisiana, the New Orleans Public School District (NOPSD) is one of the lowest-performing systems. This is the system from which the majority of our students come. It takes hard work to be successful in mentoring students with poor academic preparation in STEM. Under the conditions we have described, it is even more challenging. Notwithstanding, we have been committed to doing whatever it takes to produce competitive students in STEM for over twenty-five years. In addition to hard work, dedication, and persistence, we discovered in our mentoring work from Pre-Kindergarten (PK) to college, that a mentor needs many skills, competencies, and abilities to be successful. The ten qualities that we deemed essential are highlighted below.

The ten essential characteristics

Ability to work and collaborate across boundaries

In day-to-day human interactions, there are many boundaries to contend with. Some boundaries are subtle, some are explicit. A mentor will most likely work through some of these boundaries in her/his work. Johnson-Bailey and Cervero (2004) examined common issues and complexity in cross-cultural mentoring relationships and the resulting success in such relationships. Thomas (2001) states that many cross-race mentoring relationships suffer from "protective hesitation" – refraining from touchy issues by both parties. In Collaborate or Perish, Bratton and Tumin (2012) state that "Collaboration is about people. If it were about technology, the one with the best toys would always win." Mentoring is also about people. Mentoring relationships involve working across several boundaries such as gender, race, tradition, religion, organizational, and departmental. In order for a mentoring relationship to be successful, both parties must be able to work across these boundaries. One example that we encounter daily in our mentoring work is that of a male mentor mentoring a female student and vice versa. Another common boundary that we deal with is working with faculty and students from different countries, cultures, and traditions. We have found that while working across these boundaries, we must also respect the boundary. Some of the advantages of working across boundaries are (a) leveraging strategy and operational capabilities (American Chemical Society Workshop on Collaborating Across Boundaries (January 21, 2023), (b) holistic thinking, (c) improved product quality, and (d) exposure to alternative perspectives and methods. The authors' approach has been to focus on being friendly and approachable before the mentoring relationship starts. This method enables the mentee to feel comfortable about interacting with us as well as being assured that the mentor's goal is to help advance the mentee's career. For those mentors wishing to acquire or improve the ability to work across boundaries, Chiaet (2013) revealed that there is evidence that reading literary fiction improves a reader's capacity to understand what others are thinking and feeling. We also discovered that open dialogue with mentees about their background and the way they are used to doing things improves our boundary-to-boundary interactions.

Honesty

By definition, honesty is the quality of being honest. It is the ability to be truthful, ethical, and fair (dictionary.com). Barraclough (2016) further states that "honest behavior is about being reliable and doing what you say you will. You are honest when you keep promises." In an honest environment, both mentor and mentee are willing to admit when they are wrong, being able to speak up about their feelings, and communicate their excitement and disappointment. When both mentor and mentee perceived that the other was trustworthy and possessed integrity, the collaboration was very productive. We discovered that it is very important for the mentor to communicate with the mentee, as early as possible, important details about the work that is needed.

Such details must include how much work is needed for the project involved, important timelines and deadlines, meeting frequencies and duration, how to communicate, and what to do when a problem arises.

Ability to evaluate talent and communicate potential

Kinley and Ben-Hur (2013) stated that "Talent measurement is the use of various methods and tools to gather and use information about individuals' talents. There is no one way of evaluating talent. Some organizations rely on the intuition of their leaders and simple interviews; others employ sophisticated online tests." Most of the time, a mentee is unaware of what they are capable of, let alone what talents they possess. For this reason, it is important for a mentor to be able to identify the abilities, talent(s), and potential of the mentee. In our case, we rely on our years of experience working with students to evaluate a student's talent. In most cases, we can detect the characteristics and potential of a student when we observe the pattern and tendencies in the way a student operates as s/he takes courses from different professors in our department or participates in other activities on campus. It is equally important that the mentor communicate with the mentee about their abilities or potential. This kind of communication gives the mentee confidence and encourages her/him to strive for more. In our work, we have given opportunities to talented freshmen to conduct guided undergraduate research above their academic level. In each of those cases, we observed improvement in mentees' academic performance, research quality, confidence, openness, and persistence in subsequent semesters.

Willingness to sacrifice

Sacrifice is the giving up of something of tangible or intangible value in return for something of higher value. Mentoring is usually a voluntary service provided by the mentor. It is seldom part of the mentor's job description. For this reason, a lot of sacrifice is needed on the mentor's part. Sacrifice requires that you give up what is valuable to you (time, resources, activities, preferences, etc.) in order to accommodate others. Van Lange et al. (1997) found that "Willingness to sacrifice was associated with strong commitment, high satisfaction, poor alternatives, and high investments." We discovered that a willingness to sacrifice by the mentor creates the same ability in the mentee. In fact, we observed that mentees who observed this characteristic in a mentor tend to demonstrate the same skill over time. In other words, willingness to sacrifice, like many of the mentoring characteristics, can be passed on from mentor to mentee.

Ability to communicate

A mentor must be able to communicate effectively. McKay (2019) declares that "With Effective Communication Skills, you will gain a better understanding of not only yourself but also other people around you. This will help you become a better problem solver, build trust and respect in business." In addition, we believe that effective communication should be an ongoing process in a mentee-mentor relationship. For this reason, we actively communicate with our mentees when we evaluate their academic performance, written reports, oral presentations, application to graduate school, and daily oral and email communications. Some of the pointers given by Harvard University Professionals (Emerson, 2021) on communication skills are: prepare ahead of time, be clear and concise, watch your tone, and practice active listening. In particular, it is important for a mentor to reinforce what the mentee is doing right and the potential of the student. It is important for the mentor to remember that education is repetition. In particular, it is important for a mentor to reinforce what the mentee is doing right and the potential of the student. We have witnessed cases of students who do not believe they have the ability to earn advanced degrees from the beginning of their undergraduate program to their junior year. With proper communication of the students' abilities and potential on a regular basis, they went on to graduate schools with confidence and performed well. Lastly, it must be stated that all communications are not verbal. It could simply be the mentee observing how you do what you do each day.

Willingness to give others a second chance

It is very easy to assume that all mentoring relationships proceed smoothly from beginning to end without a hitch. This belief comes from the countless accounts of mentoring successes we read about. Contrary to this image, there are cases where the mentoring processes encounter a bump in the road. Hoke (2018) states, "we believe in second chances." Sometimes, a mentee will make mistakes that will cause the mentor to sever the relationship. In a number of these cases, we have had mentees who realized their mistakes and want to be restored. In those cases, we observed that the mentees, who were granted a second chance, were appreciative, more focused, more productive, and more hardworking than before. The important steps that we consider in giving a mentee a second chance are (a) a written explanation from the mentee about the problem that led to severance from mentorship, (b) a statement about what was learned in the process, (c) a plan of how to prevent what happened from happening in future, and (d) the mentee taking responsibility for what happened. It is very important for mentors to remember that character development is one of the cornerstones of mentoring. When you give a mentee a second chance, you grant them the opportunity to develop their character further. In addition, as was stated in Hoke (2018), a mentee who is granted a second chance is more likely going to be more empathetic, more productive, and in return, find ways to give others a second chance.

Ability to take the necessary time for human development

Human development takes time, a lot of time. Often, the time required for human development could be painfully slow. A bird's-eye view of the Human Development was given by Deneulin and Shahani (2009). For the purpose of our work, the types of development we are interested in are behavioral, cognitive, and emotional. These are the skills that a mentee will need to be able to go through college, attend graduate school, or proceed to professional life. Most of the time we spend on mentoring is devoted to supporting human development opportunities, in different situations, that mentees encounter. Those situations include interacting with classmates or research cohorts, presenting in a group setting, addressing professors properly, interacting and collaborating at conferences, etc. It is important for a mentor to address these issues on time before the student loses perspective or relevance. It should be the goal of the mentor to help the mentee grow in all aspects of human development – behavioral, social, emotional, and mental. It is our contention that the best way for this to happen is for the mentee to observe the mentor in the normal flow of life. For this reason, a mentor must model what is important for the mentee in their day-to-day interactions.

Commitment to mentee's welfare

Kohn and O'Connell (2015) emphasize the importance of being "committed to supporting the mentee's welfare and future." A mentor who is committed to the mentee's welfare will do whatever it takes to get the mentee to the finish line – graduation from high school, college, or graduate school, getting into an internship, getting a job, etc. In our program, we communicate our commitment to the students' success to our mentees. This communication gives them the assurance that they need to do a good job. In our experience, we have had many mentees requesting for us to continue the mentoring process longer than we anticipated. We take these requests as complements for the mentoring that we have done. For this reason, the duration of a mentor's work is not fixed.

Ability to listen

Banks (2021) stated that "Listening is the forgotten communication skill, but arguably, the most significant." We believe that a mentor must be an effective listener. Listening effectively enables you to hear what the speaker is saying, what the speaker is not saying, what is implied by what the speaker is saying, and what is hidden in what the speaker is not saying. By listening, a mentor is able to tell what kind of mentee s/he is dealing with. For example, the mentor would be able to detect the mentee's goals and aspirations, if the mentee wants to proceed faster in a research project, wants to be challenged more or possesses a background that allows her/him to handle special projects. We have discovered that in order to be a good listener, you must also be a good observer. Finally, good listeners ask good clarifying questions and follow-up questions.

Ability to manage multiple projects

As we stated before, mentoring responsibilities are usually not in the primary job description of the mentor. Mentoring is born purely out of compassion for the development of a fellow human being. It is an additional voluntary job taken on by the mentor. In order for the mentor to be effective, s/he must be capable of managing multiple projects. For example, it is not uncommon for a university professor to be involved in teaching, research, advising, and serving on several committees in addition to mentoring. Invariably, the ability of a mentor to manage multiple projects results from her/his time management skills. Managing multiple projects involves managing your own time, managing work requests from others, managing communication, managing schedules, and managing your environment (Harrin, 2022). The technique we have found useful is to have a timeline for each project and follow a daily *To Do List* that consists of activities from the timelines. When we write proposals, we make sure that goals, objectives, and responsibilities are well defined. These responsibilities are then communicated on a regular basis to those who are responsible for carrying them out. In addition, we solve unanticipated problems quickly before they cause more problems.

Elements of our mentoring

Listed below are activities we have found to be effective in our mentoring program:

- *Using research as a teaching tool*: Research expands the learning of students because the discoveries of the student researchers become a permanent feature of their professional development. In particular, we believe that self-generated data is more useful for students' learning than data from a textbook. A student is more passionate and more committed to the data they are responsible to collect. Consequently, these types of students tend to learn more.

- *Engaging students academically:* A student in the mentoring program becomes more structured because, as a result of the demands of the mentoring obligations, the mentee is more likely to manage his/her time better. Additionally, mentored students have more pathways to learning than their non-mentored peers.

- *Allowing students to take ownership of their own success:* An educational banner reads, "Success is a do it yourself project." This is very true in mentoring. The responsibilities given to a student in the mentoring process enable the student to be more responsible for the outcome of their education. This aspect, by itself, is leadership training for the mentee.

- *Promoting collaboration and interaction with others:* In STEM fields, the success of big projects is seldom the work of an individual. Success is attained by a group of professionals working together. Mentoring enables a student to acquire early training in collaboration and interaction. The synergy created when a group of productive students work together creates a multiplying effect on each student's development.

- *Acquiring professional development and etiquette:* As a student develops in a mentoring environment, the student is exposed to proper professional etiquette, which will follow them through the rest of their career. The earlier a student is exposed to professional etiquette, the longer they can practice this skill before they graduate. For this reason, we want our students to be exposed to mentoring as early as their freshman year.

- *Enriching and enhancing a student's academic experience:* An enriched undergraduate curriculum should include research, attending professional meetings, presentations, listening to presentations, asking questions, collaborating and networking, and community service. Students with a comprehensive academic experience are generally more outgoing and make career advancements faster.

- *Challenging a student through competition:* A challenged student is more competitive, well-rounded, more productive, and more responsible. This is the reason why we strongly encourage our students to present at local, regional, and national meetings, seminars and conferences.

- *Creating opportunities:* At conferences, our students meet with recruiters for STEM workforce and graduate schools. These interactions lead to opportunities for visits to graduate schools, applications to graduate schools, scholarships and grants offers, and employment.

Conclusion

In this paper, we highlighted what we considered the ten essential skills that an effective mentor must possess. We have made assumptions that the mentor has the necessary qualifications to serve as a mentor, is self-disciplined, hard-working, persistent, and resourceful. Although most of the authors' experiences are in academic settings where the majority of the mentees are female, these characteristics are applicable outside academia. One of the authors has implemented these characteristics successfully in a business setting. We believe, very strongly, that mentoring adds value to the human capacity. Independent of the profession or activity to which mentoring is applied, there are benefits for the mentor and the mentee. Some of the benefits we have experienced as mentors are the ability to have a more comprehensive view of our methods and operations, exposure to other cultures and values, improved leadership skills, and empathy. In our mentees, we observed improved time management skills, expanded networking ability, and the ability to make progress faster than those without mentors.

Acknowledgments

The authors would like to express their appreciation to the National Science Foundation, US Department of Education, Louisiana Board of Regents, US Department of Energy, National Institutes of Health, Louisiana Department of Health, and Centers for Disease Control and Prevention for financial support through funded grants and sub-contracts with collaborators. We thank Southern University at New Orleans for supporting our endeavor and giving us a stable base to operate from. We are very grateful to our collaborators from universities, industries, and national labs for sharing ideas and facilities and providing the type of support that we need to work successfully on teaching, research, and funded projects. We are highly indebted to our former and current students, who have responded positively to our mentoring efforts over the years, and especially to those who were inspired by our work to become mentors.

References

Adam, J. (2023, February 24). *How mentorship can benefit both the mentor and the mentee.* Retrieved from U.S. News & World Report: https://money.usnews.com/careers/articles/how-mentorship-can-benefit-both-the-mentor-and-the-mentee

Allen, T. D., Poteet, M. L. & Eby, L. T. (2004). Career benefits associated with mentoring for proteges: A meta-analysis. *Journal of Applied Psychology, 89*(1): 127–136.

Allen, T. D., Russell, J. E. A. & Maetzke, S. B. (1997). Formal peer mentoring: Factors related to protege satisfaction and willingness to mentor others. *Group & Organization Management, 22*(4): 488–507.

American Chemical Society Workshop on Collaborating Across Boundaries. (2023, January 21). https://www.acs.org/careers/leadership

Banks, R. (2021). *The art of active listening: How to listen effectively in 10 simple steps to improve relationships and increase productivity.* Nxt Level International.

Barraclough, S. (2016). *Honesty.* Capstone Publishers.

Boyle, P., and Boice, B. (1998). Systematic mentoring for new faculty teachers and graduate teaching assistants. *Innovative Higher Education, 22,* 157–179.

Bratton, W. & Tumin, Z. (2012). *Collaborate or perish!: Reaching across boundaries in a networked world.* Crown Business Publishing.

Chan, A. W. (2008). Mentoring ethnic minority, pre-doctoral students: an analysis of key mentor practices, *Mentoring & Tutoring: Partnership in Learning, 16*(3), 263-277.

Chiaet, J. (2013, October 4). *Novel finding: Reading literary fiction improves empathy.* Retrieved from Scientific American: https://www.scientificamerican.com/article/novel-finding-reading-literary-fiction-improves-empathy/

Cunningham, J. B. & Eberle, T. (1993). Characteristics of the mentoring experience: A qualitative study. *Personnel Review, 22*(4), 54–66.

Darling, N., Bogat, G. A., Cavell, T. A., Murphy, S. E. & Sanchez, B. (2006). Gender, ethnicity, development, and risk: Mentoring and the consideration of individual differences. *Journal of Community Psychology, 34,* 765–779.

Deneulin, S. & Shahani, L. (Ed.) (2009). *An introduction to the human development and capability approach.* Routledge. https://doi.org/10.4324/9781849770026

Emerson, M. S. (2021, August 30). Eight ways you can improve your communication skills. *Harvard U, Professional Development.* Retrieved July 5, 2023, https://professional.dce.harvard.edu/blog/eight-things-you-can-do-to-improve-your-communication-skills/

Feldman, D. C., Folks, W. R. and Turnley, W. H. (1999). Mentor-protégé diversity and its impact on international internship experiences. *Journal of Organizational Behavior, 20,* 597–611.

Harrin, E. (2022). *Managing multiple projects: How project managers Can balance priorities, manage expectations and increase productivity.* Kogan Page Limited.

Healey, C. C. & Welchert, A. J. (1990). Mentoring relations: A definition to advance research and practice. *Educational Researcher, 19*(9), 17-21.

Hoke, C. (2018). *A second chance: For you, for me and for the rest of us.* Do You Zoom, Incorporated.

Hollingsworth, M. A. &Fassinger, R. E. (2002). The role of faculty mentors in the research training of counseling psychology doctoral students. *Journal of Counseling Psychology, 49*, 324–330.

Johnson-Bailey, J. & Cervero, R. (2004). Mentoring in black and white: The intricacies of cross-cultural mentoring. *Mentoring and Tutoring, 12*, 7–21.

Johnson, W. B. (2002). The intentional mentor: Strategies and guidelines for the practice of mentoring. *Professional Psychology: Research & Practice, 33*(1), 88–96.

Johnson, W. B. (2003). A framework for conceptualizing competence to mentor. *Ethics & Behavior, 13*(2), 127–151.

Kinley, N. & Ben-Hur, S. (2013). *Talent Intelligence: What you need to know to identify and measure talent.* Wiley Publishers.

Kohn, S. & O'Connell, V. (2015). *9 powerful practices of really great mentors.* The Career Press.

McKay, D. (2019). *How to talk to anyone.* Amazon Digital Services LLC - KDP Print US.

National Archives. (2015). The White House, President Barack Obama. https://obamawhitehouse.archives.gov/the-press-office/2015/03/27/president-obama-honors-outstanding-science-mathematics-and-engineering-m

Ortiz-Walters, R. &Gilson, L. L. (2005). Mentoring in academia: An examination of the experiences of protégés of color. *Journal of Vocational Behavior, 67*, 459–475.

Paglis, L., Green, S. & Bauer, T. (2006). Does adviser mentoring add value? A longitudinal study of mentoring and doctoral student outcomes. *Research in Higher Education, 47*(4), 451–476.

Payne, S. C. & Huffman, A. H. (2005). A longitudinal examination of the influence of mentoring on organizational commitment and turnover. *Academy of Management Journal, 48*(1), 158–168.

Public School Rankings by State (2023). World Population Review. Retrieved August 1, 2023, from https://worldpopulationreview.com/state-rankings/public-school-rankings-by-state

Thomas, D. A. (2001). The truth about mentoring minorities: Race matters. *Harvard Business Review, 79*, 99–107.

Van Lange, P. A. M., Rusbult, C. E., Drigotas, S. M., Arriaga, X. B., Witcher, B. S., & Cox, C. L. (1997). Willingness to sacrifice in close relationships. *Journal of Personality and Social Psychology, 72*(6), 1373-1395.

Vasquez, R., & Pandya, A. G. (2020). Successful mentoring of women. *International Journal of Women's Dermatology, 6*(1), 61.

White House News Release 07-172, President Honors Mentors of Scientists and Engineers (November 19, 2007). *President Honors Mentors of Scientists and Engineers | NSF - National Science Foundation.*

SECTION.
Gender Identity and Stereotypes

This section has one chapter exploring gender identity and stereotypes that women in STEM face. These concepts provide a foundation for the remaining two book sections that will share specific programs and research about mentoring programs for women in STEM.

Chapter 2: Examining teacher perspectives of gender stereotyping in pre-college engineering education.

- Medha Dalal, Tara Nkrumah, Jennifer Kouo, Stacy Klein-Gardner

Chapter 2

Examining Teacher Perspectives of Gender Stereotyping in Pre-college Engineering Education

Medha Dalal
Arizona State University, USA

Tara Nkrumah
Arizona State University, USA

Jennifer Kouo
Johns Hopkins University, USA

Stacy Klein-Gardner
Vanderbilt University, USA

Abstract: Stereotypes, stereotype threats, and biases have contributed to gender inequities in engineering education. Mitigation initiatives tend to focus on curricular content and often ignore the societal influences that hinder equitable outcomes. Studies suggest that educators mentored to address gender stereotyping can buffer negative influences that dissuade women from pursuing engineering. Currently, pre-college science, technology, engineering, and mathematics (STEM) teacher professional learning (PL) programs minimally address gender stereotyping. Moreover, teachers' understanding of and perspectives on managing gender stereotyping are little known. This study explored gender inequity in engineering education from pre-college teacher perspectives with an aim to inform STEM teacher PL. Data were collected from three focus groups held in conjunction with a year-long teacher PL and mentorship program. Qualitative analysis uncovered deeper meanings behind teachers' perspectives of gender stereotyping. Major themes included attribution of stereotyping and implicit bias to societal norms, a sense of responsibility as a teacher to prepare women for college and engineering pathways, and frustration with systemic barriers that inhibit women's participation in engineering. The study has implications for the future design of STEM teacher PL that addresses gender stereotyping and prepares teachers to mitigate it effectively.

Keywords: Teacher professional learning, stereotype, stereotype threat, implicit bias

***

Examining teacher perspectives of gender stereotyping in pre-college engineering education

The social promotion of gender roles has contributed to gender inequity in engineering education and the workforce. Only 15% of the global engineering workforce in 2020 was women, as we wait for more women to make their way through the educational pathway (World Economic Forum, 2020). According to a report from the National Academy of Engineering and National Research Council, gender inequity has its roots in the pre-college system, where access and participation need to be expanded (Katehi et al., 2009). Next Generation Science Standards and many state standards now include engineering in pre-college curricula. As a result, the number and scores of 8th graders taking the National Assessment of Educational Progress— Technology and Engineering Literacy (NAEP-TEL) have increased. Female students outscored male students in the 2018 NAEP-TEL exams (National Center for Education Statistics, 2022).

Despite performing well in middle school, girls' interest in science, technology, engineering, and/or mathematics (STEM), particularly engineering, drops off as they enter high school (Hand et al., 2017; Sadler et al., 2012). Interestingly, the gender gap between the average number of science credits earned by high school girls and boys closed in 2019 (National Center for Education Statistics, 2022); however, the numbers are a bit nuanced. A higher percentage of females than males (87% vs 83%) completed Algebra II, and only 16% of all students completed calculus. Females completed physics at a 37% rate in comparison to a 42% rate for males (National Center for Education Statistics, 2022). Female students took a smaller percentage of Physics Advanced Placement (AP) tests. Of the students taking Physics C – Electricity and Magnetism, only 23% were female, and only 28% of those who took Physics C – Mechanics were female (College Board, 2021). Enrolling in high school physics and mathematics courses, especially calculus, is a strong predictor of persistence in engineering (Adelman, 1998). These numbers suggest that much work remains to excite young women about engineering careers and support them as they navigate the educational system.

Studies suggest that schoolteachers can encourage young women toward engineering and buffer negative influences that dissuade women from pursuing engineering (Banerjee et al., 2018; Hand et al., 2017). Yet current STEM teacher professional learning (PL) minimally addresses gender stereotyping despite the continued growth of pre-college engineering education (Dalal et al., 2021; Huang et al., 2022). PL efforts tend to focus on curricular content and ignore the mediatory roles educators play as influencers of student perceptions about the field (Kuchynka et al., 2022). This leaves a major gap in the overall education and continued learning of schoolteachers. The oversight further perpetuates narratives of fixing the individual, in particular, women students interested in engineering, instead of examining the social norms that reinforce exclusionary practices (Mondisa et al., 2021; Secules et al., 2018).

Stereotypes, stereotype threats, and biases that contribute to social norms have been documented to influence young women's educational pathways negatively (Cheryan et al., 2015; Chung & Rimal, 2016). Stereotyping starts early in schooling, wherein engineering is often portrayed as a "male-oriented" career (Bond, 2016; Cheryan et al., 2015). Teachers are less likely to talk about engineering content and careers with girl students because of their stereotypical perceptions of the abilities of different genders (Martin et al., 2013; Powell et al., 2012). These discriminatory experiences and stereotypes about who can be an engineer negatively influence the development of engineering identities and dissuade young women from engineering (Marsden et al., 2016; McKenna et al., 2018). Teachers have the ability to counter such disparities with small changes to their practice (Thomas, 2017; Underwood & Mensah, 2018).

What are teacher perspectives on gender stereotyping? How do they understand their own roles in addressing gender inequity specific to engineering? How can the STEM PL practices change to cultivate equity orientation? The current study, using multiple focus groups, explored teacher perspectives to address these questions. Specifically, we provided mentorship for secondary school STEM teachers during an engineering PL program and explored their perspectives on gender stereotyping with an aim to inform STEM teacher PL efforts. The following research questions were explored:

1. How do secondary school teachers characterize engineering stereotypes, stereotype threats, and implicit biases?

2. How do secondary school teachers perceive their roles and responsibilities and intend to address stereotypes, stereotype threats, and implicit biases in their classrooms?

3. What challenges exist as perceived by secondary school teachers specific to engineering stereotypes, stereotype threats, and implicit biases that may be beyond the classroom setting?

In the following sections, we explain theoretical underpinnings, detail the methodology, and describe the results that address a gap in understanding teacher perspectives of gender stereotyping. Next, the results are discussed in the context of current social barriers. Finally, we provide recommendations to structure PL sessions from a culturally relevant framework to confront the exclusionary practices of girls/women in engineering education.

Literature review

In this section, we first explain the phenomena of stereotypes, stereotype threat, and implicit bias. Next, we review how teacher perspectives of gender stereotypes and biases impact young women. Finally, we examine the current status of STEM teacher PL efforts.

Stereotype, stereotype threat, and implicit bias

The terms stereotype, stereotype threat, and implicit bias have been defined in various contexts. Greenwald et al. (2002) define stereotype as "the association of a social group concept with one or more attribute concepts" (p. 5). In other words, a stereotype is a widely held belief about a particular category of people. Gender stereotypes perpetuate the notion that certain behaviors are gender-specific and, hence, binary (Sagebiel, 2018). Stereotypes lead to a quick, intuitive assessment of a group and could also cause distorted judgment, leading to discrimination or biased behavior (Bordalo et al., 2016). For example, engineering is perceived and frequently portrayed as a 'masculine' discipline with pictures of men wearing yellow construction hats. This leads to a ubiquitous negative stereotype about women in engineering (Chou & Chen, 2017). When girls encounter such negative stereotypes, they may be deterred from choosing engineering pathways.

A stereotype threat is the anxiety or concern that arises from the possibility that a negative stereotype might be true about oneself. Steele et al. (2002) define the negative impact of stereotyping as a stereotype threat:

> When a negative stereotype about a group that one is part of becomes personally relevant, usually as an interpretation of one's behavior or an experience one is having, stereotype threat is the resulting sense that one can be judged or treated in terms of the stereotype or that one might do something that would inadvertently confirm it. (p. 389).

Stereotype threat can fall into categories of both self-as-source, where the concern is about confirming stereotypes in your own mind, as well as others-as-source, where the concern is about confirming stereotypes of others or representing your group poorly (Steele, 2010).

Individuals who are more likely to be affected by stereotype threats are those who are strongly invested in the domain in which they are being evaluated or are strongly committed to their group identity (Lewis Jr. & Sekaquaptewa, 2016). A young woman who either identifies strongly with being a female or who strives to be an engineer is particularly susceptible to stereotype threat because of the stereotype that girls cannot *do engineering*.

Engineering education research focused on stereotype threat provides a compelling argument to reduce stereotype threats for women students (Bell et al., 2013; Male et al., 2018). Eschenbach et al. (2014) showed that when the Fundamentals of Engineering Exam (the exam that engineers typically take at the end of the undergraduate degree and as their first step towards becoming a professional engineer) was framed as a test that is diagnostic of ability, women did worse than men. When it was framed as a non-diagnostic or exploratory examination, women performed equally well as men. Stereotype threat has been shown to lead to anxiety, raised stress, poor decision-making, and underachievement, consequently impacting one's sense of belonging and career goals (Shapiro & Williams, 2012; Steele, 2010).

Researchers have also argued for a change in the culture within the engineering field to address gendered implicit biases (Farrell & Minerick, 2018; Nakamura, 2021). Implicit biases are pre-reflective attributions that occur automatically and unintentionally to affect an individual's judgment, decisions, and behavior (Greenwald et al., 2002). Implicit biases may be contrary to one's conscious or declared beliefs. The Implicit Associations Test (Greenwald et al., 2009) has shown that stereotypical associations create implicit bias even for people who consciously seek to avoid their use. Therefore, training STEM teachers to be aware of the possibility of implicit biases influencing their behavior is crucial (Dalal et al., 2021; Holroyd et al., 2017).

STEM teacher perspectives and impact on young women

Explicit and implicit biases, stereotypes, expectations, and attributions of teachers can have an impact on student pathways (Rice et al., 2013; Thomas, 2017). Specific to STEM, teachers may perpetuate the view that STEM fields are more masculine and underestimate the abilities of women. The underestimation of women in STEM is particularly true in mathematics and engineering (Bell et al., 2013; Copur-Gencturk et al., 2021). When teachers hold an implicit STEM-is-male stereotype and a bias against the capabilities of women in STEM, the motivational beliefs and educational decisions of young women are negatively impacted (Moss-Racusin et al., 2012; Thomas, 2017). This then leads to the field being continuously male-dominated, with few female role models to inspire, attract, and support future women in STEM (Hill et al., 2010).

Teachers may not be aware that they are perpetuating gender-STEM stereotypes as they judge or treat female students differently from their male peers (Eccles, 2011). Unknowingly, "teachers may, for instance, more frequently acknowledge males' engagement or performance with gestures of approval, give males slightly more time or more hints to find an answer, and call on males for particularly demanding tasks" (Thomas, 2017, p. 41). In a study conducted by Hand et al. (2017), both high school teachers and students exhibited gender biases by associating more masculine characteristics with scientists and by conforming with stereotyped beliefs that males perform at a higher level than females in STEM disciplines. Such ideologies are oftentimes maintained within the broader school system and behaviors by peers, counselors, and school administrators (Kuchynka et al., 2022; Roarty et al., 2021).

Gender stereotypes during the critical high school period, when students are developing their identity (Rice et al., 2013), can lead women students initially interested in STEM to lower their self-esteem and self-efficacy and turn to other fields (Hand et al., 2017; Thoman et al., 2013). Addressing gender inequity in STEM thus requires appropriate and adequate teacher PL and mentoring.

STEM teacher professional learning

The general intent of STEM PL or professional development (PD) is to improve STEM instruction through a process of guiding a particular group of people (Fore et al., 2015). The term PD is often associated with one-time workshops, seminars, or lectures. In contrast, PL is a sustained training, typically customized to teachers' needs and can subsume PD (Stewart, 2014). Research on STEM teacher PL spans a wide range varying from investigating how to address what appears to be a barrier in the implementation of an integrated

STEM approach in education (Du et al., 2018; Shernoff et al., 2017), to resolving how to build cultural and linguistic competency for STEM educators to best engage diverse student groups (Charity Hudley & Mallinson, 2017). Such diverse topics reinforce the complexity of STEM education on PL models to prepare STEM educators.

STEM educators are mediators of content knowledge as well as influencers of student perceptions about the field (Christian et al., 2021; Huang et al., 2022). A well-established body of research has focused on PD and PL interventions to reform content knowledge and pedagogical skills that foster teachers' own STEM career interests (Kouo et al., 2023; Yoon et al., 2018). Studies on STEM teacher PL, for example, exploring the design of programs (Charity Hudley & Mallinson, 2017) or examining the impact on teacher STEM practices and perceptions (Du et al., 2018), imply direct correlations in teacher training and effective STEM teaching strategies as well as more positive STEM perceptions. There exist other studies directed at understanding how teachers conceptualize the integration of engineering (Christian et al., 2021), examining teacher subjectivity as a critical factor influencing what they learn from PD sessions (Fore et al., 2015) and gathering insight into how teachers' conception of integrated STEM content changes over time (Yoon et al., 2013).

Specific to pre-college engineering education, very few primary and secondary teachers have engineering backgrounds, and engineering-specific teacher preparation programs are almost non-existent (Carberry et al., 2023; Dalal et al., 2022). PL is considered an essential mechanism that provides opportunities for teachers to acquire engineering content knowledge and build positive attitudes toward and confidence in teaching engineering (Hardré et al., 2018; Utley et al., 2019). Notably, PL has been defined as a catalyst for change in STEM education, however, when addressing inequities in the field, few programs focus on developing effective approaches for working with women students (Charity Hudley & Mallinson, 2017). As more attention is given to disrupting gender inequity, this study aims to better understand teacher perspectives of gender stereotyping in an engineering PL program context.

Conceptual framework: Diffusion of innovation (DoI)

Educators respond to PL in different ways, adopting changes at varied rates and requiring additional assistance to persist through challenges (Kouo et al., 2023). Rogers (2003) examined how people process change and adopt an innovation and proposed a theory of Diffusion of Innovation (DoI). The DoI theory has frequently been used in educational research (Mayled et al., 2019; Scott &

McGuire, 2017) to examine how people undergo social change. DoI suggests that the decision process that leads to the sustained use of any innovation or a change in practice occurs in five distinct stages (Fig. 2.1):

1. Knowledge and awareness — an individual is exposed to an idea or change suggestion.

2. Interest and persuasion — the individual's interest is piqued, leading to an active pursuit of information about innovation.

3. Evaluation and decision — the individual decides to adopt or reject the innovation based on information gleaned in the first two stages.

4. Implementation and trial — those who decide to adopt change and implement it in their practice. Some might try out small-scale implementations, others might overhaul their practices and do a large-scale implementation.

5. Confirmation or adoption — individual continues and sustains, affirming the use of the innovation or change in practice.

Figure 2.1. Stages of the DoI Theory

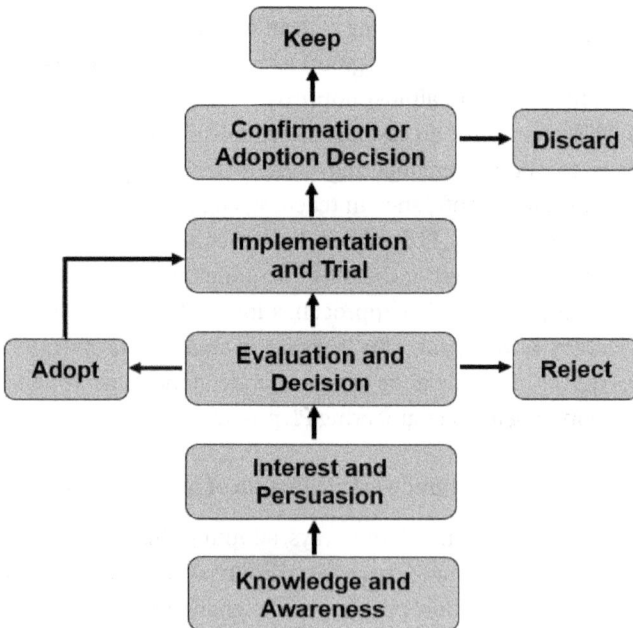

Note. Five-stage DoI Process for Sustained Use of Innovation, adapted from Mayled et al., 2019

The five stages must occur in that order because each successive stage builds off the prior. It is critical that potential adopters understand both how and why a change is suggested for them to effectively progress to the subsequent stages. Hence, the knowledge and awareness stage is the foundational building block. Appropriate mentoring, sustained PL, or a community of practice could help educators persist to the final stages of adoption (Kouo et al., 2023; Mayled et al., 2019). The DoI theory provided a lens to inform the research design and understand teachers' progress through the awareness-decision-implementation process.

Research design

A qualitative research design was used following a constructivist paradigm and thematic analysis methods. The constructivist paradigm values social context and subjectivism (Flick, 2014) and "seeks to understand a phenomenon under study from the experiences or angles of the participants..." (Adom et al., 2016, p. 5).

Context

This study is part of an ongoing nationwide effort, Engineering for US All (e4usa), that aims to make engineering education more inclusive. An introductory high school engineering course was developed to demystify and democratize engineering for students and teachers. e4usa welcomes teachers from all content backgrounds, STEM and non-STEM, to teach the course (Dalal et al., 2020). Such broadening expands the diversity of engineering teachers and encourages out-of-the-box thinking needed to "knock the walls down" on who can and cannot do engineering (Dalal et al., 2022, p.352). Enacting a broader and inclusive approach requires that teachers be supported as emerging engineering educators through appropriate PL. Accordingly, a year-long e4usa teacher PL is intentionally designed to impart curricular knowledge as well as information about stereotyping concerning engineering education.

Participants

Teachers were recruited in Spring 2019 nationwide through emails and bulletins. The open call invited all high school teachers, regardless of their STEM backgrounds and STEM teaching experience, to participate in the e4usa pilot program. The application requested an agreement from the teacher and the principal to offer the e4usa course at their school in the 2019-20 academic year.

Nine teachers teaching in public (n=8) and charter (n=1) high schools were selected in the first cohort. The nine teachers included three women and six men, three African American and six White, with teaching experience ranging from 5 to 26 years. Participating high schools were spread across the United States. All nine voluntarily agreed to take part in the current study, which was approved by the Institutional Review Board. Table 2.1 provides additional details. The geographical location (state) is intentionally not shared to protect privacy and confidentiality due to the small sample.

Table 2.1. Participant demographic information and background

Teacher Pseudonym	Gender identity	Race and ethnicity	Teaching experience (years)	Subjects taught	School Type
Ron	Man	White	23	Creative Music Arts and Sciences, Symphony Orchestra	Large city, public
Bob	Man	White	5	History	Large suburban, charter
Kim	Woman	White	13	Technology, Manufacturing	Remote rural, public
Mark	Man	White	20	Physics	Large suburban, public
Dylan	Man	White	23	Production Systems, Research Practicum	Large suburban, public
Audrey	Woman	African-American	24	Physics, Environmental Science, Chemistry	Large city, public
Chris	Man	African-American	14	Foundations of Technology, Robotics	Large suburban, public
Jeff	Man	White	24	Engineering Foundations	Large suburban, public
Sally	Woman	African-American	26	Engineering Design, Electronics, Robotics, Computer Science	Large city, public

Teacher professional learning (PL) program

The e4usa PL included: a) an in-person summer workshop, b) a follow-up online mentoring session in the fall, c) an in-person winter workshop, and d) online participation in the learning community throughout the year.

Summer workshop: The PL commenced in July 2019 with a five-day, in-person summer workshop at a large university in the northeast United States. Though the primary goal of the workshop was to provide curricular training, instilling an equity-lens for teaching engineering was equally important. Teachers were sent a copy of the book *Whistling Vivaldi - How stereotypes affect us and what we can do* (Steele, 2010) and asked to read the first three chapters. An hour-long PL session was conducted that covered the phenomena of imposter syndrome, stereotypes, biases and stereotype threats, how they promote gender disparity, and ways to promote a growth mindset (Dweck, 2015) for women students.

Fall mentoring session: In October, the founder of SciGirls Strategies: How to Engage Girls in STEM (Scigirlsconnect, 2019) conducted an online mentoring session. Teachers learned about culturally responsive education and discussed research-based strategies to create a more gender-equitable learning environment in their classrooms.

Winter workshop: A three-day, in-person workshop took place in December at a large partner university in the southwest United States. Teachers read the last three chapters of the *Whistling Vivaldi* before the workshop. In the last three chapters, the author provides practical strategies for reducing stereotype threats in the classroom and calls for educators to take the lead and use their power to diffuse these threats (Steele, 2010). A 90-minute-long session encouraged teachers to share their Fall classroom experiences and collectively agree upon strategies to address gender stereotyping in the next term.

Learning community: Throughout the year, teachers also engaged in the online learning community of peers and e4usa team members. The community was hosted on the Canvas learning management system. The project team posted weekly prompts in the discussion forum for teachers to reflect on their practices and share insights.

Data collection

Data were collected through three semi-structured focus groups. The first focus group took place for 90 minutes on the last day of the summer workshop. Seven teachers (except Bob and Mark) participated. Three prompts guided the discussion, with additional questions contingent on responses:

1. Share something that caught your attention from the first three chapters of the book *Whistling Vivaldi.*

2. How do you see stereotypes and stereotype threats as relevant to the efforts to advance engineering education in secondary schools?

3.   What have you observed regarding women students in engineering classrooms?

These questions would illuminate *knowledge and awareness,* the first phase of the DoI theory, to set the foundation and lead teachers toward the next phases.

The second focus group was conducted during the winter workshop for 90 minutes to examine how teachers perceive their own roles and intend to address gender-specific issues in engineering classrooms. All nine teachers participated, eight in-person and one online. The following questions guided the discussion:

1.   What identity threats might women students encounter in school environments that could prevent them from pursuing STEM education?

2.   What kind of messaging can teachers give to provide a positive experience for women students?

3.   What concrete ideas do you have to address the negative stereotypes and embed a sense of belonging in engineering classrooms for women students?

4.   Which of the interventions introduced in *Whistling Vivaldi* would make the most sense for you to implement?

Results would unravel teacher progression through the second (*interest and persuasion*) and the third (*evaluation and decision*) phases of the DoI model.

The third focus group was conducted online for 60 minutes at the end of the school year and was attended by all nine teachers. Teachers were asked to reflect and describe how their classroom practice had changed, if at all, considering gender stereotyping. Teachers were also asked how they would teach a session on biases and stereotypes to the next teacher-cohort. These prompts provided insights into teachers' actions to address gender stereotyping and their progression into the next two DoI phases (*implementation and trial, confirmation or adoption*).

Analysis

Transcribed focus groups were entered in Dedoose, an online tool used to facilitate qualitative analysis. Two members of the research team used a two-stage coding process, which involved structural coding followed by descriptive coding (Saldaña, 2016). Structural coding is a first-round coding method wherein a content-based code or conceptual phrase is applied to code data units in relation to the research questions (Namey et al., 2008). Saldaña (2016) states that "Structural coding both codes and initially categorizes the data corpus" and is particularly suitable for studies with "multiple participants, standardized or semi-structured data gathering protocols, hypothesis testing, or exploratory investigations" (p. 98). In the second stage, the similarly coded segments were further parsed for detailed descriptive coding. The second stage enabled researchers to understand nuances and create a set of categories. For example, teachers' descriptions of stereotypes were categorized as characterization of stereotypes. This was further parsed into descriptive codes, such as human nature, omnipresent, and a critical problem. Together, the codes and the category allowed for a more nuanced understanding of teacher perspectives, adopted solutions, and encountered challenges.

Several steps were taken to ensure robust qualitative research. A code book was developed to maintain consistent coding (Namey et al., 2008). The structural and descriptive codes were discussed by two members over bi-weekly meetings. Axial coding was used to consolidate codes into categories (Saldaña, 2016). The coding scheme was reviewed by another member and category definitions were revised where necessary. Categories were compared to identify various stages of the DoI model and the themes pertaining to the research questions. The research team often engaged in discussions about the data, interpretations, and emerging themes. Prolonged engagement and persistent observations over a year added to the trustworthiness (Lincoln & Guba, 1985). Last, member checking was done by sending teachers a draft of the manuscript to confirm data interpretations (Creswell, 2013).

Positionality

Our research team is composed of four university professors, all involved in STEM teacher PL efforts. The lead author identifies as a cisgender woman engineering education researcher of Asian descent who believes that the underrepresentation of women in engineering reflects problems with the systems and structure in the field. The second author identifies as an African American, cisgender woman, science/STEM educator with expertise in culturally relevant STEM teacher preparation and curriculum writing. The third author identifies as an Asian American, cisgender woman, and special education and engineering education researcher with a focus on inclusion in engineering education and teacher PL. The fourth author identifies as a White, cisgender woman biomedical engineer and engineering education researcher.

Findings

We describe our findings organized by research questions (Table 2.2). Attributed quotations are embedded with the focus group (FG) number in the narrative for contextual understanding.

Table 2.2. Summary of Findings

Category/Themes	Definition	Example codes	Illustrative quote
RQ 1: Characterizations of stereotypes, stereotype threat, and implicit biases			
Characterization of stereotypes	Understanding and descriptions of what stereotypes mean	Human nature; omnipresent; critical problem; taught by society	"I heard somebody saying something about how these things are inherently built into us and I agree with that."
Characterization of implicit biases	Understanding and descriptions of implicit biases	Ingrained; unintentional consciousness; difficult to change	"…how do we get away from it? It's just – it's so engrained, so baked in. It's like even if you tried to recognize, you still need it to some degree."
Characterization of stereotype threat	Understanding of what a stereotype threat is	Perceived threat; major impact; could come from own group	"…you don't understand that people may be afraid of those same things. It has a major impact."
Onus falling on the stereotyped	Recognition that marginalized populations have to fend for themselves	Need to whistle; finding whistling strategies; should not happen; shedding identity	"She felt very directly that stereotype that you know she's not going to be useful to the group…she told the story how she kind of pushed through, and it's kind of like with the whistling, you work that much harder for a while."
RQ 2: Understanding of roles, responsibilities, and intended actions			
Teacher role	Perceived teacher roles, duties, and potential actions to help mitigate stereotypes in engineering	Call out the elephant; educate about college environment; educate about stereotypes	"You know nothing changes if you don't make the step with it; and you take a small one. And if it doesn't work, you just take another one."
Women wrongly stereotyped	Teachers' observations of stereotypes against women	Noticeable participation; attention to detail; enjoy working with tools	"Three years ago, we tried to have an all-girls 10th grade engineering program…about 15 young ladies and they really enjoyed and developed confidence."

Intended actions and solutions	Suggestions for how educators can address issues related to gender stereotypes	Awareness; welcoming environment; empathy; collaborative work	"I'll have them do something like find me five engineers from five different cultures that invented something that we use today. Make sure at least two are women."

RQ 3: Implementation and on the ground challenges			
Implementation	Strategies used by the teachers in their engineering classrooms	Equity target; teamwork; ice breakers; identity building; growth mindset	"We had circles. I'll take some electrical tape out, different colors, whatever, and then, one, it'll say I'm either good at this or I'm not. I stick with what I know and my abilities or talent don't match an engineer. And then two weeks later, I'll have something else and see a little growth path. Just different activities like that, you know, just to see what they have fixed thinking thoughts on and how they've grown.
Barriers	Elements beyond classrooms that are perceived to contribute to the gender stereotypes in engineering.	Societal messages; access; guidance counselors; administrator influence	"I see issues regarding [the] influence of social media, and those kinds of stereotypes...I think that that's really what they get influenced by."
Identity cues	Framing of messages and cues that women students receive about their identity and the value of their identity	Role-models; social media; internal affirmation	"They don't identify with a lot of the figures that we might decide as adults, the things we think would motivate, don't. And then the things that probably would motivate them, we may not approve of."

Characterizations of engineering stereotypes, stereotype threats, and implicit biases

This section answers the first research question: How do secondary school teachers characterize engineering stereotypes, stereotype threats, and implicit biases? Four categories of characterization of stereotypes, characterization of stereotype threat, characterization of implicit bias, and onus falling on the stereotyped emerged that conveyed teachers' perspectives of gender stereotyping.

In just one focus group after one reading assignment, the teachers brought up issues affecting gender diversity in engineering with relative ease. There was a consensus that the problem was exacerbated in engineering because engineering is stereotyped as competitive and masculine. Kim stated, "It is definitely [an engineer's] stereotype that you have to be good in school, you have to have good grades in the math, science side of things" (FG1, 00:34:00). Everyone agreed that this kind of stereotyping particularly impacts girls, who are often stereotyped as 'girls do not like to build' or 'girls cannot do math' which then leads to girls not seeing themselves in the field of engineering. Teachers acknowledged that they often lower the bar for groups of students based on stereotypes or implicit biases; however, both stereotyping and implicit biases were attributed to human nature:

> I just felt like some of the things just can't be helped, you know, in other words, you were trying to correct something that's almost human nature. But I understand, trying to at least address some of the issues associated with the stereotype but as human beings that's the thing. Some of that is just human nature, you know, [...] not always correct, but we do stereotype. (Chris, FG1, 00:02:04)

Audrey said, "it is the physical conditioning built from all the life experiences," and others agreed that stereotypes and biases are taught by the society we live in.

While stereotypes were accepted as omnipresent, stereotype threat was a revelation for the teachers:

> What stood out to me in the first three chapters was the word threat. Everyone has a stereotype, someone for something, you know, in their life, but a perceived threat has a major impact. It is good people and the students that mean no harm. That harm happened to them. (Sally, FG1, 00:06:06)

Another revelation was the fact that the presence of stereotype threat was not understood or realized by the people on either the giving or the receiving end due to its unintentional nature and yet it influenced students' performance. This led the teachers to accept that stereotyping was a critical problem, and some, like Sally, questioned the fact that the onus of overcoming the stereotypes and stereotype threat falls on the people who are stereotyped:

Why should I always have to be the one to do the whistling to calm others, whether I wear a hoodie or a suit? But the onus goes on. It shouldn't be anyone's onus, but it seems like the onus falls on the people, people who are stereotyped [...] so what do we have to do in order to seem non-threatening? First is whistling, then what else? (Sally, FG1, 00:43:45)

Dylan remarked that women students "often work harder to prove capability and they shouldn't. That's the thing, they shouldn't have to." Others agreed that such 'whistling' should not be needed. There was a desire to learn more about biases and stereotype threats and what they could do "to make it so that all the students can learn and get the most out of the curriculum to be the best they can be" (Kim, FG1, 00:24:23). Such statements provided evidence of the *knowledge and awareness* per DoI and illustrated teacher willingness to transition toward the second phase of *interest and persuasion.*

Understanding of roles, responsibilities, and intended actions

This section answers the second research question: *How do secondary school teachers perceive their roles and responsibilities and intend to address stereotypes, stereotype threats, and implicit biases in their classrooms?* Categories of teacher roles, women wrongly stereotyped, and intended actions and solutions (Table 2.2) conveyed how teachers identified with their roles.

As focus groups progressed, Dylan pointed out that women are often wrongly stereotyped regarding their engineering interests and capabilities. A few others agreed and explained that girls also get excited to use tools and often produce superior results than boys. Chris stated:

My experience with females in the school is, it's very noticeable when they join the robotic team. I've been able to really see how much of an asset that you know female participation is and at every level, not just the mechanical, electrical, the marketing part of business, they do everything. (FG1, 00:47:07)

There was a consensus that teachers have a responsibility toward changing the prevalent stereotypes, as evident from Jeff's statement:

It is not that it is every day. But when you are presented with opportunities to kind of break those stereotypes or educate about those stereotypes, you sort of have that responsibility to do so. (Jeff, FG1, 00:31:12)

Teachers averred that girls might have more difficulty blending identities that are feminine and engineering-oriented because "They've been sort of like honed, they've been told they have to home in on a singular goal" (Dylan, FG1, 00:37:19). Discussion focused on helping women students recognize their internal drive and self-advocacy, such as finding or creating a support group. Jeff suggested that they, the teachers, could be the needed support because "[he] saw a statistic. It was something like 80% of the female engineers became engineers at the invitation of their teachers." (FG2, 00:08:04)

Mentoring young women for college was perceived as a teacher's responsibility. There was a consensus that "...college is going to be quite different; professors may not necessarily treat you as one of their own because that's not what they do" (Chris, FG2, 01:05:12). Support groups were deemed necessary for women to succeed in college as Sally said, "I would tell them to look for where the support groups are, and if there isn't one, create them" (FG2, 01:20:47). Such conversations provided evidence of the teacher's progression into the third phase (*evaluation and decision*) of the DoI.

Teachers observed that during team activities, women students often want to work in homogeneous groups. They debated that maybe high school was the right place for young women to experience teamwork in the real-world sense, wherein they don't get to pick teammates. Others seemed to agree that "the elephant [should be] called out early on" but a growth mindset should also be cultivated (Ron, FG2, 00:29:50). Overall, there was a consensus that the notion of competition in engineering is a very masculine idea and engineering classes could provide a unique opportunity to do things differently, because they are project-based. The group agreed to emphasize collaborative teamwork and problem-solving for the community in order to reduce stereotype threats for women students. Everyone agreed that the first few days of the term are crucial, and teachers could take simple steps such as, acknowledging anxiety, showing empathy, incorporating icebreakers, and team-building activities to make women students feel welcome. Reflecting on the Fall mentoring session, teachers also discussed various other actions they could take, such as engaging students in role-play activities, providing role-models and vicarious experiences, arranging buddy programs to invite women students to experience engineering classrooms, and overall creating a friendly, student-centered atmosphere.

Implementation and challenges

This section answers the third research question: What challenges exist as perceived by secondary school teachers specific to engineering stereotypes, stereotype threats, and implicit biases that may be beyond the classroom setting? Categories of implementation, barriers, and identity cues (Table 2.2) conveyed that despite implementing solutions in their classrooms, teachers struggled with the identity cues women students receive from society at large and identified multiple barriers within and outside the school systems.

Teachers' implemented solutions ranged from an acknowledgment of one's own implicit biases to the changed classroom practices. Examples included inviting women students to become peer tutors to build their confidence, arranging guest lectures with professional women engineers or school alumni, creating portfolio-based grading schemes rather than tests, and using the word *quiz* in place of *test* or *exam*. Mark enthusiastically shared his strategy and explained that such intentional approaches work well with all students, including women, first generation, and minorities:

> I started the class discussing an engineering innovation and letting students see how many different perspectives you can have on a problem [...] showing students how diversity could be a strength. I [was] very intentional in the first few days with my students, and I got a lot of feedback from them at the end of the semester that are like, I came in, not knowing if I want to be an engineer, but your first class really mellowed and made me feel like we're a team, and I'm part of the group, and I'm not going to be alone, and that was really – I really appreciated that. (FG2, 00:57:17)

Though most examples indicated small-scale implementations, moving to a portfolio-based grading was a major overhaul for Ron and Kim. The examples clearly suggested the adoption of the fourth stage *(implementation and trial)* of the DoI.

Teachers also felt they had limited influence because of often conflicting messages from within the school. The education system itself was recognized as inherently biased because it groups students into different categories for selection into certain STEM classes. Examples of school counselors sending the women students to non-STEM classes based on stereotypes were shared. Kim explained that many girls voluntarily join robotics clubs, but the number of girls in counselor-approved, elective STEM courses is always lower.

Another concern was the cues that students receive from other school sources that ultimately shape their identities, such as the quotes adorning hallways, pictures of alumni, images of engineering works and photos on classroom walls, and choices for guest lectures. Together, these send a message about what the school values, and teachers felt that they all could do a better job. A concern was expressed that many schools lack women leaders in science or technology departments.

Societal influence was identified as a prominent barrier, and Jeff expressed his dismay about "the messages that society sends to these young minds." He cited his daughter's example:

> One thing that kind of struck me as a father of a girl who you wanted to do all this wonderful stuff, you know, in engineering. My wife and I can both tell her as many times as we want, but there's a bigger society out there that she's part of. You want to buy a million LEGO sets or drop all those wonderful things you can, but at the same time, what is she receiving from society? (FG1, 00:40:37)

A concern was expressed that the use of non-digital devices used in engineering, such as carpentry tools, is decreasing among all students, and women students, in particular, do not have easy access to tools due to negative stereotypes. During the last focus group, teachers discussed ways to demonstrate to the next e4usa teacher cohort how access issues could influence students' mindsets. One strategy was to provide different materials to each team to show how access could affect their ability to build a tower. Another suggestion was to create restraining rules based on demographic factors (e.g., "If you have blue eyes, you cannot do x") to show how frustrating it could be. As Ron described, "…unless you experience it yourself, you won't realize how absurd some of these barriers are, that we as a society have put up" (FG3, 00:08:11).

Finally, teachers expressed frustration that students often enact self-fulfilling prophecies. There was a recognition that while we likely intend to disavow stereotypes, our implicit biases are reinforced through societal influences such as social media and can manifest themselves quietly and without warning. For example, when women students begin an assignment already thinking they won't be successful, they are less likely to succeed. Sounding frustrated, Audrey mentioned, "They have their own sense of stereotype, they come in with them from the experiences." Chris corroborated:

> Oftentimes it is the student who just doesn't identify with success at all, you know. And there's no – and it's not our fault. We can't change what's

been layered over early years of education and our student's life or whatever's going on at home. (FG2, 00:29:18)

Other social influences (e.g., family, friends, and media) seemed to limit what the teacher could alter, leading to feelings of diminished return among the participant group.

Discussion

Research shows that teachers play an important role in students' higher education choices and pathways (Hand et al., 2017; Martin et al., 2013). This finding has even larger implications for engineering education, which has persistently low enrollment of women students across the globe (Lucas et al., 2014; U.S. Census Bureau, 2021). Studies in engineering education tend to focus on the higher education context, examining women students' undergraduate engineering experiences or faculty perspectives (Bell et al., 2013; Farrell et al., 2018). Our study contributes to the perspectives of secondary school teachers who nurture younger students and have the agency to influence women students' higher education choices.

Findings revealed that teachers readily recognized long-standing issues affecting gender inequity in engineering. The issues have persisted through decades: societal, social, and peer influences serve to dissuade women from pursuing STEM fields (National Academy of Engineering, 2006; Thoman et al., 2013). Understanding that stereotypes exist is almost a certainty, but an appreciation that stereotypes can pose a legitimate threat was a significant realization for teachers. Many were struck by the term. Multiple studies have proved that beyond the concept of stereotypes, stereotype threats are directly applicable (Bell at al., 2013; Lewis Jr. and Sekaquaptewa, 2016), and the first step is to understand their effect and acknowledge that 'you shouldn't have to whistle' (Steele, 2010). Possibly, the greatest value of this work was the identification of the teachers themselves as advocates and agents of change. During the year, teachers implemented a few solutions to address gender stereotypes and biases in their classrooms. They also encountered multiple challenges beyond classrooms. Gender stereotypes and biases specific to engineering persist to this day in the education system at all levels—from personal biases to classroom practices, school cultures, and messages from society at large (Ross et al., 2023). Therefore, conversations and actions to enact change must continue with adequate support and training for teachers, including the intentional discussion of bias and stereotypes.

When we designed the year-long study informed by the DoI theory, our aim was to create the foundational building block of knowledge and awareness regarding gender stereotyping in engineering. Teachers acquired information and engaged in reflection. They recognized that their influence has inherent value and showed interest in further learning to adopt a change. Most PL programs are successful in assisting educators through the first two stages of the DoI to advance their understanding of the topic but falter during the third phase and beyond (Borrego et al., 2010; Mayled et al., 2019). In the case of our study, all teachers tried out small- or large-scale implementations, augmenting one or two parts of their practice and moving to the fourth phase of the DoI. Findings also revealed multiple challenges which could lead to some of them faltering in sustaining the innovative practices. The impact as it relates to the confirmation and sustained adoption remains to be examined.

The study has implications for the design of STEM teacher PL programs focusing on the grass roots solutions for gender equity at the classroom level. During the year-long PL, teachers completed *Whistling Vivaldi* readings, learned about SciGirls strategies, discussed adoption strategies, and built upon their pedagogies. Most importantly, we believe, they learned to think about gender stereotyping in connection with their instructional strategies. PL continues to be the most common and efficient means in STEM education to build content knowledge and introduce new pedagogical topics (Kouo et al., 2023; Huang et al., 2022). Arguably, perceptions of PL as highly influential in securing favorable outcomes add to the significance of having them — not only to build content knowledge but also to introduce interventions and foster pedagogy that addresses systemic gender issues in STEM education.

We proffer a few PL recommendations that embrace culturally "relevant tenets of academic" success, cultural competence, and critical consciousness (Ladson-Billings, 1995) for teachers to enact change toward mitigating gender stereotyping in STEM education. We take the culturally relevant lens because it creates a mindset that the role of a teacher as a learner is necessary to overcome gender disparities. When teachers operate in ignorance, they are equally at fault with those who are considered bystanders who witness the negative experiences of women students. Finding ways to reset engineering educational norms to be equitable takes intentionality. Teachers must (re)imagine their engagement with students as agents of change and establish an agenda within engineering education to examine and call out inequities as part of student learning. By explicitly enhancing teachers' awareness of gender-related stereotype issues in

STEM and discussing potential solutions to restructure classroom practices, the impact may be significant and far-reaching.

Recommendations: Enacting change in professional learning design

- Changing the culture of engineering education to be welcoming to women, requires designing PL to equip teachers to build authentic relationships with students to connect the engineering content to students' life experiences.

- PL can support teachers in designing assessments that acknowledge the individuals' learning styles and enable all students to experience academic success (Ladson-Billings, 1995).

- Enacting cultural competency in engineering education permits the learner, in general, to see their identity as an asset to the learning environment. PL can model instructional practices that do not marginalize non-white, male, identities as a form of knowledge production.

- Confronting stereotypes and biases requires reflexivity that examines the messages from society that shape individual impressions of self and others. Hence, PL should encourage the teachers' transformative thought processes to raise awareness of the physical and mental barriers that systematically exclude women in engineering education.

Limitations and future work

The study used a purposeful sample of secondary school teachers recruited as the first cohort of the e4usa program. Our intent was to gain deep insights through a year-long study into teacher perspectives of gender stereotyping specific to engineering education. Generalizability is a limitation of this qualitative inquiry (Flick, 2014). Considering that research on the topic of teacher PL with respect to gender inequity in engineering is narrow, this study makes a useful contribution. It should be noted that another participant group having different backgrounds or school settings could yield different results. Moreover, we did not measure the inter-teacher variability of the teacher biases to establish a baseline. Results are also contingent on the extent to which teachers were able to verbalize their own thoughts and actions.

The e4usa team continues to work with teachers. A subset of the nine participant teachers has been involved in mentoring nearly 60 teachers in the last three years. Insights continue to inform modifications to the PL to ensure all teachers feel empowered to adopt more impactful teaching practices to address the systematic exclusion of minoritized groups in STEM education. A similar PL session with school counselors was conducted in 2020-21. An effort was made to engage teachers and counselors in meaningful dialogs to take the conversations beyond the classrooms for a positive change. Similar studies with schoolteachers in other settings would provide evidence on a larger scale. e4usa future research includes classroom observations and case studies that could uncover nuances of inclusive engineering classrooms. Another area for future exploration is school administrators' perspectives on gender equity.

Closing thoughts

Engineering education, like science, math, and technology, reports on the disparities in the field to increase and retain the participation of women and girls. Prevalent stereotypes and biases hamper the participation of women in engineering. We are hopeful that the current study will contribute positively toward the motivation and design of STEM teacher PL programs emphasizing inclusive teaching practices with content expertise. The paucity of women in engineering will remain a problem until efforts are targeted at the preK-12 level and teachers are given opportunities to learn what it means to promote academic success that is inclusive and rigorous for all students.

Acknowledgments

This material is based upon work primarily supported by the National Science Foundation (NSF) under NSF Award Number EEC-1849430. Any opinions, findings, conclusions, or recommendations expressed in this material are those of the author(s) and do not necessarily reflect those of the NSF. The authors acknowledge the support of the entire project team.

References

Adelman, C. (1998). *Women and men of the engineering path: A model for analyses of undergraduate careers.* U.S. Department of Education.

Banerjee, M., Schenke, K., Lam, A., & Eccles, J. S. (2018). The roles of teachers, classroom experiences, and finding balance: A qualitative perspective on the experiences and expectations of females within STEM and non-STEM careers. *International Journal of Gender, Science and Technology, 10.*

Bell, A. E., Spencer, S. J., Iserman, E., & Logel, C. E. R. (2013). Stereotype threat and women's performance in engineering. *Journal of Engineering Education, 92*(4), 307-312. https://doi.org/10.1002/j.2168-9830.2003.tb00774.x

Bond, B. J. (2016). Fairy godmothers > robots: The influence of televised gender stereotypes and counter-stereotypes on girls' perceptions of STEM. *Bulletin* of *Science, Technology and Society, 36*(2), 91–97. https://doi.org/10.1177/0270 467616655951

Bordalo, P., Coffman, K., Gennaioli, N., & Shleifer, A. (2016). Stereotypes. *The Quarterly Journal of Economics, 131*(4), 1753-1794. https://doi.org/10.1093/q je/qjw029

Borrego, M., Froyd, J. E., & Hall, T. S. (2010). Diffusion of engineering education innovations: A survey of awareness and adoption rates in US engineering departments. *Journal of Engineering Education, 99*(3), 185-207. http://dx.doi. org/10.1002/j.2168-9830.2010.tb01056.x

Carberry, A. R., Klein-Gardner, S. S., Lottero-Perdue, P. S., & Shirey, K. L. (2023). Pre-college engineering education teacher preparation. In A. Johri (Ed.), *International handbook of engineering education research* (pp. 241-262). Routledge.

Charity Hudley, A. H., & Mallinson, C. (2017). "It's worth our time": A model of culturally and linguistically supportive professional development for K-12 STEM educators. *Cultural Studies of Science Education, 12*, 637-660. https:// doi.org/10.1007/s11422-016-9743-7

Cheryan, S., Master, A., & Meltzoff, A. N. (2015). Cultural stereotypes as gatekeepers: Increasing girls' interest in computer science and engineering by diversifying stereotypes. *Frontiers in Psychology, 6*(49), 1–8. https://doi.org /10.3389/fpsyg.2015.00049

Chou, P., & Chen, W. F. (2017). Elementary school students' conceptions of engineers: A drawing analysis study in Taiwan. *International Journal of Engineering Education, 33*(1), 476-488. https://www.ijee.ie/latestissues/Vol33 -1B/19_ijee3388ns.pdf

Christian, K. B., Kelly, A. M., & Bugallo, M. F. (2021). NGSS-based teacher professional development to implement engineering practices in STEM instruction. International *Journal of STEM Education, 8*, 1-18. https://doi.org /10.1186/s40594-021-00284-1

Chung, A., & Rimal, R. N. (2016). Social norms: a review. *Review of Communication Research, 4*, 1-28. https://doi.org/10.12840/issn.2255-4165. 2016.04.01.008

College Board (2021). *AP Summary Report.* https://securemedia.collegeboard. org/digitalServices/pdf/research/2021/2021-ap-program-summary-report.pdf

Copur-Gencturk, Y., Thacker, I., & Quinn, D. (2021). K-8 teachers' overall and gender-specific beliefs about mathematical aptitude. *International Journal of Science & Mathematics Education, 19*(6), 1251–1269. https://doi.org/10.1007/ s10763-020-10104-7

Creswell, J. (2013). *Qualitative inquiry and research design: Choosing among five approaches* (3rd edition). Sage.

Dalal, M., Carberry, A. R., & Maxwell, R. (2022). Broadening the pool of pre-college engineering teachers: The path experienced by a music teacher. *IEEE Transactions on Education, 65*(3), 344-355. https://doi.org/10.1109/TE.2022. 3141984

Dalal, M., Carberry, A.R., Warmington, D., & Maxwell, R. (2020). Work-in-progress: A case study exploring transfer of pedagogical philosophy from music to engineering. *Proceedings of 2020 IEEE Frontiers in Education Conference (FIE)*, 1-4. https://doi.org/10.1109/FIE44824.2020.9274128

Dalal, M., Klein-Gardner, S., Kouo, J., Reid, K., Beauchamp, C., O'Neal, B., Lopez-Roshwalb, J., & Pines, D. (2021). Stereotypes and implicit biases in engineering: Will students need to "Whistle Vivaldi"? *Proceedings of the Collaborative Network for Engineering and Computing Diversity (CoNECD) Conference*. https://peer.asee.org/36122

Du, W., Liu, D., Johnson, C. C., Sondergeld, T. A., Bolshakova, V. L., & Moore, T. J. (2018). The impact of integrated STEM professional development on teacher quality. *School Science and Mathematics, 119*(2), 105-114. https://doi.org/10.1111/ssm.12318

Dweck, C. (2015). Carol Dweck revisits the growth mindset. *Education Week, 35*(5), 20-24. https://www.studentachievement.org/wp-content/uploads/Carol-Dweck-Revisits-the-Growth-Mindset.pdf

Eccles J. (2011). Gendered educational and occupational choices: Applying the Eccles et al. model of achievement-related choices. *International Journal of Behavioral Development, 35*(3), 195–201. https://doi.org/10.1177/0165025411398185

Eschenbach, E. A., Virnoche, M., Cashman, E. M., Lord, S. M., & Camacho, M. M. (2014). Proven practices that can reduce stereotype threat in engineering education: A literature review. *Proceedings of the 2014 IEEE Frontiers in Education Conference (FIE)*, 1-9. https://doi.org/10.1109/FIE.2014.7044011

Farrell, S., & Minerick, A. (2018). Perspective: The stealth of implicit bias in chemical engineering education, its threat to diversity, and what professors can do to promote an inclusive future. *Chemical Engineering Education 52*(2), 129-135. https://journals.flvc.org/cee/article/view/105861

Flick, U. (2014). *An introduction to qualitative research* (5th edition). Sage.

Fore, G. A., Feldhaus, C. R., Sorge, B. H., Agarwal, M., & Varahramyan, K. (2015). Learning at the nano-level: Accounting for complexity in the internalization of secondary STEM teacher professional development. *Teaching and Teacher Education, 51*, 101-112. https://doi.org/10.1016/j.tate.2015.06.008

Greenwald, A. G., Banaji, M. R., Rudman, L. A., Farnham, S. D., Nosek, B. A., & Mellott, D. S. (2002). A unified theory of implicit attitudes, stereotypes, self-esteem, and self-concept. *Psychological Review, 109*(1), 3. https://psycnet.apa.org/doi/10.1037/0033-295X.109.1.3

Greenwald, A. G., Poehlman, T. A., Uhlmann, E. L., & Banaji, M. R. (2009). Understanding and using the Implicit Association Test: III. Meta-analysis of predictive validity. *Journal of Personality and Social Psychology, 97*(1), 17-41. https://psycnet.apa.org/doi/10.1037/a0015575

Hand, S., Rice, L., & Greenlee, E. (2017). Exploring teachers' and students' gender role bias and students' confidence in STEM fields. *Social Psychology of Education, 20*(4), 929–945. https://doi.org/10.1007/s11218-017-9408-8

Hardré, P. L., Ling, C., Shehab, R. L., Nanny, M. A., Refai, H., Nollert, M. U., Ramseyer, C., Wollega, E. D., Huang, S.-M., & Herron, J. (2018). Teachers learning to prepare future engineers: A systemic analysis through five components of development and transfer. *Teacher Education Quarterly, 45*(2), 61–88. https://files.eric.ed.gov/fulltext/EJ1175526.pdf

Hill, C., Corbett, C., & St. Rose, A. (2010). *Why so few? Women in science, technology, engineering, and mathematics.* American Association of University Women. https://www.aauw.org/app/uploads/2020/03/why-so-few-research. pdf

Holroyd, J., Scaife, R., & Stafford, T. (2017). Responsibility for implicit bias. *Philosophy Compass, 12*(3), e12410. https://doi.org/10.1111/phc3.12410

Huang, B., Jong, M. S. Y., Tu, Y. F., Hwang, G. J., Chai, C. S., & Jiang, M. Y. C. (2022). Trends and exemplary practices of STEM teacher professional development programs in K-12 contexts: A systematic review of empirical studies. *Computers & Education*, 104577. https://doi.org/10.1016/j.compedu.2022.10 4577

Katehi, L., Pearson, G., & Feder, M. (2009). *Engineering in K-12 education: Understanding the status and improving the prospects.* Committee on K-12 Engineering Education. National Academy of Engineering and National Research Council, The National Academies Press. https://nap.nationalacademies.org/ catalog/12635/engineering-in-k-12-education-understanding-the-status-and-improving

Kouo, J. L., Dalal, M., Lee, E., Berhane, B., Emiola-Owolabi, O. V., Beauchamp, C., Ladeji-Osias, J. K., Reid, K., Klein-Gardner, S. S., & Carberry, A. R. (2023). Understanding the impact of professional development for a cohort of teachers with varying prior teaching and engineering experience. *Journal of Pre-College Engineering Education Research. 13*(1), 37-54. https://doi.org/10. 7771/2157-9288.1317

Kuchynka, S. L., Eaton, A., & Rivera, L.M. (2022), Understanding and addressing gender-based inequities in STEM: Research synthesis and recommendations for U.S. K-12 education. *Social Issues and Policy Review, 16*: 252-288. https:// doi.org/10.1111/sipr.12087

Ladson-Billings, G. (1995). Toward a theory of culturally relevant pedagogy. American *Educational Research Journal, 32*(3), 465-491. https://doi.org/10.2 307/1163320

Lewis Jr, N. A., & Sekaquaptewa, D. (2016). Beyond test performance: A broader view of stereotype threat. *Current Opinion in Psychology, 11*, 40-43. https:// doi.org/10.1016/j.copsyc.2016.05.002

Lincoln, Y. S., & Guba, E. G. (1985). *Naturalistic inquiry.* Sage Publications.

Lucas, B., Claxton, G., & Hanson, J. (2014). *Thinking like an engineer: implications for the education system.* Royal Academy of Engineers. https://www.raeng.org.uk /thinkinglikeanengineer

Male, S. A., Gardner, A., Figueroa, E., & Bennett, D. (2018). Investigation of students' experiences of gendered cultures in engineering workplaces.

European Journal for Engineering Education, 43(3), 360-377. https://doi.org/10.1080/03043797.2017.1397604

Marsden, N., Haag, M., Ebrecht, L., & Drescher, F. (2016). Diversity-related differences in students' perceptions of an industrial engineering program. The International Journal of *Engineering Education, 32*(1), 230-245. https://www.ijee.ie/latestissues/Vol32-1A/20_ijee3135ns.pdf

Martin, J. P., Simmons, D. R., & Yu, S. L. (2013). The role of social capital in the experiences of Hispanic women engineering majors. *Journal of Engineering Education, 102*(2), 227-243. https://doi.org/10.1002/jee.20010

Mayled, L. H., Ross, L., Collofello, J., Krause, S. J., Hjelmstad, K. D., Sebold, B. J., & Hoyt, S. (2019, June). Coaching and feedback in a faculty professional development program that integrates the entrepreneurial mindset and pedagogical best practices into capstone design courses. *Proceedings of the 2019 ASEE Annual Conference & Exposition.* https://doi.org/10.18260/1-2--32513

McKenna, A. F., Dalal, M., Anderson, I., & Ta, T. (2018). Insights on diversity and inclusion from reflective experiences of distinct pathways to and through engineering education. *Proceedings of the 1st annual CoNECD - The Collaborative Network for Engineering and Computing Diversity Conference.* https://peer.asee.org/29548

Mondisa, J. L., Packard, B. W. L., & Montgomery, B. L. (2021). Understanding what STEM mentoring ecosystems need to thrive: A STEM-ME framework. *Mentoring & Tutoring: Partnership in Learning, 29*(1), 110-135. https://doi.org/10.1080/13611267.2021.1899588

Moss-Racusin, C. A., Dovido, J. F., Brescoll, V. L., Graham, M. J., & Handlesman, J. (2012). Science faculty's subtle gender biases favor male students. *Proceedings of the National Academy of Sciences, 109*(41), 16474–16479. https://doi.org/10.1073/pnas.1211286109

Nakamura, A. (2021). Fostering diversity and inclusion and understanding implicit bias in undergraduate chemical education. *Journal of Chemical Education, 99*(1), 331-337. https://doi.org/10.1021/acs.jchemed.1c00422

Namey, E., Guest, G., Thairu, L., & Johnson, L. (2008). Data reduction techniques for large qualitative data sets. In G. Guest & K. MacQueen (Eds.), *Handbook for team-based qualitative research* (pp. 137-161). AltaMira Press.

National Academy of Engineering (2006). *To Recruit and advance: Women students and faculty in U.S. science and engineering.* Committee on the Guide to Recruiting and Advancing Women Scientists and Engineers in Academia, Committee on Women in Science and Engineering. The National Academies Press. https://nap.nationalacademies.org/catalog/11624/to-recruit-and-advance-women-students-and-faculty-in-science

National Center for Education Statistics. (2022). *High school mathematics and science course completion.* U.S. Department of Education, Institute of Education Sciences. https://nces.ed.gov/programs/coe/indicator/sod

Powell, A., Dainty, A., & Bagilhole, B. (2012). Gender stereotypes among women engineering and technology students in the UK: Lessons from career choice narratives. *European Journal of Engineering Education, 37*(6), 541-556.

Rice, L., Barth, J. M., Guadagno, R. E., Smith, G. P. A., & McCallum, D. M. (2013). The role of social support in student's perceived abilities and attitudes toward math and science. *Journal of Youth and Adolescence, 42*(7), 1028–1040. https://doi.org/10.1007/s10964-012-9801-8

Roarty, J., Dalal, M., Ross, L., & Carberry, A. (2021). Examining the influence of a professional development program on high school counselors' practices regarding engineering. *In Proceedings of 2021 IEEE Frontiers in Education Conference (FIE)*, 1-5. https://doi.org/10.1109/FIE49875.2021.9637308

Rogers, E. M. (2003). *Diffusion of innovations* (5th edition). Free Press.

Ross, L., Dalal, M., & Carberry, A. (2023). Expanding access to STEM pathways: Professional learning for high school counselors. *School Science and Mathematics, 123*(3), 102-113. https://doi.org/10.1111/ssm.12576

Sadler, P. M., Sonnert, G., Hazari, Z., & Tai, R. (2012). Stability and volatility of STEM career interest in high school: A gender study. *Science Education, 96*(3), 411-427. https://doi.org/10.1002/sce.21007

Sagebiel, F. (2018). Gender and network awareness in/for successful leadership in academic science and engineering. *International Journal of Gender, Science and Technology, 10*(1), 24-51. https://genderandset.open.ac.uk/index.php/gender andset/article/view/519

Saldaña, J. (2016). The coding manual for qualitative researchers (3rd edition). Sage.

Scigirlsconnect (2019). SciGirls Strategies: How to engage girls in STEM. Retrieved from http://www.scigirlsconnect.org/wp-content/uploads/2019/06/SciGirls-Strategies-Guide.pdf

Scott, S., & McGuire, J. (2017). Using diffusion of innovation theory to promote university designed college instruction. *International Journal of Teaching and Learning in Higher Education, 29*(1), 119-128. https://www.isetl.org/ijtlhe/pdf/IJTLHE2457.pdf

Secules, S., Gupta, A., Elby, A., & Tanu, E. (2018). Supporting the narrative agency of a marginalized engineering student. *Journal of Engineering Education, 107*(2), 186-218. https://doi.org/10.1002/jee.20201

Shapiro, J. R., & Williams, A. M. (2012). The role of stereotype threats in undermining girls' and women's performance and interest in STEM fields. *Sex Roles, 66*, 175-183. https:doi.org/10.1007/s11199-011-0051-0

Shernoff, D. J., Sinha, S., Bressler, D. M., & Ginsburg, L. (2017). Assessing teacher education and professional development needs for the implementation of integrated approaches to STEM education. *International Journal of STEM Education, 4*(13), 1-16. https://doi.org/10.1186/s40594-017-0068-1

Steele, C.M. (2010). Whistling Vivaldi: and other clues to how stereotypes affect us. W.W. Norton & Company, Inc.

Steele, C.M., Spencer, S.J., & Aronson J. (2002). Contending with group image: The psychology of stereotype and social identity threat. In *Advances in Experimental Social Psychology, 34*, 379–440. https://doi.org/10.1016/S0065-2601(02)80009-0

Stewart, C. (2014). Transforming professional development to professional learning. *Journal of Adult Education, 43*(1), 28-33. https://files.eric.ed.gov/fulltext/EJ1047338.pdf

Thoman D. B., Smith J. L., Brown E. R., Chase J., Lee J. Y. K. (2013). Beyond performance: A motivational experiences model of stereotype threat. *Educational Psychology Review, 25*(2), 211–243. https://doi.org/10.1007/s10 648-013-9219-1

Thomas, A. E. (2017). Gender differences in students' physical science motivation: Are teachers' implicit cognitions another piece of the puzzle? *The American Educational Research Journal, 54*(1), 35–58. https://doi.org/10.310 2/0002831216682223

Underwood, J. B., & Mensah, F. M. (2018). An investigation of science teacher educators' perceptions of culturally relevant pedagogy. *Journal of Science Teacher Education, 29*(1), 46-64. https://doi.org/10.1080/1046560X.2017.142 3457

U.S. Census Bureau (2021). *American community survey: Industry and occupation changes.* Retrieved from https://www.census.gov/programs-surveys/acs/technical -documentation/user-notes/2019

Utley, J., Ivey, T., Hammack, R., & High, K. (2019). Enhancing engineering education in the elementary school. *School Science & Mathematics, 119*(4), 203–212. https://doi.org/10.1111/ssm.12332

World Economic Forum. (2020). *Global gender gap report 2020* http://reports. weforum.org/global-gender-gap-report-2020/dataexplorer

Yoon, S. Y., Diefes-Dux, H., & Strobel, J. (2013). First-year effects of an engineering professional development program on elementary teachers. *American Journal of Engineering Education (AJEE), 4*(1), 67–84. https://doi.org/10.19030/ajee.v4i 1.7859

Yoon, S. Y., Kong, Y., Diefes-Dux, H. A., & Strobel, J. (2018). Broadening K-8 teachers' perspectives on professional development in engineering integration in the United States. *International Journal of Research in Education and Science, 4*(2), 331–348. https://doi.org/ 10.21890/ijres.409263

SECTION.
Mentoring Young Women in STEM

This section has four chapters, three on K-12 programs and one for undergraduate students. Chapter 3 brings new perspectives from a program in South Africa; Chapter 4 shares longitudinal research on a mentoring program in the southern United States with K-12 students, while the program's impacts on undergraduate women in STEM is covered in Chapter 6. Chapter 5 describes longitudinal research through a lens of young Black women in STEM.

K-12 research section

Chapter 3: Mentorship and support for young South African women advancement in mathematical-related careers

- Zingiswa Jojo

Chapter 4: Mentoring K-12 students in STEM education

- Dr. Phyllis Okwan, Dr. Joe Omojola, and Dr. Murty Kambhampati

Chapter 5: "What we really need": How the women in natural sciences (WINS) program supports culturally sustaining mentorship and STEM career opportunities for women of color

- Jacqueline Genovesi, Ayana Allen-Handy, Kimberly Sterin, Kimberly Godfrey, Dominique

Undergraduate programs research section

Chapter 6: Impact of effective mentoring on stem minority and women undergraduates

- Murty S. Kambhampati, Joe Omojola, and Phyllis Okwan

Chapter 3

Mentorship and Support for Young South African Women Advancement in Mathematical-Related Careers

Zingiswa Jojo

Rhodes University, Eastern Cape, South Africa

Abstract: Globally, women have been historically underrepresented in the Science, Technology, Engineering, and Mathematics (STEM) professions. Consequently, the underrepresentation of women in STEM is substantial in South Africa, and it translates into a loss of a critical mass of talent, thoughts, and ideas, which hinders the country from reaching its maximum development potential. This chapter chronicles initiatives on mentorship in which the role of Mathematics Education in empowering young South African Women and girls to advance to mathematical-related careers has been explored. Women's empowerment can be viewed as a continuum of several interrelated and mutually reinforcing components. The present chapter shares the experiences of initiatives taken towards developing skills among girls through STEM women role models and intellectual traditions of Mathematics. First, stereotypes on gender issues in following STEM careers are discussed and challenged. This is followed by suggestions on self-confidence boosters, perseverance activators that enable women in STEM to continue trying, refining strategies, solving problems, posing explanations, and moving to the next challenges.

How role modeling by women in STEM-related careers encourages mentees to pursue mathematics and be empowered is discussed. The program-related mentoring outcomes of STEM activities conducted with mentees and mentors in schools are presented. Consequently, how mentors became trusted confidantes who share wisdom, support, and knowledge over an extended period in the role of mathematics education in empowering women helps female mentees to understand the relevance of STEM subjects to their own personal and professional pursuits. To debunk the myth that mathematics is a difficult subject, and that STEM careers are only meant for men, the intervention methods followed were geared towards making sure that the mentees find it easy to solve mathematics problems in a relaxed and conducive environment in the program. Finally, the chapter proposes a mentorship program that ensures that mathematics in schools is popularized for the mentees such that girls have confidence, vision, and focus on following STEM-related fields.

Keywords: Mentorship, women, mathematics, girls, STEM fields, role models

***

Mentorship and support for young South African women advancement in mathematical-related careers

Mae Jemison, the first African American woman astronaut in space, warns, "Don't let anyone rob you of your imagination, your creativity, or your curiosity. It's your place in the world; it's your life. Go on and do all you can with it and make it the life you want to live." (Lynch, 2015, para. 1). This is a woman who followed her childhood dreams and grew to become an accomplished woman as a chemical engineer, scientist, physician, and astronaut while having made her mark in the history books as the first African American woman to travel into space. This is an excellent indication that, ideally, this is a world in which every woman and girl can create the kind of life she wishes to lead, unconstrained by harmful norms and gender stereotypes.

In South Africa, Chauke (2022) complains that despite the government's call for students to pursue science, technology, engineering, and mathematics in the era of the Fourth Industrial Revolution (4IR), the gender gap in Science, Technology, Engineering, and Mathematics (STEM) education is still of significant concern in the country. Consequently, the underrepresentation of women is substantial in South Africa in STEM and translates into a loss of a critical mass of talent, thoughts, and ideas, which hinders the country from reaching its maximum development potential. This is also observed globally where women have been historically underrepresented in the STEM professions. This chapter chronicles initiatives on mentorship in which the role of Mathematics Education in empowering young South African women and girls to advance to mathematical-related careers has been explored. The department of education (2012) defines mathematics as a language that makes use of symbols and notations to describe numerical, geometric and graphical relationships. Osei-Tutu and Ampadu (2017) define empowerment as the gaining of power in particular domains of activity by individuals or groups and the processes of giving power to them or processes that foster and facilitate their taking of power. Women's empowerment can be viewed as a continuum of several interrelated and mutually reinforcing components. Those components could involve activities shared by prominent women mentors in STEM fields with girls as mentees. Osei-Tutu and Ampadu (2017) further put emphasis on empowerment through the role of mathematics in the life of an individual learner and its impact on their school and wider social life, both in the present and in the future. In addition, **Gurjar (2018) suggests that empowering women would enhance their self-esteem, confidence, and help them to realize their potential and develop their collective bargaining power.** Osei-Tutu and Ampadu (2017) distinguished between (i) mathematical empowerment, which concerns the gaining of power over the language, skills and practices of using and applying mathematics, (ii) social empowerment through mathematics, which concerns the ability to use mathematics to better one's life chances in study and work and to participate more fully in society through critical mathematical citizenship, and (iii) epistemological empowerment that concerns the individual's growth of confidence not only in using mathematics but also a personal sense of power over the creation and validation of knowledge. All those kinds of empowerment are crucial for the total support needed by young women to gain confidence and follow STEM-related careers.

In South Africa, the Curriculum Assessment Policy Statement (CAPS) defines mathematics as a human activity that involves observing, representing, and investigating patterns and quantitative relationships in physical and social phenomena and between mathematical objects themselves. It helps to develop mental processes that enhance logical and critical thinking, accuracy and problem-solving that will contribute to decision-making (Department of Education (DBE), 2012, p. 13). Consequently, the South African education policy prescribes that all learners must enroll in mathematics or mathematical literacy because the subject **determines the success of schools and governments, and it is also used as a yardstick to indicate the state of a nation.** However, Rühle (2022), in her paper on Mind the gap – an analysis of gender differences in mathematics and science achievement in South Africa, recalls U.S. senator Kirsten Gillibrand's words, who said: **"My hope is that in the future, women stop referring to themselves as 'the only woman' in their physics lab or only one of two in their computer science jobs. "**

I submit in this chapter that the author's wish can come into existence when young South African women enjoy mentorship and support to advance to careers in mathematical-related careers. To remain globally competitive, all South African citizens have a right to learn. Precisely, Spaull and Makaluza (2019) acknowledge that although South African women are better educated than South African men, they remain underrepresented in the labor market, particularly in higher-skilled occupations. Those include STEM-related careers and fields. In South Africa, women constitute more than half of the population, yet there is an under-representation of the female gender in science, technology, engineering, and mathematics (STEM) fields. This scenario needs to be reversed such that women are empowered to bring about their upliftment in social, economic, and political spheres where they can play roles at par with men in society. Researchers (Khatum, 2023; Madusise, 2018; Gradín, 2021) note that there is a dearth of studies globally, in Africa and locally that offer an account of gender equality and women empowerment in STEM. What is lacking is how young women can be mentored and supported to venture into STEM-related careers in higher education. The main purpose of this chapter is to offer insight into how mentorship and support of young women can help them advance to mathematical-related fields. The study was guided by the question: How can young women be supported to venture into mathematical-related fields?

In relation to this question, the UNESCO Institute of Statistics asserts that in higher education, women represent just over 35 percent of graduates in STEM-related fields. Moreover, Cham, Sok, and Hay (2021) recall that before she followed her career as an environmental analyst, she was told not to major in STEM-related fields because it was a difficult path for women. She also believes that there are many women and girls out there who were told the exact same thing because of gender stereotypes in career development but hopes that her experience can inspire and encourage more women and girls to take part in the science world (Cham, et, al., 2021). I am therefore convinced that sharing mentorship and support will play a bigger role in empowerment and increasing the number of young women who venture into STEM-related fields. In the next section, I highlight the sources of gender gaps in mathematics achievement as this determines entry affordance to STEM fields.

Gender gaps in mathematics achievement in schools.

In South Africa, the National Developmental Plan has set a goal that, by 2030, women and Black Africans should make up more than 50% of research and training staff. However, the path toward a PhD in mathematical sciences and beyond remains challenging, and many young women get lost along the way. In academia, the dropout of women is attributed to socio-cultural and institutional factors. Mathekga et al. (2022) reveal that South African women have a ten-percentage point lower labor force participation rate compared to their counterparts and are still more likely to be unemployed or participate in unpaid work. This, Sheperd (2017) associates with women's underrepresentation in management and leadership positions in several occupations and, especially in STEM fields which tend to be better paid. Ironically, studies reflect comparatively better performance in mathematics and science for girls than boys in school education, although this does not lead to a female advantage in the labor market and underrepresentation of women in STEM fields.

Some studies (Abiam & Odok, 2006; Mahlomaholo & Sematle, 2005; Opolot-Okurut, 2005; Zhu, 2007) have been carried out to understand the sources of gender gaps in mathematics achievement (Else-Quest et al., 2010). For example, Meinck and Brese (2019) asserted that international boys often report having more positive attitudes towards mathematics and science despite having similar mathematics and science achievements. Moreover, the PISA study reveals that there is a pro-boy gap in 32 countries and a pro-girl gap in 14 countries (OECD, 2019). This clearly indicates that the gender gaps in mathematics performance and achievement do not favor girls.

Factors that influence gender differences in mathematics achievement

Asante (2010) asserts that gender differences in mathematics achievement and ability have remained a source of concern as scientists seek to address the under-representation of women at the highest levels of mathematics, physical sciences, and Engineering.

Previously, when researchers (Jungwirth, 1991; Waiden & Walkerdine, 1985) tried to make meaning of the experiences of girls and boys in mathematics classrooms, and interpret male-female power relations, they found that girls are often marginalized and given subordinate status in the mathematics class. Perhaps this is because of the perceptions of teachers who assume that girls' performances in mathematics depend on rote learning, hard work, and perseverance rather than natural talent, flexibility and risk-taking, which are the learning styles of boys. Contrastingly, Ajai and Imoko (2015) argue that performance is a function of orientation and not gender because there was no significant difference in girls and boys in mathematics achievements, but rather their findings indicated that boys and girls can compete and collaborate in mathematics. This should be considered as a foundation to believe that girls can do well in mathematics just like boys in schools.

Based on Paechter (1998), who argues that male and female students experience the world in different ways, the following factors associated with gender differences in mathematics achievement are listed: Male and female students (i) are differently positioned in society (ii) perceive and process reality differently and (iii) have different learning styles (Ajai & Imoko 2015). Buhl-Wiggers et al. (2021) suggest that some family factors, like socio-economic status, are likely to influence gender differences in mathematics achievement. Studies from South Africa (Shepherd, 2017; Spaull & Makaluza, 2019; Zuze et al., 2017) mention that wealthier families have access to a larger variety of schools and that they tend to send their children to schools with higher quintiles that are better equipped (van Dyk et al., 2019; Zuze and Beku, 2019). Moreover, (Buhl-Wiggers et al. (2021) assert that the aspirations of girls are usually raised by educated mothers. In addition, Ogbonna and Umeh (2020) note that usually the occupation of mothers is an important factor affecting the mathematics achievement of students in mathematics courses. Consequently, mothers with higher levels of education could be a role models for their children to accomplish high levels of achievement in mathematics courses (Ogbonna & Umeh, 2020). Unfortunately, in South Africa, there is a low percentage of mothers who might be in occupations that could affect students' attitudes, needs, interests and other characteristics for learning and studying mathematics. From a different angle, Zuze and Beku (2019) caution that in rural areas, cultural practices might be more restrictive for the education of girls who are usually involved in time-consuming activities. This is because, traditionally, the rural communities have no belief that girls can outperform boys in some trades. They also perceive that some careers are meant for boys and not girls.

Some studies (Buhl-Wiggers et al., 2021; Jones & Dindia, 2004) reveal that teachers' academic expectations are different and hence treat girls and boys differently. In addition, researchers (Hofmeyr, 2020; Mullis et al., 2020; Zuze & Beku, 2019) cite school factors such as differences in bullying, sense of belonging, class behavior and teacher gender as likely to influence gender differences in achievement. Usually, it is boys who suffer bullying, while girls are usually subjected to sexual violence (Burton U Leoschut, 2013; Popp et al., 2014). While girls often report having lower self-efficacy and self-concept, valuing mathematics and science less and having higher levels of mathematics and science anxiety (Else-Quest et al., 2010; OECD, 2015, 2013), boys often report having more positive attitudes toward mathematics and science (Meinck & Brese, 2019) and hence are likely to pursue STEM-related careers.

Stereotypes on gender issues in following STEM careers

Study.com Online (2003) defines gender stereotyping as an over-generalization that is usually negative about the characteristics of an entire group based on gender that highlights the role of males and females in society. Consequently, women tend to rate themselves as more communal than men, whereas men tend to rate themselves as more agentic than women (Obioma et al., 2022). The authors further note that women tend to adopt more communal goals, such as working with people or caring for others, whereas men tend to adopt more agentic goals, such as power, mastery, and self-direction. Since 2012, the South African Government has been aware that the success rate and enrolment of female students at institutions of higher learning, particularly at technical and vocational education and training (TVET) colleges, was lower than that for male students (Chauke, 2022). Consequently, the National Youth Policy (2020) states that to increase young people's interest in STEM education, the government needs to ensure that young girls are mentored to learn science, technology, engineering, and mathematics with an environmental focus.

This is supported by global research, which found that on screen, engineers, scientists, and mathematicians are largely played by men, with seven times more male STEM roles in movies than female roles (World economic forum, 2023). In fact, in that country, only 12% of characters are recorded with identifiable STEM jobs (World economic forum, 2023). Meanwhile, Sub-Sahara countries, as reflected in the UNESCO Science report in Figure 3.1, indicate less than 35% of girls involved in STEM careers while South Africa records only 28% of those.

Figure 3.1. UNESCO Science Report: Towards 2030, 2015

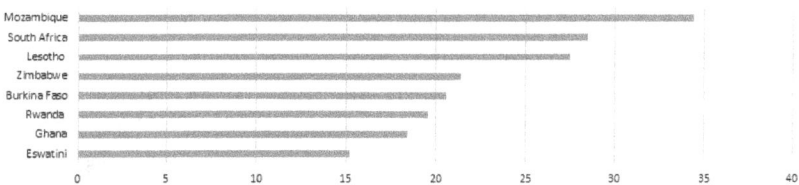

While girls' secondary education enrolment is higher than that of boys in Sub-Sahara countries in secondary education, there seems to be a leaky pipeline leading to few women in STEM careers. Furthermore, World Bank (2021) reports that of those who complete secondary education, many lack the required proficiencies in numeracy, science and the digital skills required to enroll and/or excel in STEM-related programs at the tertiary education level. Consequently, Hammond, Rubiano, Beegle and Kumaraswamy (2020) report that gender norms, stereotypes, biases, and sexual harassment emerge as key drivers of low representation of women in male-dominated STEM fields. Moreover, the World Bank (2021) notes that gender biases and expectations for different genders, set by families, society, culture, and the media, tend to propagate stereotypes, discriminatory practices and policies that deter girls from pursuing STEM careers and lead to women leaving STEM careers. Surely, this created vicious circle must be disrupted since these challenges limit the chances of girls' exposure to STEM fields and thus discourage more girls from pursuing STEM careers. This disruption should focus on incorporating gender-responsive and integrated STEM education in the pre-tertiary education curricula, providing mentorship and hands-on training opportunities for girls and young women in collaboration with STEM industries and promoting flexible and family-friendly workplace policies (World Bank, 2021).

Akinlolu and Haupt (2022) assert that gender stereotypes predict career choice and guide students toward careers that are deemed appropriate to their gender. For example, social norms and unconscious biases have been found to reinforce the perception that construction is more appropriate for men than for women (Powell & Sang, 2015). Haupt and Madikizela (2009) note that women had a role to play in the construction industry and that they could build successful careers within that sector. However, the authors cite various barriers to entry into the construction industry, such as gender-based discrimination against women, the harsh work environment of construction, lack of sufficient knowledge about the industry and the lack of successful women in construction as role models. When girls are rarely encouraged to enter male-dominated professions (Mujtaba & Reiss, 2013: 2980), those stereotypes become deeply rooted. However, there are initiatives suggested by Ellis (2022) to ensure that girls and women follow STEM-related careers. Those include (i) the connection of female role models in STEM careers who can serve as both mentors and examples of success stories, (ii) creation of learning resources that portray the girl child in STEM, among others (iii) encouraging girls to have interest in STEM early in education, (iv) girls must be able to access digital literacy—meaning the government must bridge the digital divide early in their education, during primary school and (v) teachers need to be intentionally equipped with strategies that encourage collaboration rather than competition, peer teaching, hands-on activities, mentoring by role models (Ellis, 2022). These are some of the suggestions on self-confidence boosters, perseverance activators that can enable women in STEM to continue trying, refining strategies, solving problems, posing explanations, and moving to the next challenges.

Role modeling by women in STEM-related careers

Gladstone and Cimpian (2021) define role models as individuals who can positively shape a student's motivation by acting as successful exemplars. Researchers (Crosby, 1999; Downing et al., 2005; Gibson, 2004) distinguish role models from mentors and sponsors because although they are all career guides, they need not (and in fact often do not) have any prior relationship with the students whom they are influencing. Contrastingly, mentors and sponsors must have a prior relationship and set goals with the student. Wooll (2021) asserts that a sponsor advocates for one and his/her career development sees potential and wants those sponsored to succeed in their careers, puts his/her name in for promotions, recommends one for a raise, or provides one with other similar opportunities. While mentors support mentees through formal or informal discussions about building skills, qualities, and confidence for career advancement, a sponsor is someone in a position of power who uses their influence to endorse and advocate on your behalf by communicating with other high-status leaders in the company (Bates et al., 2023). The latter could also be anyone who is able to influence others and who knows one well enough to use his/her power and political capital for one's benefit. Consequently, Gladstone and Cimpian (2021) argue that the features of a role model that are key for boosting students' expectancies for success in STEM and their STEM subjective value are the perceived competence of the role model, students' perceived similarity to the model and the perceived attainability of the model's success. Sáinz (2020) asserts that the effectiveness of the female role-model-oriented intervention depends on several indicators, such as the scope of the intervention, the theoretical background inspiring it, the design, measures, and tools to evaluate its impact, educational agents involved and its sustainability. In addition, Johnson et al. (2020) expounds that not only do role models and mentors help broaden the perspectives of those who can work in the STEM field, but they also expand students' perceptions of their own potential. A teacher is mostly an instructor, can be a role model, but not necessarily a mentor.

At the school level, Fergeson (2008) suggests that to serve as a STEM role model, one needs a growth mindset that believes in learning, trying, doing, and accomplishing new things. Thus, STEM teachers may need to model and share authentic passion that can ignite passion while leading to passionate students. It is also important for the teacher to humble him/herself in front of students to not only admit, but transparently demonstrate, areas where she might not be proficient. This is one way in which the students can watch how the role model deals with failure. In teaching STEM subjects, it is important to always highlight everyday STEM examples for students. Those could assist reluctant STEM students in engaging with STEM applications as solutions that help others to clean drinking water, clean and affordable energy, local environmental conservation, delivery of life-saving medical supplies, prevent loss of life from local natural disasters, and so many other examples. It is also critical for STEM instructors to bring in a variety of STEM professionals from various fields to interact with students. Those professionals can also do classroom presentations, guest-teaching lessons, respond to question-and-answer sessions with students, ongoing mentoring, interactive online sessions, serve as an audience for student presentations, share about personal or historical STEM heroes and many more. This can assist students to see themselves reflected in examples, such that they can dream about becoming something that they do not know exists. These suggestions are valid because there is evidence that passionate people imbue passion in others. Also, when humility is modeled, it grants permission to fail and allows people to permit themselves to try new things. Thus, when students witness teachers and/or role models fail, but do not give up, they are likely to learn and re-learn new skills. It's up to us, as educators, to lead, teach, model, invite and motivate every child to become a STEM professional our that choice by example.

Mentoring for STEM young women

Women need mentoring and leadership training to take decisive action and express themselves forthrightly in advancing the Sustainable Development Goals (SDGs), which include equity, diversity, and justice and to educate children, especially girls (Steinke, 2017; UNDESA, 2017). While mentoring success is best facilitated by structured programs that match mentees with mentors and offer training, support and programming, the availability of those programs to women in mathematical sciences is limited. In South Africa, as early as grade 10 students need to choose relevant subjects that will be required by their careers that they intend to follow post school. This is usually determined by their performance in mathematics in their grade 9 which indicates whether they would enroll for mathematics or mathematical literacy in the following year and henceforth. The involvement of women in mathematics requiring careers and STEM-related career paths in South Africa has undergone a re-examination in recent times. A new look was required in how the education fraternity can assist girls in crafting their future careers along these avenues. Girl learners have diverse and unique abilities needed in the mathematics classroom, of which both teachers and learners must be aware of, and act upon. In South Africa, despite improvements over the past decades, women continue to be underrepresented in tertiary studies and professional careers in the field of mathematical sciences.

In ensuring mentorship and increasing the number of young women who follow STEM-related careers, there is a need to establish a project that looks at the role of mathematics education in women's empowerment to encourage more girls to pursue STEM careers. Such a project should focus on:

- Combating stereotypes about gender and intellect,
- Pointing girls toward women role models in STEM,
- Showing girls that STEM is about trial-and-error,
- Prioritizing mentoring moments,
- Providing opportunities for girls to build their confidence in doing mathematics and
- Creating an environment that promotes the teaching of mathematics.

In this section, I share how experiences on mentorship relationships of schoolgirls which were built with mathematics education lecturers in our institution. First, we worked with girls enrolled for further education and training (FET) (Grades 10-12) in two secondary schools. Activities conducted with the girls included events on the celebrations and observation of the International Day of Women and Girls in Science held in their schools. In those events, mathematics education lecturers would make various presentations outlining STEM-related careers while encouraging girls to master mathematics and science subjects upon which they would be eligible to enroll in STEM fields. Secondly, we exposed the schoolgirls to various women role models in the STEM fields in South Africa. We conducted activities that observed the National Science Week, role modelling campaigns and were visible in those high schools for girls to break the man, power, dominance. This is also supported by Thompson and Thompson (2023), the Global Goals Ambassador

& Gender Equality Advocate, who echo that by providing guidance and support, mentors help females overcome obstacles, navigate their careers, and shatter the glass ceiling. The author further advocates for reverse mentorship in which mentees can teach their mentors the latest trends and platforms and help them navigate new tools by providing them with fresh perspectives on their work (Thompson & Thompson, 2023). In addition, mentors can receive training on diversity and inclusion from mentees, including best practices and strategies for creating an inclusive work environment with increasing cultural, social, racial and gender awareness.

However, in higher institutions, the experiences of initiatives taken towards developing skills among the girls through STEM women role models and intellectual traditions of mathematics take another format. This may be because girls already enrolled in STEM-related fields face other challenges. Thus, mentorship becomes crucial. Girls in higher institutions need mentors who provide 1) support and encouragement, thereby creating an emotional safety net, and 2) constructive feedback as the student explores career options and sets goals (Bastos et al., 2020). To prevent the loss of a critical mass of talent, thoughts, and ideas, which hinders countries from reaching their maximum development potential, and the decline in the number of women learning university STEM degrees as they move through the educational ladder, the leaking pipeline must be closed. Thompson and Thompson (2023) suggest the creation of intergenerational collaborations, which can be an innovative approach that brings together the perspectives and experiences of mentees and mentors to work on common goals. The result of such collaborations would be the formation of mentoring circles, joint projects, and collaborative teams, which can be used to strengthen a mentorship culture in which the younger generation learns from, the older one and gain experience together with skills for future role models. Since socio-economic factors, the masculine image of science, lack of mentoring, role models, and confidence in mathematics are some of the factors contributing to the underrepresentation of women in STEM, informed by literature, the following is then the model proposed for mentoring of STEM women:

1. Identification and ensuring that female academics serving in STEM-related fields in higher institutions in the country extend their networks to young women doing mathematics in all schools and institutions for engaged scholarship (Wang & Degol 2017),

2. Collaboration of schools with at least one female STEM academic serving in higher institutions in the country (González-Pérez et al., 2020),

3. Compilation of a list of young women registered for STEM subjects' higher institutions in the country so that they can be paired with women serving in STEM careers (Stevens, 2023).

4. Outsourcing from the Department of Basic Education excelling students in STEM subjects with potential to follow STEM fields as future careers (Hira & Hynes, 2018)

5. Explore working together with the Department of Higher Education and organizations to drive Girl Learner Intervention Programmes in STEM across the country (Hira & Hynes, 2018) and

6. Pairing of mentors with mentees in their relevant STEM fields (Kupersmidt et al., 2018).

Thus, how mentors can become trusted confidantes who share wisdom, support, and knowledge over an extended period in the role of mathematics education in empowering women helps female mentees to understand the relevance of STEM subjects to their own personal and professional pursuits. To debunk the myth that mathematics is a difficult subject and that STEM careers are only meant for men, the model proposed is geared towards making sure that girls find it easy to pursue STEM-related fields. Perhaps, the last question is, which mentorship program can ensure that mathematics in schools is popularized for the girl child to follow STEM-related careers?

The mentorship program should:

1. Expose young girls to STEM by correcting the negative perceptions that girls develop at a young age so that they are led to embrace mathematics and science when they reach high school rather than avoid the subjects (Wang, 2017),

2. Motivate young girls to explore typically male-dominated STEM fields by taking a girl-child to work or encouraging them to do job shadowing (Genoways, 2017),

3. Expose young women to specific programs that encourage young girls to maintain their interest in STEM fields,

4. Team a young woman with a mentor as a career strategy that can bring huge benefits, especially to women in unbalanced work environments in STEM-related fields (Torres-Ramos, 2021) and

5. Take charge and educate girls to access websites of multiple professional organizations to learn about what it's like to be a woman in a specific STEM profession and about career opportunities (González-Pérez, 2020).

Conclusion

This chapter sought to understand how mentorship and support for young South African women can empower them to advance to mathematical-related careers, drawing from literature and the outcomes of projects carried out in South Africa. The program-related mentoring outcomes of STEM activities conducted with young girls and women in schools were presented. Consequently, how mentors became trusted confidantes who share wisdom, support, and knowledge over an extended period in the role of mathematics education in empowering women helps female mentees to understand the relevance of STEM subjects to their own personal and professional pursuits.

Mentorship appears to be one of the promising possibilities that can improve the gender balance in STEM careers. It has been shown in this chapter the creation of platforms where women are prevalent in STEM careers, more young girls may begin to recognize the STEM career opportunities open to them. This can also help in exposing young women to more growth and development through access to existing support structures for women in STEM fields. To debunk the myth that mathematics is a difficult subject, and that STEM careers are only meant for men, the intervention methods followed were geared towards making sure that the girls find it easy in school to solve mathematics problems in a relaxed and conducive environment in the program. Finally, the chapter proposed a mentorship program that ensures that mathematics in schools is popularized for the girl child such that girls have confidence, vision, and focus on following STEM-related fields.

References

Abiam, P. O., & Odok, J. K. (2006). Factors in students' achievement in different branches of secondary school mathematics. *Journal of Education and Technology, 1*(1), 161-168.

Ajai, J. T., & Imoko, B. I. (2015). Gender differences in mathematics achievement and retention scores: A case of problem-based learning method. *International Journal of research in Education and Science, 1*(1), 45-50.

Akinlolu, M., & Haupt, T. C. (2022). Tertiary students career choices in construction disciplines: Are the predictors the same for men and women? *Choice 4*(5), 6-7.

Asante, K. O. (2010). Sex differences in mathematics performance among senior high students in Ghana. *Gender and Behaviour, 8*(2), 3279-3289.

Bates, C. R., Bakula, D. M., Egbert, A. H., Gerhardt, C. A., Davis, A. M., & Psihogios, A. M. (2023). Addressing barriers to career development awards for early career women in pediatric psychology. *Journal of Paediatric Psychology, 48*(4), 320-329.

Buhl-Wiggers, J., Jones, S., & Thornton, R. (2021). Boys lagging behind: Unpacking gender differences in academic achievement across East Africa. *International Journal of Educational Development, 83*, 102382.

Bastos, M. L., Tavaziva, G., Abidi, S. K., Campbell, J. R., Haraoui, L. P., Johnston, J. C., ... & Khan, F. A. (2020). Diagnostic accuracy of serological tests for covid-19: systematic review and meta-analysis. *BMJ, 370*.

Burton, P., & Leoschut, L. (2013). School violence in South Africa: Results of the 2012 National School Violence. *Study centre for justice and crime prevention monograph series*, no 12. Cape Town, March.

Cham, S., Sok, N., Hay, V., & Ir, P. (2021). Factors determining the use of modern contraceptive among married women in Cambodia: Does their decision-making matter? *Cambodia Journal of Public Health (CJPH) of the School of Public Health at NIPH, 2*(4).

Chauke, T. A. (2022). Gender differences in determinants of students' interest in STEM Education. *Social Sciences, 11*(11), 534.

Crosby, F. J. (1999). The developing literature on developmental relationships. *Mentoring dilemmas: Developmental relationships within multicultural organizations*, 3-20.

Department of Basic Education. (2012). *Integrated strategic planning framework for teacher education and development in South Africa*. Pretoria: Department of Basic Education.

Downing, R. A., Crosby, F. J., & Blake-Beard, S. (2005). The perceived importance of developmental relationships on women undergraduates' pursuit of science. *Psychology of Women Quarterly, 29*(4), 419–426.

Ellis, S. B. (2022). *An exploratory quantitative study of the impact of stem-focused middle schools on student persistence and performance in STEM* (Doctoral dissertation, Gardner-Webb University).

Else-Quest, N. M., Hyde, J. S., & Linn, M. C. (2010). Cross-national patterns of gender differences in mathematics: a meta-analysis. *Psychological bulletin, 136*(1), 103.

Ferguson, C. (2008). The School-Family connection: Looking at the larger picture. A review of current literature. *National Center for Family and Community Connections with Schools*.

Genoways, S. K. (2017). The experiences of female high school students and interest in STEM: Factors leading to the selection of an engineering or computer science major. *Student Work*, 3650. https://digitalcommons.unomaha.edu/studentwork/3650

Gibson, D. E. (2004). Role models in career development: New directions for theory and research. *Journal of Vocational Behavior, 65*(1), 134–156.

Gladstone, J. R., & Cimpian, A. (2021). Which role models are effective for which students? A systematic review and four recommendations for maximizing the effectiveness of role models in STEM. *International Journal of STEM education, 8*(1), 1-20.

Gradín, C. (2021). Occupational gender segregation in post-apartheid South Africa. *Feminist Economics, 27*(3), 102-133.

González-Pérez, S., Mateos de Cabo, R., & Sáinz, M. (2020). Girls in STEM: Is it a female role-model thing? *Frontiers in Psychology, 11,* 2204.

Gurjar, M.K. (2018). The role of mathematics education in women empowerment. - *International Journal of Research and Analytical Reviews, 5*(4), 353-355.

Hammond, A., Rubiano Matulevich, E., Beegle, K., & Kumaraswamy, S. K. (2020). *The equality equation. Advancing the participation of women and girls in STEM.* The International Bank for Reconstruction and Development.

Haupt, T., & Madikizela, K. (2009). Why do South African women choose careers in construction? *Acta Structilia: Journal for the Physical and Development Sciences, 16*(2), 46-68.

Hira, A., & Hynes, M. M. (2018). People, means, and activities: A conceptual framework for realizing the educational potential of makerspaces. *Education Research International,* 2018.

Hofmeyr, H. (2020). *South Africa's Pro-Girl Gap in PIRLS and TIMSS: How Much Can be Explained?* Department of Economics, University of Stellenbosch.

Jones, S. M., & Dindia, K. (2004). A meta-analytic perspective on sex equity in the classroom. *Review of educational research, 74*(4), 443-471.

Jungwirth, H. (1991). Interaction and gender—findings of a micro ethnographical approach to classroom discourse. *Educational Studies in Mathematics, 22*(3), 263-284.

Khatun, J. (2023). Reflecting the major issue of women empowerment with respect to gender socialization and gender equality in Indian scenario. *International Journal of Multi-disciplinary Research, 5*(6), 93-97.

Kupersmidt, J., Stelter, R., Garringer, M., & Bourgoin, J. (2018). STEM Mentoring. Supplement to the "Elements of Effective Practice for Mentoring." MENTOR: *National Mentoring Partnership.*

Lynch, K. (2016, February 17). BHM Highlight: Dr Mae Jemison, first African American woman to travel in space. Liberty Science Center. Retrieved from https://lsc.org/news-and-social/news/bhm-highlight-dr-mae-jemison-first-african-american-woman-to-travel-in-space

Madusise, S. (2018). Women empowerment for sustainable development through stem subjects: A case of mathematics. *Journal of Humanities & Social Sciences, 23*(2), 3.

Mahlomaholo, S., & Sematle, M. (2005). *Gender differences and black students' attitudes towards mathematics in selected high schools in South Africa.* Retrieved on October 31, 2009.

Mathekga, J., Mahlaela, A., & Maciko, L. (2022). Evidence of Sasol Limited's Contribution to Skills Development in Democratic South Africa. *African Journal of Employee Relations, 46.*

Meinck, S., & Brese, F. (2019). Trends in gender gaps: Using 20 years of evidence from TIMSS. *Large-Scale Assessments in Education, 7*(1), 1-23.

Mullis, I. V. S., Martin, M. O., Foy, P., & Hooper, M. (2016). TIMSS advanced 2015 international results in advanced mathematics and physics. *Boston: Boston College TIMSS & PIRLS International Study Center.* http://timss2015.org/advanced/

Mujtaba, T., & Reiss, M. J. (2013). What sort of girl wants to study physics after the age of 16? Findings from a large-scale UK survey. *International Journal of Science Education, 35*(17), 2979-2998.

National Youth Policy. 2020. *National Youth Policy 2020–2030: A decade to accelerate positive youth development outcome.* Available online: https://www.gov.za/sites/default/files/gcis_document/202103/nationalyouthpolicy.pdf (accessed on 17 August 2022).

Obioma, I. F., Hentschel, T., & Hernandez Bark, A. S. (2022). Gender stereotypes and self-characterizations in Germany and Nigeria: A cross-cultural comparison. *Journal of Applied Social Psychology, 52*(8), 764-780.

OECD (2013) *PISA 2012 results: Ready to learn: Students' engagement, drive and self-beliefs* (volume III): Preliminary version. Paris: OECD.

OECD, O. (2019). *Social Impact Investment 2019.* The Impact Imperative for Sustainable Development. OECD.

Ogbonna, C. & Umeh, E.C. (2020). Girl child Mathematics Education: An imperative for women empowerment and sustainable development. *International Journal of Gender & Women's studies, 1.* 46-54.

Opolot-Okurut, C. (2005). Student attitudes towards mathematics in Ugandan secondary schools. *African Journal of Research in Mathematics, Science and Technology Education, 9*(2), 167-174.

Osei-Tutu, E. M., & Ampadu, E. (2017). Domestic violence against women in Ghana: The attitudes of men toward wife-beating. *Journal of International Women's Studies, 18*(4), 106-116.

Paechter, C. (1998). Educating the other: Gender, power and schooling. London: Falmer Press.

Popp, J., MacKean, G. L., Casebeer, A., Milward, H. B., & Lindstrom, R. R. (2014). *Inter-organizational networks: A review of the literature to inform practice.* Washington, DC: IBM Center for the Business of Government.

Powell, A., & Sang, K. J. (2015). Everyday experiences of sexism in male-dominated professions: A Bourdieusian perspective. *Sociology, 49*(5), 919-936.

Rühle, R. (2022). Mind the gap: An analysis of gender differences in mathematics and science achievement in South Africa. *Department of Economics,* University of Stellenbosch.

Sáinz, M. (2020). Brechas y sesgos de género en la elección de estudios stem. *Por qué ocurren y cómo actuar para eliminarlas?* [Gender Gaps and Biases in the Choice of STEM. Why They Occur and How to Act to Eradicate them?]. Sevilla: Centro de Estudios Andaluces.

Shepherd, L. J. (2017). *Gender, UN peacebuilding, and the politics of space: Locating legitimacy.* Oxford University Press.

Spaull, N., & Makaluza, N. (2019). Girls do better: The pro-female gender gap in learning outcomes in South Africa 1995–2018. *Agenda, 33*(4), 11-28.

Steinke, J. (2017). Adolescent girls' STEM identity formation and media images of STEM professionals: considering the influence of contextual cues. *Frontiers in Psychology, 8,* 716.

Thompson, S., & Thompson, N. (2023). *The critically reflective practitioner.* Bloomsbury Publishing.

Torres-Ramos, S., Fajardo-Robledo, N. S., Pérez-Carrillo, L. A., Castillo-Cruz, C., Retamoza-Vega, P. D. R., Rodríguez-Betancourt, V. M., & Neri-Cortés, C. (2021). Mentors as Female Role Models in STEM Disciplines and Their Benefits. *Sustainability, 13*(23), 12938.

UNDESA/United Nations Department of Economic and Social Affairs (2017), World Population Prospects: The 2017 Revision, https://esa.un.org/unpd/wpp

UNESCO. (2015). *Gender and EFA 2000–2015. Achievements and challenges.* Paris: UNESCO.

UNESCO. (2016). Global education monitoring report. *Gender Review Creating Sustainable Futures for All,* UNESCO, Paris.

UNESCO. (2017). *Global education monitoring report 2017/18.* Accountability in Education: Meeting our Commitments UNESCO, Paris.

Van Dyk, N., Behan, F. P., & Whiteley, R. (2019). Including the Nordic hamstring exercise in injury prevention programmes halves the rate of hamstring injuries: a systematic review and meta-analysis of 8459 athletes. *British journal of Sports Medicine, 53*(21), 1362-1370.

Walden, R., & Walkerdine, V. (1985). Girls and mathematics: From primary to secondary schooling (*Bedford Way Papers 24.*) London: Institute of Education, University of London.

Wang, M. T., & Degol, J. L. (2017). Gender gap in science, technology, engineering, and mathematics (STEM): Current knowledge, implications for practice, policy, and future directions. *Educational Psychology Review, 29,* 119-140.

World Bank (2021), "Country Grouping Classifications," in Ndiamé Diop, Daniela Marotta and Jaime de Melo, eds., Natural Resource Abundance, Growth, and Diversification in the Middle East and North Africa: *The Effects of Natural Resources and the Role of Policies,* Washington, World Bank, p. 199-201, http://hdl.handle.net/10986/11956

Wooll, M., 2021. *Mentor vs. sponsor: Why having both is key for your career.* [Online]

World Economic Forum. (2023). Enabling the economic integration of refugees: lessons learned on refugee employment and employability from the rapid response to Ukraine. *World Economic Forum,* Geneva, Switzerland.

Zhu, Z. (2007). Gender differences in mathematical problem-solving patterns: A review of literature. *International Education Journal, 8*(2), 187-203.

Zuze, T. L., & Beku, U. (2019). Gender inequalities in south African schools: New complexities. In *South African Schooling: The Enigma of Inequality*, 225-241.

Zuze, L., Reddy, B. V., Visser, M., Winnaar, L., & Govender, A. (2017). *TIMSS 2015 Grade 9 national report: Understanding mathematics and science achievement amongst Grade 9 learners in South Africa*. Cape Town: HSRC Press.

Chapter 4

Mentoring K-12 Students in STEM Education

Phyllis Okwan
Southern University and A&M College, Baton Rouge, USA

Joe Omojola
Southern University at New Orleans, USA

Murty Kambhampati
Southern University at New Orleans, USA

Abstract: Science, Technology, Engineering, and Mathematics (STEM) mentoring, particularly for females and underrepresented students, needs to begin as early as elementary school through high school, and ultimately through college. The reason for this is that many young students are turned off from STEM very early in grade school due to a lack of its awareness and significance to other fields. The shortage of workers in STEM originates from a lack of interest in early elementary school. To bridge this gap, the mentoring program in this chapter describes mentor programs for students through various educational programs to motivate and enable students to think about the pursuit of STEM degrees. This mentoring program, through various hands-on, minds-on activities in the form of academic enhancement, and enrichment, excites students' interest to excel in STEM fields throughout their educational careers. This approach can instill a love of STEM in young people at an earlier age. A successful mentor must possess (1) self-discipline, (2) empathy, and (3) support, and this chapter outlines those key attributes.

Keywords: STEM, Elementary and High School Students, Underrepresented and Minority Students, Females, Workers, Mentoring

***

Mentoring K-12 students in STEM education

Mentorship is prioritized by programs that aim to increase diversity and support future leadership in STEM fields (Atkins et al., 2020). Crisp and Cruz defined mentoring as a one-on-one relationship between an experienced and less experienced person for the purpose of learning or developing specific competencies (Crisp & Cruz, 2009). This definition is in alignment with our approach of mentoring students through academic enhancement and enrichment programs. In his book, (mentoring students and young people), Miller (2004) attributes mentoring to be:

1. Simple: complex social issues can be tackled by focusing on the needs of an individual.

2. Direct: mentoring enables an adult to give direct help to a young person in order to make a difference in their lives.

3. Cheap: mentoring is a low-cost alternative to expensive government programs and to the work of public institutions.

4. Sympathetic: to be called a mentor is a kind of honor that links to a noble tradition.

5. Flexible: in that, it can be used for a range of purposes and appeals to all shades of political opinion.

Nora and Crisp (2007) and Cohen and Galbraith (1995) defined mentoring to comprise six dimensions. (1) Relationship emphasis: encompasses the mentor exhibiting a genuine acceptance of the student's feelings; (2) Information emphasis: involves the mentor providing accurate and sufficient advice to the student; (3) Mentor as facilitator: entails the mentor guiding students through a review and exploration of their abilities, interests, and beliefs; (4) Confronting function: involves the mentor assisting students in recognizing nonproductive behaviors, such as focusing on unrealistic goals; (5) Mentor model: The mentor shares his or her experiences with the student in an attempt to develop the relationship; and (6) Student vision: The underlying premise of this dimension of mentoring is that students' critical thinking skills are stimulated by the mentor (Miller, 2004; Galbraith & Cohen, 1995). Evidence from various research publications found that the difference between mentors and non-mentors is not who they are but in what mentors do in the mentoring relationship. Research suggests that mentors increase the competence and performance of mentees by actively demonstrating trust and confidence in their mentees, praising and encouraging mentees, explaining to mentees those behaviors that are desirable within the system, and also protecting mentees from unjust verbal attacks when necessary (Slicker & Palmer, 1993). Mentoring has been shown to be a mechanism that may assist underrepresented students in persisting and help remedy the negative experiences of underrepresented students. However, research studies lack an in-depth examination of what occurs in the mentoring processes that enhance student success (Mondisa, 2018). In our case, we found limited in-depth research on mentoring K-12 students and a lack of awareness.

Framework

The goal of our programs was to mentor K-12 students through hands-on, minds-on activities in Science, Technology, Engineering, and Mathematics (STEM) in order to excite them at a younger age to think about STEM fields as a career choice. In this paper, we described the programs, methods, and activities that enabled us to achieve our desired goal of mentoring these students, especially young girls, in order to encourage them to aspire to become scientists and engineers. For example, investing to ensure a pipeline of workers skilled in STEM competencies is a big issue currently affecting the workforce. Therefore, to optimize the return on these investments, the most effective strategy is to cultivate these skills in young children from an early age (Chesloff, 2013). These are some of the reasons why we use our programs to mentor younger students, especially younger girls, to encourage, nurture, and engage them at an early stage of their educational journey to pursue STEM degrees and to become STEM professionals.

The National Assessment of Educational Progress (NAEP, 2022), in its report, stated that the average fourth-grade mathematics score decreased by 5 points and was lower than all previous assessment years going back to 2005; the average score was one point higher compared to 2003. The average eighth-grade mathematics score decreased by 8 points compared to 2019 and was lower than all previous assessment years going back to 2003. In 2022, fourth- and eighth-grade mathematics scores declined for most states/jurisdictions as well as for most participating urban districts compared to 2019. In its 2009 report, NAEP indicated that just over a third (34 percent) of US fourth graders are proficient in science, 30 percent in eighth grade, and only 21 percent in twelfth grade. (NEAP, 2009 & 2023)

Women are vastly underrepresented in STEM jobs and among STEM degree holders despite making up nearly half of the U.S. workforce and half of the college-educated workforce (Beede et al., 2011). Their research further stated that although women fill close to half of all jobs in the U.S. economy, they hold less than 25 percent of STEM jobs. We think, this is so because, for centuries, STEM disciplines have been attributed as disciplines for men, not for women, and most importantly, not for women of color. This is the more reason why we are interested in mentoring underrepresented female students to think STEM at an early age. The majority of the students we mentor are females, and about 95% are underrepresented females. In 2019, the *Trends in International Mathematics and Science Study* (TIMSS) educational survey assessment report indicated that, in the United States, fourth-grade boys scored 11 points higher on average than fourth-grade girls on the TIMSS mathematics (540 vs. 529 points, respectively). The 2007 TIMSS report also makes the point: in fourth grade, US students, on average scored 539 on the test (ranking eighth among the countries tested), compared with an international average of 500. By eighth grade, they averaged only 520 and were ranked 11th. Since 1995, fourth-grade scores have slightly declined (by 3 points) and in eighth grade increased marginally (7 points), although neither of these trends is statistically significant. The US ranking has declined since 1995 for fourth graders, falling from second place and rising slightly (from 12th) for eighth graders. The TIMSS has a different threshold for its "advanced" level, with 15 percent of fourth graders and 10 percent of eighth graders, numbers that are greater than the international median but that these have both declined since 1995 (Gonzales et al., 2009 & TIMSS, 2019).

In our programs, we employed mentoring through the lens of STEM to encourage and entice underrepresented students, in particular, young women, by engaging them in hands-on and minds-on activities over the summer. These programs were geared toward K – 12 students. These programs were also specifically targeted to run during the summer months for students completing second through the fourth grades and 10th and 11th grades.

Our STEM mentoring programs for young students range from two to six weeks. These mentoring programs were created to address the problem of declining interest in STEM at the elementary school level. The first STEM mentoring program for young students on our campus was established in 2008 through a "Presidential Awards for Excellence in Science, Mathematics and Engineering Mentoring (PAESMEM)" grant. This came about when one of the authors was recognized by President Bush at the White House for his exceptional mentoring efforts that increased the involvement of diverse and underrepresented student groups in Science, Technology, Engineering, and Mathematics (STEM) fields. A commemorative certificate and a grant (to encourage the author to advance his mentoring work) accompanied the award.

The grant was used to launch a Mathematics and Science Kamp for Beginners (MSKB) – Kamp, a hands-on program for third-, fourth-, and fifth-graders. Kamp program was intended to increase the interest of urban elementary school students in science and mathematics through mentoring.

Since the inception of the mentoring programs in 2008, we have served over 400 elementary through high school students. How did our mentoring programs work? Our mentoring programs for elementary school students employed the services of STEM faculty members (including the authors) who created hands-on and minds-on exercises at the students' level. We mandated that the exercises comply with three criteria: (1) They must be innovative, hands-on and minds-on, (2) They must be exciting and fun, and (3) They must inspire the students to want to become STEM professionals. Before the programs began each summer, selected faculty members, including the authors of this paper, met every week to discuss and design the curriculum with mentoring as the main focus. We also emphasized that the curriculum incorporates the three criteria mentioned above.

We were aware that some of the students participating in our mentoring programs would not immediately proceed to the university to major in STEM. However, we expected that the interest kindled in these programs would keep the students seeking knowledge in STEM until they get through high school and college. In other words, by addressing the lack of interest in STEM at its root - the elementary school, and in the most cost-effective way, we can create life-long adherents to the field and assist in addressing the shortage of workers in STEM. According to Badmus and Omosewo (2020), the presence of STEM in the classroom is to train individuals with up-to-date knowledge in the related disciplines to meet the current demands of society and to shift the limit of human thinking and problem-solving ability, which may result in meaningful development and improved living. To address the shortage of workers in STEM, the United States Senate introduced a landmark comprehensive immigration reform bill that has the potential to increase skilled foreigners working in specialty occupations and shift the U.S. employment-based visa system to a more merit-based scheme that favors science, technology, engineering, and mathematics (STEM) workers (Rothwell & Ruiz, 2013). Rothwell and Ruiz further stated in their paper that businesses say they cannot find the skills they need from the domestic labor pool and need access to a global pool of skilled workers. Their statement attests to why we want to instill STEM in young children at an early age through mentoring in order to activate their interest before they are turned away from STEM-related disciplines. Children turn away from STEM-related disciplines because of a lack of interest. But if their interests are tapped into at an early age, they will grow to love the subject and pursue a career in STEM fields. It is becoming increasingly difficult to define a STEM "job." Regardless of the industry –manufacturing, utilities, construction, technology, or financial services, employers are looking for a talent pipeline that can produce workers proficient in the STEM disciplines (Chesloff, 2013). Concepts at the heart of STEM—curiosity, creativity, collaboration, and critical thinking—are in demand. They also happen to be innate in young children (Chesloff, 2013). In particular, our mentoring program at the elementary school level takes advantage of the curiosity of children.

According to ManpowerGroup, a global leader that connects human potential to the power of business, their talent shortage survey found 36 percent of employers globally reported talent shortages in 2014, the highest percentage in seven years and in 2023, their third quarter survey indicated that demand for talent surpasses supply where 78% of organizations report difficulty finding the talent they need. (ManpowerGroup, 2014 & 2023). Our mentoring programs are geared towards developing talents at an early age in order to bridge the shortage of talent gap. Even though the news release article by the Bureau of Labor Statistics U.S. Department of Labor recorded the unemployment rate at 3.5 percent (Bureau of Labor Statistics, 2023), the United States is still facing a critical workforce shortage, and employers find it difficult to find applicants who meet all critical job requirements (Zender, 2014).

Failure to equip rising generations with the knowledge and skills required for available jobs could lead to further disintegration of our nation's economy as well as increased unemployment. However, one solution has been put forward: combine the hands-on approach of a vocational program with the convenience and cost-effectiveness of online education to gear modern learning towards addressing the skills gap (Yashchin, 2014).

Program overview

Elementary school programs
Mathematics and science kamp for beginners (MSKB)
MSKB originated from a PAESMEM award that specifies a Mathematics and Science Kamp for Beginners (MSKB). During the summer of 2008, the authors used the award money from PAESMEM to start a summer mentoring program. That year, the program recruited students completing second through fifth grade for a two-week hands-on and minds-on STEM mentoring activities. The

program was very successful and exceeded the expectations of the parents. The next year, parents requested that we continue this mentoring program to enhance their children's interests in STEM.

Gateway for excellence in mathematics and science (GEMS)

We wrote a National Science Foundation (NSF) grant into which we incorporated the elementary school students' mentoring program. The grant was funded, and we continued the elementary school students' mentoring program through the grant. We changed the name of the program to Gateway for Excellence in Mathematics and Science (GEMS). The main goal of both MSKB and GEMS was to mentor elementary school students by providing them with hands-on and minds-on inquiry-based instruction in Mathematics and Science. The initial idea was to bring in 25 elementary school students, from different schools, to participate in a two-week mentoring program. The program became so successful and in demand that upon requests from the parents, we started hosting two sessions of the program during the summer in order to accommodate the ever-growing number of parents who wanted this program for their children. In spite of increasing to two sessions, we had waiting lists for students who were unable to get in.

Become excellent in science and mathematics by training (BEST)

BEST is the offspring of the GEMS Camp. BEST Camp is a two-week (math and science) summer program for elementary school students (second to fourth graders). BEST is similar to GEMS, but it has more activities built into it. One of the examples from the curriculum is the Global Positioning System (GPS), where students go outside and are taught how to use to cartesian coordinates (North, South, West and East) system to physically navigate from one location to another. The reason for this exercise is for students to understand how GPS works and also how to read maps. Another Physics-related topic is Newton's third law of motion, where students were able to examine forces, differentiate between push and pull, and how visualize why action and reaction are equal but opposite. Like many other topics for students in this age range, we designed this topic to take advantage of the multiple permutations of hands-on activities that students can take part in. In their biology class, faculty members introduced students to DNA and how to extract DNA from strawberries. Another popular topic in Biology is dissection. In chemistry, students were taught how to make perfume by extracting the scent from red roses. They were also taught how to make soap and to observe the chemical changes that take place in the process. In mathematics, students were able to sort out the different colors in Skittles to construct histograms, and examine probabilities, just to mention a few of the activities in the curriculum. In the case of the Skittles, their reward is eating the Skittles at the end of the activities.

Testimonies

We provide here a few testimonies from students who participated in our mentoring programs and why we felt the need to continue the programs.

"The greatest camp! Each teacher inspires me to do my best; the teachers inspire me to be anything I want to be; the lab teacher inspires me to discover things other people have not discovered. I wish I will never leave; I wish I could stay here forever." (*MSEIP BEST participant*)

"I did not like the program, I LOVED it!!! My favorite part was meeting new people. I made good friends too. I learned about light, construction work, math, enzymes, speed, and forces. I learned how light goes through different shapes of mirrors and lenses. We learn about forces and push and pull. This program was amazing. The program continued my learning life and kept me busy this summer instead of staying home and being lazy." (*MSEIP BEST participant*)

"The great camp helped me learn reading and math. I love that when we learn we get to do fun things too. I have made five friends so far. I love my special teacher. I love that we get to do science here. I get to learn so I can get smarter." (*MSEIP BEST participant*)

"I like this camp because I made friends, I like the food, and the best part is when we did the experiment with chicken liver and soap and peroxide, and I learned to do the math. I like the GPS experiment, we did the north, east south, and west, and we were running in all directions. This camp was fun." (*MSEIP BEST participant*)

"The BEST camp ever... (*MSEIP BEST participant*)

High school program
Summer Enrichment Program (SEP)

We mentored high school students through the Summer Enhancement Program (SEP). This mentoring program started in 2001with the focus on (1) increasing the "pipeline" flow of minorities from high schools to science, mathematics, and computer technology fields, (2) to sustain the increase of high school students, especially minorities and female students, in science and mathematics and (3) to improve the quality of graduating high school students who are entering college. The high school mentoring program was designed to introduce students to college life while building up their ACT test-taking skills and STEM skills to finish high school strong. In addition, we introduce students to research by assigning each student an independent research project. We assisted the students in completing the projects which they presented on the last day of the program. Students were also able to use these projects at Science Fair competitions during the following academic year. SEP became one of the signature summer educational enhancement and enrichment programs on our campus and the New Orleans metropolitan area as well. At the end of 2009, the SEP mentoring program came to an end, but parents, high school principals, and counselors wanted the program to continue because they saw the impact the mentoring program had on their students when they went back to school in the fall. In particular, parents and teachers noted that these students were more focused and more productive. Under a new grant proposal titled Enhancement, Enrichment, and Excellence in Mathematics and Science program (E^{3}MaS), we continued SEP.

The goals of the outreach to the high school portion of E^{3}MaS were to improve the educational quality of incoming high school students through the Summer Enrichment Program (SEP), Early Career Awareness, Science Fair, and developing high school Mathematics and Science Teachers through hands-on activities and enhancement workshops. We believe that improving the educational quality of incoming high school, students will reduce science and mathematics anxiety and subsequently lead to increased enrollment in STEM majors, and ultimately improving the STEM workforce. SEP was a six-week intensive mentoring program consisting of hands-on instructions in college-level Science, Mathematics, English, Research, and ACT preparation. Our aim for the summer enrichment program was to train and equip students with the necessary tools to succeed in high school and be better prepared for college.

During this period, the delivery of instructions through mentoring focused on topics that enable students to develop skills that are needed to be successful in STEM fields. In addition, technical writing, including research methods, is taught to the students. The students were introduced to the college environment while they were on our campus. Their daily activities started at 9:00 o'clock in the morning. Each class was designed to last for 50 minutes with transitional 10-minute intervals. At the beginning of the program, an ACT pre-test was administered to the students to assess their current knowledge level.

At the end of the program, a post-test was administered to students. The two test scores were then compared to determine the effectiveness of our instructions. About 90% of the students' post-tests showed a significant increase over the pre-test. The same is found to be true for their understanding and proficiency in science and mathematics subjects. The SEP courses were taught by university professors, including the authors of this paper, while undergraduate students served as assistants to the instructors in the classrooms. The undergraduate students assisted the professors in working one-on-one with high school students who needed additional assistance in understanding the concepts being taught in class. One of the reasons the program was so successful is the small group setting with a low student-teacher ratio and one-on-one instructions and hands-on activities. The program provided all the instructional materials for students. Students were also given stipends upon successful completion of the program.

Another aspect of SEP was the recreational activities that the program offered to students. These activities include field trips to places such as NASA and the Laser Interferometer Gravitational-Wave Observatory (LIGO) supported by the NSF and operated by Caltech and MIT. These field trips were designed to expose students to STEM applications, enhance their curiosity and inspire them to want to learn more. During a visit to LIGO, the students were welcomed by the LIGO scientists and staff. Students were ushered into an auditorium where the staff made a presentation to the students about their work. Students were then taken to tour the facility and also to interact with the scientists at their workplaces. After the tour, students went to the exhibition hall to explore the hands-on activities at the hall. SEP also had talent search activities that students performed at the end of the program.

SEP personnel designated Fridays as research mentoring and talent development days. SEP instructional days were Monday through Thursday. On Fridays, students checked in and went to their mentors to work on their research projects. At this point, the undergraduates working under the same mentor served as peer mentors to the high school students. The undergraduate peer mentors' responsibilities were to make sure the high school students were following proper research protocols and also to talk to the high school students about their own research projects and about available opportunities in STEM-related fields. At noon, the high school students met in a central place to work on their chosen talent show program. This aspect of the program is spear-headed by the undergraduate mentors. Students perform during the closing ceremony to the faculty, parents, high school counselors, principals, and the university community at large. Awards were given to the best group. Another fun part of the program was that every Friday, the personnel selected the student of the week, the best-behaved student, and the overall best student in mathematics, biology, chemistry, etc. This was done to encourage students to be active and perform their best in the program.

At the beginning of the program, students were assigned research topics in the STEM subjects that they were being taught. They were also assigned research mentors. These mentors were STEM faculty members of the university. The assigned mentor worked with the group of high school students assigned to her/him on individual projects (one-on-one basis) by teaching and guiding the student step-by-step on how to do scientific research. Each faculty mentor is paired with an undergraduate student who serves as a research assistant. In addition to serving as mentors to the high school students, the undergraduate students were also conducting their own research under the same mentor. These pairs are strategically chosen in order for the high school students to have a role model. The high school students were required to prepare an abstract and a PowerPoint presentation of the results of their research. The last day of the program was devoted to students' presentations and competitions for monetary awards at their own grade levels. Parents and family members, school counselors, principals, and the university community were invited to the presentations and award ceremony.

Career Awareness was one of the components of our K-12 mentoring program. Two career awareness seminars were provided every year. These seminars were designed to inform students about career options in STEM fields. Students were introduced to materials and information that emphasize career opportunities in STEM and STEM-related fields. During the months of February and March, undergraduate students and program personnel visited high schools in the New Orleans metropolitan area to host career awareness seminars in the form of recruitment activities for our summer programs. These seminars were mainly conducted by undergraduate student mentees to high school students. This interaction allows the undergraduate students to share their college experience and available opportunities with the high school students and encourages them to go to college. It is also for the high school students to ask the undergraduate students any question that comes to mind.

Every year, in collaboration with our Office of Enrollment and Retention Management, STEM faculty hosts an annual science fair competition involving students from high schools with a focus on the feeder high schools. Also, at the time of the science fair competition, we conduct an Open House during which

STEM majors provide guided tours of the science laboratories and departments to the high school students and their teachers. During the science fair, students from different high schools in the metropolitan area come to our campus to make poster presentations of their research. The majority of the high school students who participated in our summer enrichment program also came to the science fair to present their research. Each participant received a certificate of participation, and the winners received monetary awards in the form of checks or gift cards.

Science enrichment for teachers

In order to propagate the benefit of mentoring to high school students during the school year, we added the SET component to the program. This aspect of the program was to improve the teaching quality of K-12 mathematics and science teachers through two weeks of intensive hands-on pedagogy activities geared toward enhancing their teaching skills and their ability to improve students' performance. In addition, we trained these teachers on how to assist their students in completing scientific research projects.

In Schmidt et al. (2013) paper, *On the Road to Reform: K–12 Science Education in the United States*, they reported that the US science curriculum is "a mile wide and an inch deep," covering a large number of topics in a scattershot, shallow fashion rather than systematically and in-depth. According to them, many teachers are not adequately prepared to teach science. The results of the NCES Schools and Staffing Survey indicated that, although 76 percent of high school biology teachers have a major or minor in biology, much smaller proportions of teachers of chemistry (25 percent), earth science (33 percent), physical science (49 percent), or physics (58 percent) have the same level of training (Schmidt et al. 2013). It is hard to expect teachers to implement a strong science curriculum if they are insufficiently prepared and limited in the required subject matter. Consequently, we expect that engaging high school teachers in hands-on and minds-on pedagogy activities will boost their confidence in teaching STEM subjects and being able to assign and guide their students through simple projects.

Our goal was to improve the teaching quality of science and mathematics teachers in our region through content enhancement workshops, Summer Enrichment Programs, and software and technology training. Specifically, the content enhancement workshops were given by faculty members in Biology, Chemistry, Mathematics, Computer Science, Technology, and Physics. During summer, the two-week paid intensive workshops on how to teach science and mathematics more effectively were conducted on our campus. We provided these teachers with Computer Aided Instruction (CAI) software to facilitate their teaching. Once these teachers returned to their various schools, they used the knowledge learned in the program to assist their students in the classrooms. After the workshops, the teacher participants were able to effectively conduct hands-on science projects with their students. These projects prepared students to take part in our annual high school science fairs. These teachers also served as ambassadors for our programs by becoming the points of contact in their schools for our program. In addition to being ambassadors, these teachers also served as recruiters for our summer enrichment programs and undergraduate programs. Finally, SET trained the teachers to become effective mentors to their students. The program personnel worked with the high school teachers to ensure they were implementing the lessons learned from the workshops to mentor their students.

Summer training and enrichment program (STEP)

STEP is another high school summer enrichment program. STEP is an offspring of SEP. The purpose of STEP is to mentor and prepare students with the necessary tools that will help them to succeed in college. This summer mentoring program was designed to serve high school students. STEP enabled us to bring in identified high school students to our campus for a five-week intensive program. During this time, instructors focus on topics that enable students to develop skills that are necessary for students to be successful in science and mathematics. Participants were exposed to intensive, innovative, hands-on instructions in biology, chemistry, mathematics, physics, research, ACT preparation, and applications of STEM.

Mentor attributes

As narrated above, we have mentored hundreds of elementary school and high school students through funded summer academic enhancement and enrichment programs. Through our experience, we discovered that a successful mentor should have several attributes, including (1) self-discipline, (2) empathy, and (3) supportive.

Self-discipline

Merriam-Webster defines self-discipline as a correction or regulation of oneself for the sake of improvement. A successful mentor should have the ability to control his or her feelings and overcome any weakness arising from mentoring students or their own weaknesses. For us to be self-disciplined and effective mentors for our program, we set weekly meetings where we talk about ways and strategies we have employed to mentor our individual mentees. This approach creates checks and balances for us to stay focused on the goals of our mentoring program. Research shows that successful mentoring can lead to greater student achievement, retention, and knowledge-sharing (Vasquez & Pandya, 2020). In his book, *Embrace the Suck: The Navy SEAL way to an extraordinary life*, Gleeson talks about "learning to effectively lead yourself and others all come down to discipline. Happiness, success, and fulfillment stem from focus and self-control" (Gleeson, 2021). Gleeson further listed the eight most powerful things to do to master self-discipline: 1) Know your strengths and weaknesses; 2) Remove temptations; 3) Set clear goals and have an execution plan; 4) Practice daily diligence; 5) Create new habits and rituals; 6) Change your perception about willpower; 7) Give yourself a backup plan; and 8) Find trusted coaches and mentors.

As mentors, we are always constantly using ourselves and methods to make sure that we are disciplined in our mentoring processes. For example, we are committed to making sure our mentees are getting what they need to make them successful not only in their educational journey but in life as a whole. We also follow a timeline to help us avoid unnecessary distractions. For the most part, we make use of both internal and external advisory committees to evaluate our mentoring programs, including student performances, curriculum quality, and commitment and performance of mentors, every year, to make sure we are following the three criteria that govern our programs: (1) They must be innovative and hands-on, (2) They must be exciting and fun, and (3) They must inspire the students to want to become STEM professionals. For the summer mentoring programs, students complete a survey to evaluate the curriculum, social activities, instructors, and mentors at the end of the program. These feedbacks help us to improve our goals, objectives, activities, and methods, and to eliminate any identified weakness that may undermine our performance and outcomes.

Empathy

Mentoring is a caring business. Dictionary.com defines empathy as the psychological identification with or vicarious experiencing of the emotion, thoughts, or attributes of another. A successful mentor should be empathetic to his or her mentees. That is, s/he should be understanding and sensitive to his or her mentees' feelings. In our program, we show empathy to our mentees. As a result, they developed trust in us. Not only do they share their academic and professional experiences with us, they voluntarily share their personal life stories and experiences with us. They do so because they trust that we will understand them, help them, or direct them to where they can get the necessary resources to overcome any problems. Our mentees know that they can always count on us to be there for them when they need us. According to Mondisa's research, mentors use listening skills and empathy, and they also recognize the individuality of their protégés. In addition, mentors are flexible, open, and receptive. They use their own experiences to relate to their protégés (Mondisa, 2018). Empathy is thought to facilitate the development of a meaningful relationship through which an array of positive youth outcomes may be promoted (i.e., social-emotional, cognitive, and identity development) (Rhodes, 2002; Spencer et al., 2020). In our mentoring programs, we are developing young minds in order to encourage them to become STEM professionals. We do this by creating a positive environment for them. The empathy chart below (Figure 4.1) demonstrates how we mentor K-12 students. We reinforce positive behavior, correct negative behavior, and create trust and lasting relationships through all the activities that permeate our programs. These activities help us to create a mentor-mentee quality relationship. In the context of youth mentoring, a mentor's ability to demonstrate empathy to a mentee is a core indicator of relational competence (Doty et al., 2019; Deane et al., 2022).

Figure 4.1. Mentoring With Empathy Chart

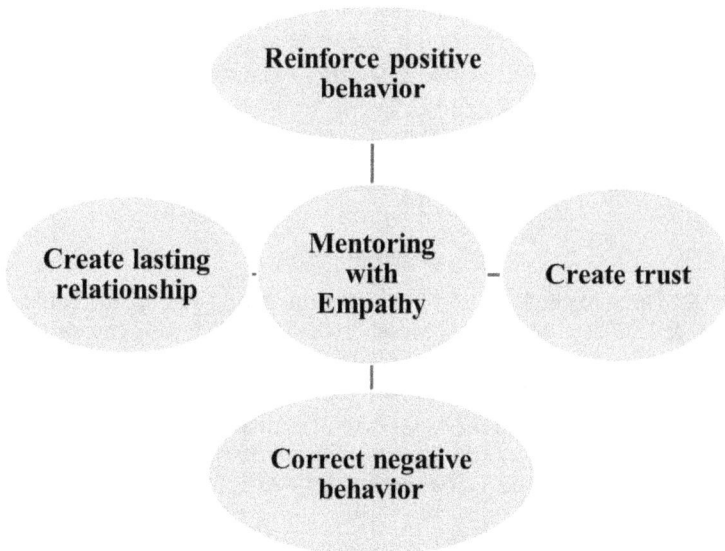

Supportive

A successful mentor should be supportive of their mentees. The relationships that develop between a mentor and mentee are aimed at improved role of understanding, successful role transition, and completion of goals and objectives (Barrett et al., 2017). Formal mentoring programs strive to provide young people with an ongoing relationship with a supportive, non-parental adult. Such relationships have been found to promote a more positive social, emotional, behavioral, and academic functioning for youth (Spencer et al., 2020). Providing emotional support is arguably the foundation upon which all other aspects of mentoring rest, and an emotionally supportive relationship is crucial and without this, it is hard to envisage effective mentoring (Gakonga, 2019). Successful youth-adult mentoring relationships exhibit qualities of emotional closeness, support, and mutual respect (Shelmerdine & Louw, 2008; Weiss et al., 2019).

Conclusion

Mentoring K-12 through summer STEM enhancement and enrichment programs has proven to be beneficial for students and high school teachers and, more importantly, for underrepresented females and women of color, as outlined in this paper. Although it is time-consuming, it is a very important endeavor to take in order to develop leaders of tomorrow.

Acknowledgments

The authors would like to express their appreciation to the National Science Foundation and the US Department of Education for funding our mentoring endeavors over the years. We thank Southern University for supporting our professional undertakings and for giving us a stable base from which to operate. We are highly indebted to the parents and students who have responded positively to our mentoring efforts since the inception.

References

Atkins, K., Dougan, B. M., Dromgold-Sermen, M. S., Potter, H., Sathy, V., & Panter, A. T. (2020). "Looking at Myself in the Future": how mentoring shapes scientific identity for STEM students from underrepresented groups. *International Journal of STEM Education, 7*, 1-15.

Badmus, O., & Omosewo, E. O. (2020). Evolution of STEM, STEAM and STREAM education in Africa: The implication of the knowledge gap. *International Journal on Research in STEM Education, 2*(2), 99-106.

Barrett, J. L., Mazerolle, S. M., & Nottingham, S. L. (2017). Attributes of effective mentoring relationships for novice faculty members: Perspectives of mentors and mentees. *Athletic Training Education Journal, 12*(2), 152-162.

Beede, D. N., Julian, T. A., Langdon, D., McKittrick, G., Khan, B., & Doms, M. E. (2011). Women in STEM: A gender gap to innovation. *Economics and Statistics Administration Issue Brief,* (04-11).

Bureau of Labor Statistics (2023). *News Release.* Retrieved August 1, 2023, from https://www.bls.gov/news.release/pdf/empsit.pdf

Chesloff, J. D. (2013). STEM education must start in early childhood. *Education Week, 32*(23), 27-32.

Crisp, G., & Cruz, I. (2009). Mentoring college students: A critical review of the literature between 1990 and 2007. *Research in Higher Education, 50,* 525-545.

Deane, K. L., Boat, A. A., Haddock, S. A., Henry, K. L., Zimmerman, T. S., & Weiler, L. M. (2022). The comparative roles of mentor self-efficacy and empathy in fostering relationship quality with youth. *Journal of Youth and Adolescence, 51*(4), 805-819.

Doty, J. L., Weiler, L. M., Mehus, C. J., & McMorris, B. J. (2019). Young mentors' relationship capacity: Parent–child connectedness, attitudes toward mentees, empathy, and perceived match quality. *Journal of Social and Personal Relationships, 36*(2), 642-658.

Galbraith, M. W., & Cohen, N. H. (1995). *Mentoring: New strategies and challenges.* Jossey-Bass.

Gakonga, J. (2019). Mentoring and mentor development. *The Routledge Handbook of Language Teacher Education,* 432-445.

Gleeson, B. (2021). Embrace the suck: The Navy Seal way to an extraordinary life. *Hachette Go.*

Gonzales, P., Williams, T., Jocelyn, L., Roey, S., Kastberg, D., & Brenwald, S. (2009). Highlights From TIMSS: Mathematics and Science Achievement of U.S. Fourth and Eighth-Grade Students in an International Context (NCES 2009-01 Revised). *National Center for Education Statistics, Institute of Education Sciences, U.S. Department of Education. Washington, DC.*

ManpowerGroup Talent Shortage Survey. (2014). *Wayback Machine.* Retrieved August 1, 2023, from http://web.archive.org/web/20151029214731/ http://www.manpowergroup.us/campaigns/talent-shortage-2014/assets/pdf/2014_Talent_Shortage_WP_US.pdf

ManpowerGroup Employment Outlook Survey (2023). *Global hiring plans cool for summer, yet talent shortages remain.* Retrieved August 1, 2023, from https://go.manpowergroup.com/hubfs/MPG_MEOS_Report_Q3_2023.pdf

Miller, A. (2004). *Mentoring students and young people: A handbook of effective practice.* Routledge.

Mondisa, J. L. (2018). Examining the mentoring approaches of African-American mentors. *Journal of African American Studies, 22*(4), 293-308.

National Assessment of Educational Progress. (2023). *The Nation's Report Card.* Retrieved July 23, 2023, from https://www.nationsreportcard.gov/highlights/mathematics/2022/

Nora, A., & Crisp, G. (2007). Mentoring students: Conceptualizing and validating the multi-dimensions of a support system. *Journal of College Student Retention: Research, Theory & Practice, 9*(3), 337-356.

Rhodes, J. (2002). Older and wiser: The risks and rewards of mentoring today's youth. *Harvard University Press.*

Rothwell, J. T., & Ruiz, N. (2013). *H-1B visas and the STEM shortage: A research brief.* Available at SSRN 2262872. http://dx.doi.org/10.2139/ssrn.2262872

Slicker, E. K., & Palmer, D. J. (1993). Mentoring at-risk high school students: Evaluation of a school-based program. *The School Counselor, 40*(5), 327-334.

Schmidt, W. H., Burroughs, N. A., & Cogan, L. S. (2013). On the road to reform: K-12 science education in the United States. *Bridge, 43*(1), 7-14.

Shelmerdine, S., & Louw, J. (2008). Characteristics of mentoring relationships. *Journal of Child and Adolescent Mental Health, 20*(1), 21-32.

Spencer, R., Pryce, J., Barry, J., Walsh, J., & Basualdo-Delmonico, A. (2020). Deconstructing empathy: qualitative examination of mentor perspective-taking and adaptability in youth mentoring relationships. *Children and Youth Services Review, 114,* 105043.

Trends in International Mathematics and Science Study (TIMSS). National Center for Education Statistics (NCES) Home Page, a part of the U.S. Department of Education. (n.d.). https://nces.ed.gov/timss/results19/index.asp#/science/achievement

Vasquez, R., & Pandya, A. G. (2020). Successful mentoring of women. *International Journal of Women's Dermatology, 6*(1), 61.

Weiss, S., Harder, J., Bratiotis, C., & Nguyen, E. (2019). Youth perceptions of a school-based mentoring program. *Education and Urban Society, 51*(3), 423-437.

Yashchin, A. (2014, February 17). Redefining education to close the workforce skills gap. *Huffington Post.* Retrieved August 1, 2023, from https://www.huffpost.com/entry/redefining-education-to-c_b_4676818

Zender, F. (2014). An IPPD approach providing a modular framework to closing the capability gap and preparing a 21st century workforce. http://hdl.handle.net/1853/51822

Chapter 5

"What we Really Need": How the Women in Natural Sciences (WINS) Program Supports Culturally Sustaining Mentorship and STEM Career Opportunities for Women of Color

Jacqueline Genovesi
The Academy of Natural Sciences of Drexel University, USA

Ayana Allen-Handy
Drexel University, USA

Kimberly Sterin
Drexel University, USA

Kimberly Godfrey
The Academy of Natural Sciences of Drexel University, USA

Dominique Thomas
The Academy of Natural Sciences of Drexel University, USA

Janai Keita
The Academy of Natural Sciences of Drexel University, USA

Katie Mathew
Drexel University, USA

Tajma Cameron
Drexel University, USA

Abstract: In this chapter, the authors illuminate 40+ years of findings and best practices from the implementation of the Women in Natural Sciences (WINS) program. WINS is much more than an out-of-school time, STEM enrichment program for young women. The WINS program demonstrates a strong interconnection between Critical Race Feminism, Ecological Systems Theory, Yosso's Community Cultural Wealth, and Culturally Sustaining Pedagogies in guiding the program's impact on Women of Color in their pursuit of STEM opportunities, development of self-efficacy, STEM careers, and supportive relationships. This comprehensive framework ensures that the program supports the holistic development of these students within the STEM field. Findings garnered from over forty years of implementation and investigation of the impact of the program have pointed to how the program specifically supports women of color from low-income backgrounds in three major ways: (1) Culturally Sustaining STEM Opportunities Help Develop Self-efficacy for Women of Color; (2) Culturally Sustaining STEM Mentorship Supports Pursuit of STEM Careers; and (3) The WINS Web of Supportive Relationships.

Keywords: WINS, Critical Race Feminism, Critical Race Theory, Ecological Systems Theory, Yosso's Community Cultural Wealth, and Culturally Sustaining Pedagogies, STEM, Mentors

***

"What we Really Need": How the Women in Natural Sciences (WINS) Program supports culturally sustaining mentorship and STEM career opportunities for women of color

As a quiet young girl who faced a significant amount of bullying in school with inadequate access to the needed academic and social-emotional support at home and in my community, WINS represented an opening to gain the necessary tools to thrive academically and socially. Throughout my K-12 schooling years, standard classroom settings never seemed to hit the mark in nurturing a holistic learning environment. Unfortunately, this resulted in feelings of isolation, invisibility, and fear, so learning about the WINS program sparked excitement. The impact WINS continues to have in my life cannot be fully put into words. For me, WINS was more than an academic enrichment program focused on honoring and increasing the visibility of women in science; it saved my life.

- Maleka Diggs (Gilbert), WINS Alumna, 1991

Women in Natural Sciences (WINS), the only all-female science program of its type in the region, serves young women from the School District of Philadelphia (SDP) who represent almost every zip code in the city. The program's mentoring and support have resulted in 100% of the young women graduating from high school, with 97% of these graduates continuing to a college or university, and more than 60% majoring in a STEM (Science, Technology, Engineering and Mathematics) discipline. The program provides students with information, encouragement, and opportunities to shape their futures.

Originally conceived in 1982 as a free after-school enrichment program by Carol Williams Green, Russel Dawes, and Patricia Clifford, WINS has grown into an eight-year (high school and college years) comprehensive STEM enrichment and positive youth development program. WINS is designed to improve participants' understanding of basic ecological principles, scientific methods, techniques, and terminology; to provide hands-on, engaging activities that foster personal achievement, self-confidence, and communication skills; and to encourage students to enter science fields by identifying science-related career paths, advising them in college selection and assisting them in developing skills such as interviewing, and resume development. However, the heart of what WINS is all about is best told through the words of the young Black and Brown women whose lived experiences tell us a more complex and interesting story of the true impact of out-of-school time (OST) STEM programs that center supporting the person first and STEM learning second.

> What is WINS? For some, it's known as the Women in Natural Sciences Program through The Academy of Natural Sciences but for me, it's the people that MADE me. WINS has been my saving grace and my home away from home since the summer of 2006. After losing my mom earlier that year, being around a group of girls for hours at a time multiple days a week was not even imaginable. However, after week one I knew that my life had changed forever for the BETTER. WINS has changed my life in ways I couldn't imagine. They gave me a family, a home, and WINS gave me LIFE. I never knew as a 14-year-old girl from Philly that I would be able to explore the world, discover many talents I have for earth, and space sciences, especially PALEONTOLOGY!
>
> - Shanaya Shoats, WINS Alumna, 2010

In this chapter, we begin by sharing background related to the WINS program, including research related to participating women's outcomes. Next, we describe the theoretical frameworks that guide the implementation of the program and the exploration of women of color's experiences in the program. Then, we amalgamate over 40 years of findings related to the program to describe three major themes that have emerged from the WINS approach. Finally, we conclude with how the WINS program fits into the larger scope of work related to supporting women of color in STEM. Throughout the chapter, we highlight the voices of WINS participants and alumnae. We aim to demonstrate how culturally sustaining STEM opportunities and relationships cultivated during an OST STEM program can be understood as a mechanism for change regarding the underrepresentation of women of color in STEM fields.

Background on the WINS program

WINS is renowned among teachers and counselors in Philadelphia's public middle schools. These professionals work with parents, guardians, and students through a series of essays and interviews with museum educators to help select a new WINS class every year. There are 25-30 "seats" for each cohort, and every year the program is over-subscribed. WINS staff do not necessarily select science-motivated students or those with the highest grades. They prioritize geographic distribution and the enrollment of rising 9th graders who have the fewest enrichment opportunities. Upon enrollment, most students have a "B" average; only half intend on a STEM career. Rather than only offering this opportunity to those students already achieving at the highest levels, the intention is to identify those students who may most benefit from the network of support the WINS program provides and open possibilities for them to flourish.

WINS has slightly over 1,000 participants to date and their demographics align with program goals. From 2010 to 2020, 79% of WINS participants identified as Black and 16% as bi- or multi-racial. 67% of WINS students come from single-parent or guardian homes; 78% of their households have incomes under $40K a year; 36% have household incomes of less than $20K per year. Thus, the majority of WINS students identify as Black and come from low-income households. The success of the program derives in large part from direct student feedback and the acuity of staff knowledge about culturally sustaining pedagogies centered on minoritized women's distinct ways of knowing and being. Extended engagement over four summers and afterschool year-round in grades 9th–12th has combined with 40 years of iterative evaluation to create a finely-honed enrichment program for low-income Black women in urban public high schools.

WINS student recruitment process

Eighth-grade teachers and counselors in public and charter schools make initial recommendations and contact guardians. In Philadelphia, there are approximately 180 public and charter schools with 8th-grade students, and WINS staff personally reaches out to encourage these professionals to nominate their students regardless of interest. Prior to WINS, some students expressed little to no interest in STEM or had a real understanding of what it means to be a scientist based on limited exposure. They just wanted to try something new. Due to this, before application submissions, WINS provides an overview to share a small snapshot of what WINS looks like for nominees to gain an understanding of the hands-on science they could possibly experience throughout their time in WINS. This is done by allowing nominees to participate in activities like dissecting squids as well as holding hissing cockroaches.

> I vividly remember walking through the museum's side entrance doors with excitement, curiosity, and fluttering nervousness. Seeing a beautiful rainbow of primarily black and brown girls gathering in the meeting space planted a beautiful seed around the power and importance of centering identity, culture, and belonging in our academic and community-building practices.
>
> - Maleka Diggs (Gilbert), WINS Alumna, 1991

Maleka's memory of her first introduction to WINS highlights how it's not *just* the innovative STEM activities nor *just* the gathering of a group of women of color – but the intentional combination of the two that makes the WINS program an opportunity that these young women deem worthy of their time, worthy of taking a risk for, as they can already see themselves in its future.

What makes WINS an exemplar

WINS databanks and prior published research documents show that WINS alumnae outperform national averages on all metrics related to STEM advancement up through college graduation.

This same WINS research highlights some important foundational components that contribute to the success of OST STEM programs. These components include a clear mission for the program; reliable and sustainable funding and fundraising capacity; organizational buy-in, staff support, and reciprocity among host institution and program participants; positive program culture including mutual respect and collaboration; and strong program leadership and stability (Research for Action, 2017).

However, WINS goes beyond these foundational components to provide ecosystems of support (Sterin et al., 2023). These ecosystems provide opportunities to explore STEM identities and build STEM self-efficacy while exploring possible selves and STEM careers in a supportive environment of mentors and peers (See Figure 5.1).

Figure 5.1. Building an ecosystem of STEM opportunities and support for women of color

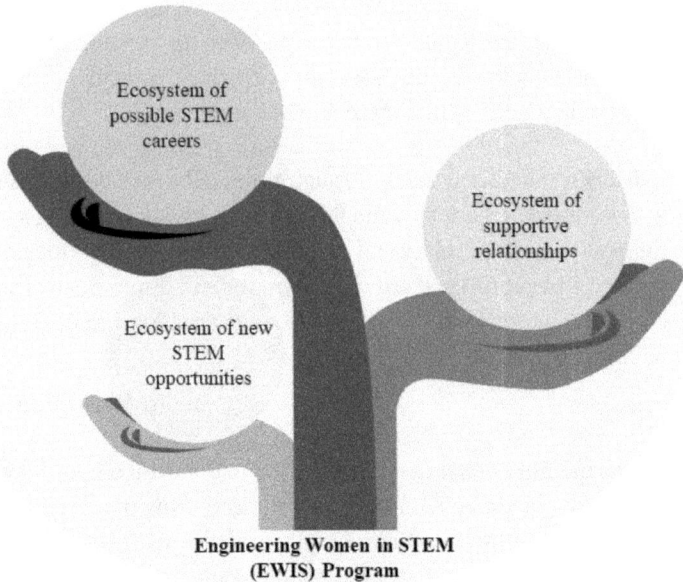

Source: Sterin et al., 2023

Data on WINS' long-term success

WINS women are surveyed about career aspirations three times during high school and twice in college. Data collected from 2009-2016 WINS cohorts show that 49% of incoming rising 9th graders in WINS already aspire to a STEM career. Of this 49%, a large fraction (32.5%) envisions a career in medicine. WINS has been highly successful in diversifying young women's interests in STEM. By the end of high school, 17% of WINS students who initially indicated a preference for medical careers had shifted their interests to another STEM field. Upon graduation from high school, the total number of students focused on STEM careers rises by nearly 20%. The impact the WINS program has on these young women of color is evident from their college matriculation and graduation rates, especially when situated in juxtaposition to the rates for public school students at-large in the city of Philadelphia. While only 51% of graduating seniors from the School District of Philadelphia attend college, WINS students matriculate at a rate of 97%, almost doubling the rate of their peers. Furthermore, follow-up surveys found that 88.5% of WINS alumnae earned four-year college degrees, and over 60% of these are STEM degrees, as compared to only 1% of all Black students, male and female, who earn STEM degrees after graduating from the SDP (NSCH, 2018). These stark differences in successful pursuits of higher education demonstrate the life-changing outcomes the WINS program has generated for many of its participants.

The WINS archive of 40+ years of quantitative data, student journals, and artifacts has been studied by some of the nation's leading figures in young women's engagement with OST STEM learning. Fadigan and Hammrich (2004) tracked the career trajectories of WINS alumnae who enrolled in the early decades of the WINS program. Susan Foutz (unpublished report, 2009), at the Institute for Learning Innovation, underscored the criticality of belonging to a community of like-minded women. McCreedy and Dierking (2013) won NSF support (#0452419) to study how WINS and other OST STEM programs for minoritized women use Community of Practice (interpersonal) frameworks to increase self-efficacy and persistence in STEM.

In early 2021, the authors received internal funding from Drexel University School of Education and experimented with an innovative life narrative approach to exegesis of WINS program impacts in the post-college adult years. Findings from this pilot study consistently point to factors outside of widespread assumptions in the OST STEM field that are as or even more highly valued by WINS alumnae. To summarize, these salient components are the revelational impacts of novel experiences as impetuses for identity shifts; the in-group solidarity of the WINS sisterhood as a primary driver for self-efficacy and skill development; the enduring impacts of relations with museum educators rather than mentors from industry and academia; the importance of the WINS "clubhouse" as a haven where students can re-imagine themselves in new social STEM-rich contexts.

What is WINS? In an alumna's own words

To understand the impact of WINS on participating women's lives, it is helpful to hear about their experiences in their own words. In the following vignette, Janai Keita reflects on her experiences in the WINS program as well as how those experiences shape the way she approaches her current role as the WINS Coordinator:

Being nominated for WINS felt like such an accomplishment and it was really a weight off my mother's shoulders. Looking back on middle school, I was afraid to step into new spaces and was always scared I would not fit in or make friends. The very first day of WINS I made some friends that would carry me into my late twenties. I spent my summers and even most days after school with these young women. I grew up with them and experienced life changes with them by my side.
The WINS program afforded me opportunities that a lot of my high school peers had not gotten a chance to tap into. Ms. Betsy [WINS Manager] pushed us outdoors and helped us see things differently than what was in our neighborhood park. My eyes were opened to what it meant to really appreciate natural sciences and the world we live in while also learning how to keep a small ecological footprint.
The Academy of Natural Sciences became a place that held space for me to be my "nerdy" self, and the WINS office became a safe place that felt like home. Working as an explainer was my first real job. I received an internship and simultaneously worked as the WINS I assistant and even won an award for the best big sister (this is something that, to this day, I pride myself on). WINS taught me the importance of mentorship.
When I graduated high school, I remember being sad that my time with WINS had come to an end. I made my way through college but was surprised at how the sisterhood and bonds that I held carried me during one of the toughest times of my life. When I was in college, I was diagnosed with Multiple Sclerosis and in the same year, I lost my father. My WINS sisters lifted me up in ways that I could never thank them enough for.
WINS has impacted my life by allowing me to find sisterhood and the power in it. It helped me have the ambition and drive to complete any goal that comes to my mind. -Janai Keita, WINS Alumna, 2010 and WINS Coordinator

As Janai described, the opportunity to join the WINS program drastically changed her summer (and future) from one of potential familial burden and social seclusion to one of exciting academic growth and long-lasting camaraderie. Janai's journey resembles that of many other WINS alumnae who have continued to return to the Academy of Natural Sciences for internships, volunteer engagements, and even careers. Because WINS provides holistic support and mentoring for these young women of color from the start, their appreciation for the program extends beyond the benefits of the curriculum and is often embodied by a reciprocal commitment to the encouragement of culturally sustaining pathways for Black and Brown women in STEM.

Guiding conceptual and theoretical frameworks

The following conceptual framework reviews previous research related to access for and persistence of women of color in the STEM fields. The theoretical framework provides a description of the ideologies that guide the WINS program and the analysis of the data.

Conceptual frameworks

Stark inequities, evident in the extremely low representation of Black women in STEM, persist despite considerable investments in the diversification of the STEM pipeline. The National Science Foundation and the National Council of Educational Statistics recently reported that between 2008-2018, participation rates by Black women measured only 4-5% of all degrees in the biological and physical sciences, only 2-3% of degrees in computer sciences and math, and slightly more than 1% in engineering (NSF, 2021). Black women make up only 2.5% of career positions in STEM-related fields (Catalyst, 2020). These numbers suggest that Black women in STEM chronically experience stalled professional advancement.

Barriers to women's participation in STEM are well documented. Factors range from male-dominated stereotypes of who is and can be a scientist, a lack of girls' playthings that foster spatial reasoning and experimentation, a lack of role models and mentors, pedagogies that favor abstract modes of thinking, while women prefer content that has relevance, overt and subtle aggressions against women in STEM, and young women's low self-assessments of their innate abilities (Tate & Linn, 2005; Eccles, 2007; Pajares, 2005; Zimmerman, 2000; Zeldin & Pajares, 2000; Aronson, Fried & Good, 2002). To combat these barriers, WINS adopts a growth mindset through which coordinators focus on building students' self-efficacy within a community of practice.

All WINS programming is grounded in a growth mindset. This approach means viewing intelligence and skills as malleable attributes that can be acquired through effort (Dweck, 2006). This mindset is likely to lead to greater persistence in the face of adversity and inoculate women against negative stereotypes (Dweck, 2009; Blackwell et al., 2007). Stereotypes can also be combatted by acknowledging them and exposing students to role models and mentors (Aronson et al., 2002; Good et al., 2003; Johns et al., 2005). Researchers agree that effective mentors instill growth mindsets, self-efficacy, and goal-setting among those considering careers in STEM (Cheryan et al., 2021; Stout et al., 2011; Stoeger et al., 2013). The WINS mentors help reinforce a culture characterized by a growth mindset within which the students are immersed.

When designing WINS, coordinators further understand the importance of intentionally building self-efficacy and implementing a Community of Practice among the women of color participating in their STEM program. In large sample surveys conducted for the WINS program, 71% of WINS students credited their mentors with enhancing their self-efficacies and abilities to persist in their studies (Research for Action, 2016 & 2017). Zeldin & Pajares (2000) report that the most influential sources of self-efficacy in STEM for women are relevant experiences, social cohesion, and encouragement from others. A large study of self-efficacy indicators among STEM students finds that self-efficacy is a stronger predictor of vocational choice for women than it is for men (Larose et al., 2006). As a program designed for women, WINS' focus on self-efficacy has been integral to its success.

Since 1982, the social-cultural context of learning within a Community of Practice has helped WINS women develop self-efficacy and persistence in STEM (Wenger, 2011). WINS has a significant body of research on its own Community of Practice (CoP). Simply put, learning within a CoP arises through three elements of shared engagement and participation: 1) the collective development of a common domain of knowledge, often driven by a large question or goal; 2) a network of people with differing talents and skill levels who are engaged in the pursuit of the knowledge domain; and 3) investigative activities that bind the community together through shared experiences (Lave & Wenger, 1991; Wenger, 2011). Starting in the summer before students enter 9th grade, the WINS program fosters sisterhood and a CoP among each cohort by celebrating womanhood, learning with others about the natural world, and collectively confronting the barriers and biases that face women in STEM, particularly women of color.

Theoretical frameworks

We reject what Bang et al. (2012) call "settled" epistemologies as we re-examine long-held notions about effective factors in the design of OST STEM programs for minoritized women in high school. We will refocus extant literature through the combined lenses of Critical Race Feminism (CRF), Ecological Systems Theory (EST), and Community Cultural Wealth (CCW). Critical Race Theory (CRT) analyzes the endemic nature of racism in social systems; here, we examine its legacies in OST STEM education (Ladson-Billings & Tate, 1995; Leonardo, 2013; Solorzano & Delgado Bernal, 2001; Bonilla-Silva, 2015). CRT is defined by Howard and Navarro (2016) as: a) centering race and racism, b) being interdisciplinary, c) challenging the dominant perspective, d) committing to social justice, and e) valuing experiential knowledge. Other axes of oppression regarding gender and class distinctly complicate the barriers facing Black women in STEM. While not all WINS participants share this identity, Black women are the most marginalized within the program, and therefore, we view the data through this lens to amplify both their needs and assets. Our research and findings are more specifically grounded in Critical Race Feminism (Evans-Winters & Esposito, 2010; Wing, 1997). As a practice-based theory, CRF uses life-story narratives to study the multi-dimensional identities of women of color (Berry, 2010). Berry et al. (2016) assert that centering stories of lived experiences illuminate the distinct experiences of Black women as they navigate through the oppressions of racism, sexism, and classism. In our study, Critical Race Feminism is used to examine the unique challenges and oppression that Black women face in STEM education and their efforts to overcome them. By entering the life-story narratives of Black women within the WINS program, we are able to highlight the complex interplay of racism, sexism, and classism that shapes their experiences.

Viewing identity development as the intersection of multiple experiences, environments, and factors that are mutually influential (Patton & Ward, 2016), CRF is aligned with mainstream research on intersectionality (Patton, 2009). This approach allows us to go beyond a one-dimensional analysis and explore the nuances of how these intersecting identities impact the identity development, persistence, and self-efficacy of Black women in STEM fields. We assume that WINS' experiences are the intersecting influences of school, home, and WINS environments that paint a rich portrait of OST program features that positively affect Black women in adulthood (Patton, 2009). Ecological Systems Theory (Bronfenbrenner, 2001), in tandem with Community Cultural Wealth (Yosso, 2005), thus frames how we view the multiple systems in Black women's lives (e.g., financial resources, family support, socio-political events, popular culture, and personality characteristics such as persistence and self-efficacy). An ecological framing helps illustrate how elements of the WINS program intersect with other significant influences within the larger contexts of Black women's lives. Our study employs Ecological Systems Theory to understand the broader contexts that impact the experiences of Black women in the WINS program. The various systems, such as family, school, community, and the WINS program itself, are interconnected and mutually influential. By examining how these different systems interact, we can better understand how the experiences within the WINS program intersect with other significant factors in the lives of Black women. This allows us to portray a more comprehensive picture of the influences that shape WINS alumnae identity development, including financial resources, family support, socio-political events, and cultural factors. Next, we utilize Yosso's Community Cultural Wealth to help acknowledge and appreciate the unique cultural assets that Black women bring to their STEM education experiences. By valuing and understanding the richness of their cultural backgrounds, our study sheds light on how these assets contribute to their identity development and success within the WINS program. This perspective challenges deficit-based narratives that might overlook the strengths and contributions of Black women and emphasizes the importance of recognizing and building upon their cultural wealth.

Culturally sustaining pedagogies (CSP)

This study also utilizes culturally sustaining pedagogies (CSP) as a guiding framework to explore and comprehend the distinct ways of knowing and being exhibited by Black and Brown women who participated in WINS. Culturally sustaining pedagogies (CSP) are educational approaches that seek to validate, support, and enhance the cultural identities and knowledge of marginalized or minoritized groups rather than assimilate them into dominant cultural norms (Alim et al., 2020; Marshall, 2023). In the context of minoritized women in STEM, culturally sustaining pedagogies focus on acknowledging and honoring their distinct ways of knowing and being, which have often been overlooked or marginalized in STEM educational settings. Within their curriculum and activities, WINS' incorporation of elements that resonate with participants' cultural experiences, histories, and interests represent a hallmark of culturally sustaining pedagogies, with participants connecting their identities with STEM learning.

Black and Brown women encompass a range of intersecting identities (Minnett et al., 2019; Simpson & Bouhafa, 2020). These identities shape their experiences, perspectives, and ways of engaging with the world. Culturally sustaining pedagogies in this context affirm and celebrate the cultural identities and histories of Black and Brown women, recognizing their ways of knowing and being as a legitimate form of knowledge. Furthermore, CSP recognizes that Black and Brown women's distinct ways of knowing and being often arise from their lived experiences. Thus, in our study, Black and Brown women's personal narratives and stories provide rich perspectives of their ways of knowing and being and recenters and redefines what it is to be Black and Brown women engaging in STEM. As CSP recognizes that there are diverse ways of knowing beyond traditional academic approaches (Alim et al., 2020), WINS participants were given the opportunities to express their understanding of STEM through a variety of mediums, providing an environment for Black and Brown women to express multiple ways of knowing.

Culturally sustaining pedagogies also prioritize students' agency and empower them to actively shape their learning experiences (Alim et al., 2020). Reflecting on their participation in the WINS program and the mentoring they received, WINS alumnae expressed how the program encouraged self-efficacy, leadership, and a sense of ownership over their STEM journeys. Additionally, CSP calls for the inclusion of diverse perspectives and voices in pedagogical approaches and encourages long-term impact and sustainability (Alim et al., 2020; Ginsberg et al., 2020). Thus, the culturally sustaining approach contributed to the alumnae's ongoing engagement in STEM and their professional trajectories.

Employing culturally sustaining pedagogies as a guiding framework provides a rich and holistic understanding of the WINS program's impact on alumnae's academic and personal development and highlights how this form of mentorship fosters a sense of belonging, peer support, and effective strategies for supporting minoritized students in STEM fields.

Findings from over 40 years of the WINS program

Findings garnered from over forty years of implementation and investigation of the impact of the WINS program have pointed to how the program specifically supports women of color from low-income backgrounds in three major ways: (1) Culturally Sustaining STEM Opportunities Help Develop Self-efficacy for Women of Color; (2) Culturally Sustaining STEM Mentorship Supports Pursuit of STEM Careers; and (3) The WINS Web of Supportive Relationships.

Culturally sustaining STEM opportunities help develop self-efficacy for women of color

Self-efficacy is the belief in one's ability to complete tasks or influence events that have an impact on one's life (Bandura, 1986). Previous research has shown that students are more likely to pursue postsecondary education in STEM fields if they have high self-efficacy in math (Wang, 2013) or science (Scott & Mallinckrodt, 2005). Accordingly, the WINS program has conducted mixed methods research to better understand how participation in WINS has influenced students' self-efficacy specifically in regard to the STEM fields. One study included both quantitative surveys and semi-structured interviews and focused on WINS students' development of STEM self-efficacy during their first year in the program from two cohorts, the 2020-2021 and 2021-2022 school years. Results from the *Student Attitudes Toward STEM* (S-STEM) survey, an instrument that assesses middle and high school students' confidence and self-efficacy in the areas of mathematics, science, engineering, technology, and twenty-first-century learning (Friday Institute for Educational Innovation, 2012), showed that, descriptively, the WINS students' mean self-efficacy ratings on science, engineering and technology, and twenty-first century increased from the beginning to the end of the program, whereas mean self-efficacy ratings on mathematics decreased slightly across the year (see Table 5.1). A dependent samples t-test showed that the only change that approached statistical significance was the change in women's science self-efficacy (t (35)= -1.40, p =0.09). While not all aspects of students' STEM self-efficacy increased, most of the factors trended towards significance, with science self-efficacy standing out among them.

Table 5.1. Pre and Post S-Stem Survey Results

Subscale	Pre-survey M (SD)	Post-survey M (SD)	t(35)	P
Mathematics	3.67 (0.61)	3.57 (0.63)	0.88	0.19
Science	3.67 (0.65)	3.86 (0.55)	-1.40	0.09
Engineering & Technology	3.74 (0.57)	3.80 (0.59)	-0.49	0.31
21st Century Learning	4.12 (0.45)	4.22 (0.38)	-1.03	0.16

Note. Standard deviations are presented in parentheses.

Complementing these results, the qualitative findings from the study provide a more nuanced understanding of how the participants make sense of their experiences in the WINS program and particularly how they story their STEM self-efficacy as women of color. When reflecting on how socio-environmental factors have influenced their STEM self-efficacy, participants highlighted the lack of representation of women in the STEM ecosystem, Bianca (Pseudonym) explained:

> It's like every time when I see something about someone becoming a doctor or you're going to school for something, you never really see women on a poster of anything. You always see a white man on a poster and it's either a doctor or engineer. But you never really see women, Black or Brown, or white women in general.

Participants noted how the absence of women of color in STEM career field messaging has influenced their sense of STEM identity but quickly referenced how their experiences in the WINS program have started to counteract those narratives. Dominique explains how her experiences in WINS opened her to these new STEM opportunities:

> As a teenager, I knew that I really loved science, but through WINS I was able to gain firsthand experience and exploration beyond what I had experienced from my school curriculum. I love that WINS fostered an opportunity for continued exploration and passion to continually learn about the environment, travel to new places, meet new people and learn new cultures. But more importantly, encourage opportunities where I could support young people from my community as they strive towards reaching their highest potential.
>
> - Dominique Thomas, WINS Alumna, 2012 and WINS Coordinator for Social Justice Programs

Exposure to novel STEM experiences in a culturally sustaining and supportive environment helps WINS students leverage their curiosity, develop STEM identities, and increase their STEM self-efficacy. The first mentors for many of the WINS students are the managers and coordinators of the WINS program. As stated previously, many of the WINS coordinators are WINS alumnae. They understand the challenges faced by many WINS students but also respect and nurture students' unique abilities and assets. WINS staff serving as first mentors specifically design activities to leverage the social and environmental capital of students.

It's something that WINS does because that's the way it's evolved and why WINS works. Because we do have this sort of asset-based [approach], we're looking at the curriculum [in the context of] students' neighborhoods and what's available in Philadelphia. It revolves around the students bringing in their knowledge.

– Kimberly Godfrey WINS Manager

Recognizing the women of color as knowers and experts of their own lived experiences demonstrates how WINS enacts a CRF philosophy by amplifying the women's stories as well as drawing on the ecological approach by incorporating evidence from their surrounding environments in the STEM lessons and activities. While this acknowledgment and inclusion of the local environment may seem like a simple or even obvious way to support and engage these students in STEM learning, the field has a history of failing to activate students' prior knowledge and using exclusionary cultural norms and practices (Brown, 2019; Wade-Jaimes et al., 2019). This "traditional" approach has had an especially disparate effect on Black students living in urban environments (Seiler, 2001). WINS' asset-based approach, steeped in the lived contexts of its participants, runs counter to the norms in STEM education.

Angie Albarouki, WINS alumna (2021), talks about the STEM opportunities and learning about the impact women like her have had in STEM:

WINS has opened many opportunities for me, whether interning at the USDA or going to Montana to learn about geology. WINS helped me realize how big of an impact women have in science, and of all the possibilities and opportunities for young women.

Angie's reflection shows how central the discussion of women's role in STEM was during her experience in WINS. Not only did she get to experience new STEM learning and career opportunities, but she was also engaged in understanding the gendered and racialized pathways that have been both withheld and subsequently created for women, and specifically women of color. Analysis shows how a CRF lens has undergirded WINS' multilayered approach as Angie and other WINS students experienced STEM opportunities in a way that did not shy away from the barriers they would likely face in the field while also encouraging them to persist in forging STEM's future.

Culturally sustaining STEM mentorship supports pursuit of STEM careers

Motivated by a goal to increase access to STEM career pathways for women of color, providing the opportunity to explore a wide variety of STEM careers is an important component of the WINS program. As noted, not all WINS students express a strong desire to pursue STEM careers from the start of the program and some are committed to other career pathways; however, the research has found that participation in WINS has encouraged many students to either choose a STEM path or to find a way to combine their passions and integrate their STEM knowledge and skills into their career. For example, Jah'ya describes her path toward conceptualizing herself as an environmental lawyer:

> Prior to joining the Women in Natural Sciences Program, I wanted to be a lawyer. That did not change, but I was exposed to all different types of science. A passion for environmental science had formed. After my freshman year, I participated in Women on Water and Drexel Environmental Science Leadership Academy at Barnegat Bay. After graduating from Central High School and WINS, I became a student at Spelman College majoring in Political Science and minoring in Environmental Studies. Then, I was recommended to my position as the Alliance for Watershed Education Fellow at John Heinz National Wildlife Refuge at Tinicum. As an AWE Fellow, I promote watershed stewardship and community engagement of the 23 centers along the Delaware River Watershed. With my real experiences in environmental science and conservation, I now hope to become an environmental lawyer, who advocates for the protection and preservation of natural lands. This all started because I joined WINS.
>
> - Jah'ya Gale Cottries, WINS Alumna, 2020

Like Jah'ya, many students express that the WINS program exposed them to unknown STEM careers and that the mentorship experiences built up their confidence and skills. One student mentioned that they are thinking about a career in engineering and specifically that the WINS internship experience at the College of Engineering significantly increased their interest and confidence in computer science.

Before a WINS student graduates high school, they will have been introduced to over 100 STEM professionals through lectures, workshops, field trips, internships, and research opportunities. Many of the students will work alongside one of these scientists in what, for many, is their first job. Some of these STEM professionals agree to become formal mentors for WINS students in an ongoing research-based capacity. Survey findings indicate that the following actions have helped STEM mentors develop positive relationships with their WINS mentees:

1. understanding that each WINS student is an individual that comes with their own strengths and challenges;

2. taking time to get to know each student, both directly and by reaching out to the WINS staff;

3. offering choices in the types of projects that students can participate in during their research experiences, especially ones that leverage students' experiences;

4. being sure to scaffold projects and presentations – especially when it is the student's first time participating in these types of activities;

5. positioning themselves as learners and sharing their own experiences in their fields of study.

These five recommendations from STEM mentors about approaches to developing positive working relationships with WINS students show how all aspects of WINS programming are rooted in a CRF framework and reinforced with culturally sustaining practices. The STEM mentors' recommendations repeatedly include actions that demonstrate value for the individual, such as their suggestions to take time to get to know each student and to recognize their unique strengths and challenges. These recommendations demonstrate an intersectional understanding of the WINS women of color working with them as their mentees because the actions allow for a deeper understanding of each person to develop and contribute to a reciprocal relationship between mentor and mentee. Professional STEM working spaces have often been described as sterile spaces that suppress conversations about identity and culture (McGee & Bentley, 2017). By actively encouraging these conversations and honoring the experiential knowledge each WINS student brings with them to the lab, these STEM mentors are using culturally sustaining practices to disrupt normalized STEM spaces to better include women of color who have been historically marginalized from STEM careers.

It is important to note that mentors provide culturally sustaining and supportive STEM environments for students to thrive while exploring different STEM careers. Students were especially appreciative of mentors who provided the following while they were exploring STEM careers:

- being understanding of their scheduling needs;

- offering future support through reviewing presentations, writing recommendation letters and offering advice on college and major selection;

- being patient when lab trials didn't turn out as expected;

- communicating in a variety of ways, including frequent in-person check-ins, group chats, email, and Zoom, a web-based video conferencing platform (Research for Action, 2022).

The most important component of successful STEM career exploration and supportive mentoring experience was providing an environment where women of color feel a sense of belonging. The WINS program and the STEM mentors intentionally create and maintain welcoming spaces where young, talented women of color are challenged to explore the intersectionality of their lives and the potential of their future-selves. As Saieda Bethea (WINS Alumna, 2010) explained it, *"WINS showed me that Black and Brown girls can thrive in STEM regardless of how and where we come from!"* And Lynn Larabi (WINS Alumna, 2020) remembers, *"I would not have known about the intersections of gender, environmental sustainability and international development if not for WINS. I wouldn't have had the courage to be in South Korea doing sustainability work if it weren't for WINS.* The WINS program provided culturally sustaining mentorship which helped both Saieda and Lynn unlearn harmful narratives about women of color's ability to belong and thrive in the STEM fields by nurturing inclusive STEM learning environments and helping students envision intersectional STEM careers. These examples show how the WINS program is striving towards its goal of rectifying the current imbalance of racialized and gendered representation in the STEM field.

The WINS web of supportive relationships

We found that the network of supportive relationships the WINS program provides proved to be integral to the women of color's success and persistence in STEM fields. Like a web, once a student is "caught" or welcomed into the WINS network of relationships, they are supported throughout their time in the program and beyond into college and career. This network of support includes relationships with WINS program staff, STEM professionals, WINS Alumnae and among the WINS students themselves.

WINS program staff

WINS students credit supportive relations both within the program and in their lives to their successes. There are many different supportive relationships that run throughout the fabric of WINS. The first is the relationship that is built with the WINS staff itself. The staff not only teach the lessons and chaperone the field trips, but they also continuously check in with participants about academic progress and what support they need. They serve as counselors when participants are not sure how to address or cope with life experiences, like trauma in their homes or conflicts with peers, and connect them with the support they need outside of school and WINS. If WINS staff are not able to provide support, they work directly with participants to locate and connect them to these supports. One student described how she experienced the support from WINS program staff as found in Sterin et al.'s (2023) study: "*... and they don't just help you with stuff in WINS, they can help you with stuff outside of WINS – school, your personal life. You can go to them and actually talk to them... it's bigger than just WINS.*"

This student's description that the program is "bigger than just WINS" shows how she felt a holistic level of support from the staff. As a culturally sustaining practice, the WINS program staff aims to see and support the whole student.

Close relationships often form among cohorts and WINS staff, which is at the heart of what makes WINS so successful. Staff members who see the students day-to-day often support them with job applications, homework, and college and financial aid forms. Over the 40+ years of the program, WINS has only had five managers, with many WINS alumnae holding coordinator positions. This low turnover rate, in conjunction with alumnae participation in leadership positions, continues to highlight the importance of consistency to ensure meaningful connections.

STEM professionals

Scientists serve as secondary mentors to WINS students. Many Academy scientists have supported numerous students. They have high expectations and levels of trust in WINS students, recognizing students' strengths and potential. After serving as a WINS summer internship mentor one STEM professional offered the following praise of the WINS students:

> The students that come through WINS are as good or better than the [undergraduates we] get from colleges. It's hard to believe some of them

are high school students... the maturity and the ability; the willingness to just dive right into things.

- Academy of Natural Sciences' Scientist

Scientists and other STEM mentors successfully integrate WINS students into their teams, having participants work on major projects and giving them credit for their work on these projects. One STEM professional shares how their approach to mentorship was guided by the idea that they could learn from and with the students, debunking traditional hierarchies of knowledge:

I feel like sometimes when people see scientists and talk to scientists, it's like, 'Oh, I know everything, and you don't know anything.' It's like, 'No, I'm just like you. That's why I'm a scientist to figure it out, to learn more about it.' So, I think my demeanor, personality, and approach was very relatable to them.

- WINS Mentor

The WINS Program similarly enacts this spirit of academic inclusion and professional empowerment through the ways they integrate students into museum activities. If you visit the Academy of Natural Sciences, you will likely meet a WINS participant in the exhibit spaces leading the visitor engagement. WINS have been credited for photography of Academy specimens, data collection in the field, and have their names listed in credits for research publications. Upon completion of their initial internships, WINS students have developed advanced STEM literacy and research skills. Many go on to represent their lab and/or collection's team, presenting at national and international conferences such as the National Science Teachers Association, American Educational Research Association, and the American Society for Engineering Education. The WINS students' conference presentations promote the visibility of high-achieving women of color in STEM as well as build the students' self-efficacy and STEM field experiences.

WINS alumnae

WINS alumnae also provide mentorship to others, including new cohorts of WINS sisters. The WINS program coordinators, both alumnae, work directly with each cohort not only to introduce them to STEM but also to use their lived experiences as anchors. This provides WINS students with a continuous visualization as well as a tangibility of what women of color in STEM look like.

Jakiah McDonald, WINS Alumna (2019), shares how her WINS experience has influenced her ability to mentor young women in a similar capacity: "*WINS has helped me learn to talk with other young women. I currently work helping young women choose career paths. WINS also helped me understand the importance of mental health and self-care.*" Jakiah's reflection further emphasizes the ways that WINS supported students both in their academic pursuit of STEM knowledge and skills as well as in their personal growth and wellbeing. Kiambi Bruce, also a WINS alumna (2015), talks about the impact of WINS and giving back to young girls in Philadelphia:

> I was able to pass down my love of STEM to many elementary-aged girls throughout the city of Philadelphia as a program facilitator. WINS also equipped me with the skills to give and receive professional and emotional support from my peers and other adults. The concept of community support to foster youth's future was never lost throughout the entire WINS program.

Kiambi expressed that WINS helped her understand how to enact and value two-way supportive relationships through developing the ability to both "give and receive" support while in the program. Her reflection as a WINS alumnae deeply illustrates the connection between the web of supportive relationships to the larger program goals of promoting the future of women of color in STEM. Another WINS Alumna describes the lasting impact the program has made for her:

> This program has shaped my life forever. It has shown me that, ... I am strong, and nothing will bring me down...WINS has given me wings to fly very high.
>
> -WINS Alumna and DREAMer

The WINS sisterhood

WINS students gain lifelong friendships beyond their years as participants in the program. These positive peer experiences are fostered through the programs' Big WINS Little WINS components, where older students provide peer mentorship to younger participants. They have opportunities to engage in activities around self-care, such as mindful conversations fostering positive youth development and community building. WINS encourages a community of like-minded young people where they can feel safe to be their authentic selves. More importantly, these friendships strengthen throughout the years as participants transition into adulthood. WINS students hold on to experiences gained while in the program but can also count on sisterhood as they gain new experiences or changes in life. Jiciana Knight (WINS Alumna, 2016) discusses what the WINS sisterhood means to her, *"WINS impacted my life by allowing me to find sisterhood and the power in it. It helped me have the ambition and drive to complete any goal that comes to my mind."*

Jiciana's description of WINS as a driving force encouraging her to achieve her goals has been echoed by many other participants and alumnae. Maiya couples the way WINS has acted as both a home and a launching pad for her development as a STEM professional:

> When I describe the WINS program, I often say that it is like my second home. It is indescribable what WINS has given me. I was able to come out of my shell, find my passion for my future career, and gain a sense of family in the WINS program. WINS has always pushed me and supported me in gaining new opportunities and pushing me out of my comfort zone. I have truly grown throughout my time in the WINS program, and I am very grateful for every experience I have had in the program.
>
> - Maiya Mangum, WINS Alumna, 2022

Whether the support comes from the WINS program staff, the STEM professional, the WINS Alumnae, or the sisterhood of peers, the WINS web of supportive relationships provides a strong foundation for these women of color to grow and thrive within a STEM environment.

Conclusion

WINS is more than a STEM program; it is what the field really needs – especially right now. For a STEM mentorship program to be successful, it must be more than just the STEM. It must support the individual as a whole person and in a culturally sustaining way, not just fostering their interests in STEM in a vacuum. While providing access to opportunity is important, it is equally, if not sometimes more important, to provide all the other supports that young women of color need to navigate life in general. Building lifelong friendships means that WINS students are always there to elevate one another and celebrate successes, but they are also there to support each other during the most challenging times. Of all the knowledge that a WINS girl gains, they learn what it means early to "spot" the next person who comes after them. A WINS' journey includes a series of opportunities guiding them from one doorway to the next. WINS staff open the first of those doors, followed by Big WINS supporting new cohorts, STEM mentors in the Academy, and finally Alumnae that go on to open doors for current participants and other alumnae alike. We conclude with a statement in a WINS alumna's own words:

> WINS is where I grew to love myself as a whole and I met my life long best friend, Saieda. I have gained a host of new sisters from throughout the city! Today, I have a daughter who will know what WINS is and how much it means to her Mommy. WINS is a program to you, but for us .... it's a sisterhood and a bond that can't be broken. WINS is a safe haven and within OUR sisterhood everyone knows that once you're a WINS girl you are ALWAYS a WINS GIRL!
>
> - Shanaya Shoats WINS Alumna, 2010

The analysis of the findings from the WINS program demonstrates a strong interconnection between Critical Race Feminism, Ecological Systems Theory, Yosso's Community Cultural Wealth, and Culturally Sustaining Pedagogies in guiding the program's impact on Women of Color in their pursuit of STEM opportunities, development of self-efficacy, STEM careers, and supportive relationships. This comprehensive framework ensures that the program supports the holistic development of these students within the STEM field.

STEM opportunities and development of self-efficacy

The WINS program adopts a CRF lens by recognizing the systemic barriers faced by Women of Color in STEM and actively countering these barriers through inclusive curriculum and experiences. Within the WINS program, the CSP approach fosters an environment that validates and incorporates students' cultural backgrounds, allowing them to develop STEM identities and self-efficacy within a context that resonates with their lived experiences. The CCW framework highlights the unique strengths, skills, and experiences that Women of Color bring to the STEM field, emphasizing the importance of acknowledging and valuing their cultural assets.

Additionally, the WINS program integrates ecological systems by recognizing the influence of the students' surrounding environments and experiences on their STEM self-efficacy. This approach counters the history of exclusionary norms in STEM education.

STEM careers

The WINS program aligns with CRF by addressing the historical and ongoing marginalization of Women of Color in STEM careers, empowering them to envision and pursue STEM career pathways. Through CSP, the WINS program offers mentorship and experiences that align with students' cultural backgrounds, enabling them to connect their passions and talents to STEM careers. The CCW framework acknowledges the role of community and cultural connections in shaping career aspirations. The WINS program provides role models and mentorship from within the community to inspire students to pursue STEM careers. Lastly, the WINS program leverages ecological systems by providing exposure to a diverse range of STEM professionals, integrating students into real STEM projects, and offering opportunities for hands-on experiences.

Supportive relationships

By centering the experiences and narratives of women of color, the WINS program enacts CRF principles, valuing and amplifying their stories and perspectives. CSP creates a supportive network where students' cultural identities are affirmed, allowing for the development of strong relationships with peers, mentors, and program staff.

The WINS program aligns with CCW by recognizing the importance of community and family connections in students' success. The supportive relationships fostered within the WINS program mirror the concept of "social capital" in CCW. The WINS program integrates ecological systems by understanding that students are influenced by various layers of support, including peers, mentors, and program staff. The holistic web of relationships nurtures students' growth.

In conclusion, the analysis and findings from the WINS program alumnae underscore the profound connections among Critical Race Feminism, Culturally Sustaining Pedagogies, Yosso's Community Cultural Wealth, and Ecological Systems Theory in shaping the program's impact on Women of Color in their pursuit of STEM opportunities, self-efficacy, careers, and relationships. This comprehensive framework ensures that the WINS program not only addresses the systemic barriers faced by these students but also empowers them with the necessary tools, support, and cultural validation to succeed and excel in the STEM field.

I don't think there is enough space or time to talk about my experience with WINS. I started WINS in 1989 and didn't leave until 2001! We were

WINS girls who never wanted to leave the program or the Academy. We were embraced by a program, an institution, and people who... ignited and fueled a desire to change the world around us, learning concepts that seemed beyond an inner-city girl.

WINS is special because it looks for girls with potential, not limitations. It embraces girls for who they are and can be, not for what they don't have. And it places girls in the bosom of safety. First in a program, then in an institution and makes them realize they can conquer the world!

- Ninette LaDeva (Cooper) Bennett, WINS Alumna

Acknowledgments

This material is based upon work partially supported by the National Science Foundation (NSF) under NSF Award Number DRL-1849735. Any opinions, findings and conclusions, or recommendations expressed in this material are those of the author(s), and do not necessarily reflect those of the NSF. The authors acknowledge the support of the entire project team, WINS alumnae, Carol Inman and Laurie Smith.

References

Alim, H. S., Paris, D., & Wong, C. P. (2020). Culturally sustaining pedagogy: A critical framework for centering communities. In *Handbook of the cultural foundations of learning* (pp. 261-276). Routledge.

Aronson, J., Fried, C. B., & Good, C. (2002). Reducing the effects of stereotype threat on African American college students by shaping theories of intelligence. *Journal of Experimental Social Psychology, 38*(2), 113–25.

Bandura, A. (1986). *Social foundations of thoughts and action: A social cognitive theory.* Prentice Hall.

Bang, M., Warren, B., Rosebery, A. S., & Medin, D. (2013). Desettling expectations in science education. *Human Development, 55*(5-6), 302-318.

Berry, T.R. (2010). Engaged Pedagogy and Critical Race Feminism. *Educational Foundations, 24*, 19–26.

Blackwell, L. S., Trzesniewski, K. H., & Dweck, C. S. (2007). Implicit theories of intelligence predict achievement across an adolescent transition: A longitudinal study and an intervention. *Child Development, 78*(1), 246–63.

Bonilla-Silva, Eduardo (2015). More than prejudice: Restatement, reflections, and new directions in critical race theory. *Sociology of Race and Ethnicity, 1*(1), 73–87, https://doi.org/10.1177/2332649214557042

Bronfenbrenner, U. (2001). The bioecological theory of human development. In N.J. Smelser & P.B. Baltes (Eds.), *International Encyclopedia of the Social and Behavioral Sciences* (Vol. 10, pp. 6963 - 6970). Elsevier.

Brown, B. A. (2019). *Science in the city.* Harvard Education Press.

Catalyst (2020). Women in science, technology, engineering, and mathematics (STEM): Quick take. https://www.catalyst.org/research/women-in-science-technology-engineering-and-mathematicsstem/

Cheryan, S., Drury, B. J., & Vichayapai, M. (2012). Enduring influences of stereotypical computer science role models on women's academic aspirations. *Psychology of Women Quarterly, 37,* 72–79.

Dweck, C.S. (2006). Is math a gift? Beliefs that put females at risk. In S. J. Ceci & W. M. Williams (Eds.), *Why aren't more women in science? Top researchers debate the evidence* (pp. 47–55). American Psychological Association.

Dweck, C.S. & Master, A. (2009). *Handbook of motivation at school.* Routledge.

Eccles, J. S. (2007). Where are all the women? Gender differences in participation in physical science and engineering. In S. J. Ceci & W. M. Williams (Eds.), *Why aren't more women in science? Top researchers debate the evidence* (pp. 199–210). Washington, DC: American Psychological Association.

Evans-Winters, V. E., & Esposito, J. (2010). Other people's daughters: Critical race feminism and Black girls' education. *Educational Foundations, 24,* 11-24.

Fadigan, K. A., & Hammrich, P. L. (2004). A longitudinal study of the educational and career trajectories of female participants of an urban informal science education program. *Journal of Research in Science Teaching, 41*(8), 835-860.

Foutz, S. (2009). Women in natural sciences: Academy of natural sciences evaluation study of current and alumnae WINS participants (Unpublished report). The Academy of Natural Sciences of Drexel University.

Ginsberg, A., Gasman, M., & Castro Samayoa, A. (2020). "A learning process versus a moment": Engaging black male teacher education candidates in culturally sustaining pedagogy at Jackson State University. *The Teacher Educator, 56*(2), 171-193.

Good, C., Aronson, J., & Inzlicht, M. (2003). Improving adolescents' standardized test performance: An intervention to reduce the effects of stereotype threat. *Applied Developmental Psychology, 24,* 645–662.

Howard, T.C. & Navarro, O. (2016). Critical race theory 20 years later: Where do we go from here? *Urban Education, 51*(3), 253–73, https://doi.org/10.1177/0042085915622541

Johns, M., Schmader, T., & Martens, A. (2005). Knowing is half the battle: Teaching stereotype threat as a means of improving women's math performance. *Psychological Science, 16*(3), 175–79.

Ladson-Billings, G. & Tate IV, W.F. (1995). Toward a critical race theory of education. *Teachers College Record, 97*(1), 47-68.

Larose, S., Ratelle, C. F., Guay, F., Senécal, C., & Harvey, M. (2006). Trajectories of science self efficacy beliefs during the college transition and academic and vocational adjustment in science and technology programs. *Educational Research and Evaluation, 12,* 373–393.

Lave, J., & Wenger, E. (1991). *Situated learning: Legitimate peripheral participation.* Cambridge University Press.

Leonardo, Z. (2013). *Race frameworks: A multidimensional theory of racism and education*. Teachers College Press.

Marshall, S. (2023). But what does it look like in maths? A framework for culturally sustaining pedagogy in mathematics. *International Journal of Multicultural Education, 25*(1), 1-29.

McCreedy, D., & Dierking, L. D. (2013). *Cascading Influences: Long-Term Impacts of Informal STEM Experiences for Girls*. Retrieved from https://www.fi.edu/sites/default/files/cascadinginfluences.pdf

McGee, E. O., & Bentley, L. (2017). The troubled success of Black women in STEM. *Cognition and Instruction, 35*(4), 265-289.

Minnett, J. L., James-Gallaway, A. D., & Owens, D. R. (2019). Help a Sista Out: Black Women doctoral students' use of peer mentorship as an act of resistance. *Mid-Western Educational Researcher, 31*(2).

NSF- National Science Foundation (2021, November 16). Women, minorities, and persons with disabilities in science and engineering. https://ncses.nsf.gov/pubs/nsf21321/report/field-of-degreeintersectionality

Pajares, F. (2005). Gender differences in mathematics self-efficacy beliefs. In A. M. Gallagher & J. C. Kaufman (Eds.), *Gender differences in mathematics: An integrative psychological approach* (pp. 294–315). Cambridge University Press.

Paris, D. (2012). Culturally sustaining pedagogy: A needed change in stance, terminology, and practice. *Educational Researcher, 41*(3), 93-97.

Patton, L.D. (2009). My sister's keeper: A qualitative examination of mentoring experiences among African American women in graduate and professional schools. *The Journal of Higher Education, 80*(5), 510–537, https://doi.org/10.1080/00221546.2009.11779030

Patton, L.D. &Ward, L.W. (2016). Missing Black undergraduate women and the politics of disposability: A critical race feminist perspective. *The Journal of Negro Education, 85*(3) 330–49, https://doi.org/10.7709/jnegroeducation.85.3.0330

Research for Action (2016). *Perspectives on the women in natural sciences program: Phase 1 research memo* (Unpublished memo). The Academy of Natural Sciences of Drexel University.

Research for Action (2017). *Perspectives on the women in natural sciences program: Phase 2 research memo.* (Unpublished memo). The Academy of Natural Sciences of Drexel University.

Research for Action (2022). *ANS EngWINS Year 3 evaluation.* (Unpublished Report). The Academy of Natural Sciences of Drexel University.

School District of Philadelphia (2018, January 11). District Scorecard. https://www.philasd.org/performance/programsservices/school-progress-reports/district-scorecard/

Scott, A., & Mallinckrodt, B. (2005). Parental emotional support, science self-efficacy, and choice of science major in undergraduate women. *Career Development Quarterly, 53*, 263-273.

Seiler, G. (2001). Reversing the "standard" direction: Science emerging from the lives of African American students. *Journal of Research in Science Teaching, 38,* 1000–1014.

Simpson, A., & Bouhafa, Y. (2020). Youths' and adults' identity in STEM: A systematic literature review. *Journal for STEM Education Research, 3,* 167-194.

Solorzano, D.G. & Delgado Bernal, D. (2001). Examining transformational resistance through a critical race and latcrit theory framework: Chicana and Chicano students in an urban context. *Urban Education, 36*(3), 308–342, https://doi.org/10.1177/0042085901363002

Sterin, K., Mathew, K., Manongsong, A., Allen-Handy, A., Genovesi, J., Walker, S., Peter, N. Godfrey, K., Thomas, D. (2023). Stepping out and stepping up: Narratives of women of color in an urban STEM OST Program. Journal of Urban Learning, Teaching, and Research.

Stoeger et al. (2013). Stoeger, H., Duan, X., Schirner, S., & Greindl, T. (2013). *Computers and education: The effectiveness of a one-year online mentoring program for girls in STEM* Pergamon Press. doi:10.1016/j.compedu.2013.07.032

Stout, J. G., Dasgupta, N., Hunsinger, M., & McManus, M. A. (2011). STEMing the tide: Using ingroup experts to inoculate women's self-concept in science, technology, engineering, and mathematics. *Journal of Personality and Social Psychology, 100,* 255–270.

Tate, E.D. & Linn, M.C. (2005). How does identity shape the experiences of women of color engineering students? *Journal of Science Education and Technology, 14*(5), 483- 493.

Wade-Jaimes, K., Cohen, J. D., & Calandra, B. (2019). Mapping the evolution of an after-school STEM club for African American girls using activity theory. *Cultural Studies of Science Education, 14*(4), 981-1010.

Wang, X. (2013). Why students choose STEM majors: Motivation, high school learning, and postsecondary context of support. *American Educational Research Journal, 50,* 1081-1121.

Wenger, E. (2011). *Communities of practice: A brief introduction.* New York: Cambridge.

Wing, A.K. (1997). *Critical Race Feminism: A Reader.* NYU Press.

Yosso, T.J. (2005). Whose culture has capital? A critical race theory discussion of community cultural wealth. *Race Ethnicity and Education, 8*(1), 69–91, https://doi.org/10.1080/1361332052000341006

Zeldin, A. L., & Pajares, F. (2000). Against the odds: Self-efficacy beliefs of women in mathematical, scientific, and technological careers. *American Educational Research Journal, 37,* 215–246.

Zimmerman, B. J. (2000). Self-efficacy: An essential motive to learn. *Contemporary Educational Psychology, 25,* 82–91.

Chapter 6

Impact of Effective Mentoring on STEM Minority and Women Undergraduates

Murty S. Kambhampati
Southern University at New Orleans, USA

Joe Omojola
Southern University at New Orleans, USA

Phyllis Okwan
Southern University A & M College, Baton Rouge, USA

Abstract: The severe shortage of manpower in Science, Technology, Engineering, and Mathematics (STEM) fields, especially among the minority population and women, is well documented. The authors of this article are aware of this shortage and that the origin of this problem, no doubt, can be traced to science education in the early elementary years. As a result of our mentoring efforts amongst the poorest minority population, we are presenting a review and summary of our experiences at Southern University at New Orleans (SUNO) on the Impact of STEM Programs and Effective Mentoring on Minority and Women Undergraduate Students. Out of all Louisiana's public-school districts, the New Orleans Public Schools District (NOPSD), containing about ten percent of all public schools' students, is one of the lowest performing districts. This is the population where Southern University at New Orleans (SUNO) recruits its students. On average, these students are enrolled in remedial education for an average of one academic year in college. These are the types of students we have been mentoring and turning into competitive students who go on to graduate or professional schools and become contributing members of society.

Keywords: Women and Minorities, STEM Education, Mentoring and its Impact, Funded Grants

***

The impact of effective mentoring on STEM minority and women undergraduates

In this chapter, we will discuss details on the mentoring of minority and women undergraduate students in STEM. We present an overview effect of mentoring in the state of Louisiana and the national level on: (a) the need, (b) evidence of mentoring effectiveness, (c) mentoring programs and activities, (d) STEM mentoring objectives, (e) funded grants and plan to sustain the mentoring activity, (f) mentoring methods and procedure, (g) building faculty/student relationships, (h) quantitative and qualitative assessment, and (i) overall measurable impact. To begin with, we will provide our background and training as a backdrop.

Mentors' background and training

The authors are tenured faculty members in biology, mathematics, and physics at two institutions within the Southern University System. In addition to their full-time teaching, university and community service, professional development, scholarship activities and other responsibilities, they are actively engaged in mentoring and writing, securing and managing state and federal grants such as Louise Stokes-Louisiana Alliance for Minority Participants (LS-LAMP), Louisiana Board of Regents Support Fund (LABoR-SF), Historically Black Universities and Colleges Undergraduate Program (HBCU-UP), Scholarships for Science, Technology, Engineering, and Mathematics (S-STEM), Minority Science and Engineering Improvement Program (MSEIP), etc., for over two decades (SUNO, n.d.). They also received supplemental grants to the NSF HBCU-UP grant to provide opportunities for minority students to participate in summer undergraduate research in Faculty and Student Team (FaST) and Summer Undergraduate Laboratory Internships (SULI) at Brookhaven National Laboratory (BNL) and to purchase pieces of replacement research equipment that were lost due to hurricane Katrina.

   Due to these multiple funded grants and supplemental funding from NSF-HBCU-UP grants, more than one hundred biology and mathematics undergraduate students participated and conducted 8 to 10-week summer research at SUNO and at its collaborative research institutions and national laboratories such as Tulane University, Louisiana Universities Marine Consortium, Louisiana State University, Brookhaven National Laboratory, Southern University at Baton Rouge, Iowa State University, Northern Iowa University, for over two decades. These efforts have strengthened their undergraduate mentoring activities and increased the admission of students to graduate and or professional schools.

Two of the authors have received several academic and mentoring awards, including two Presidential Awards for Excellence in Science, Mathematics, and Engineering Mentoring (PAESMEM) and the Proclamations from the City Council of New Orleans for their excellence in STEM Mentoring over the years. We have been identified as ideal STEM mentors because of the rare combination of our collegiate personalities and a wonderful set of desirable characteristics of effective mentors. Among those characteristics are hard work, humility, dependability, honesty, and the courage to work across multiple boundaries. These qualities have paid off well for us (White House News Release, 2007; National Archives, 2015).

The need

The authors are aware of the severe shortage of manpower in the sciences, especially among the minority population (Blacks in Undergraduate Science and Engineering Education, 1992; Hill, 1992a & b; Women and Minorities in Science and Engineering, 1992; Institute for Higher Education Policy, 2004; American Institutes for Research, 2005). Throughout their careers, the authors have addressed this problem through mentoring Minority and Women Undergraduate STEM majors. From the year 2009 to 2018, the rate of STEM graduates among women increased by 60% compared to their male counterparts' increase of 66% (USAFacts, September 28, 2020). College graduates among blacks increased from 39% to 45% compared to whites increase of 58% to 67% from the year 2002 to 2020 (USAFacts, n.d.). Nkrumah and Scott (2022) provided a detailed review of college graduates in STEM fields among women of ethnic diversity and summarized that the percentage of minority women was very low (Black women 6.3%, Hispanic/Latino women 7.0%, and Asian women 2.6%) compared to white women (34.5%). They discussed the role of women of color in mentoring minorities and its impact on nurturing and producing a competitive workforce (Hill, 2000; National Science Foundation, Committee on Equal Opportunities in Science and Engineering, 2005; Nkrumah & Scott, 2022).

On a positive note, the graduation rate and the college entry rate in New Orleans public schools have increased from 54% to 78% and 37% to 56%, respectively, from 2014 to 2021 (NOLA Teacher Fest, 2023) compared to the relative time period on national graduation rate increase from 82.3% in 2014 to 85.3% in 2019 (Public high school adjusted cohort graduation rate - USAFacts) and the decline of college entry rates from 66% in 2014 to 62% in 2021 (IES NCES Fast Facts: Immediate transition to college (51). For instance, during this period, more than 100 of our STEM mentees, mostly women from Southern

University at New Orleans (SUNO), graduated with a BS degree in STEM fields. Some of them earned graduate and professional degrees. Some of the recent graduates are currently enrolled in graduate or professional schools.

Evidence of mentoring effectiveness

Throughout our careers, we have collaborated with colleagues, collaborators, and students. Our efforts have impacted hundreds of students and resulted in several awards (White House News Release, 2007; Tantillo, 2018; National Archives, 2015). Several of our mentees are in the STEM workforce working as dedicated STEM teachers in New Orleans parish and Jefferson parish and in neighboring states such as Georgia and Texas, serving as university faculty, administrators such as chairs, deans, national organizations such as the National Science Foundation, private business entrepreneurship, etc. These former mentees are impacting hundreds of thousands of students and faculty members across the nation.

Mentoring programs/activities

Our mentoring method requires a sustained effort to consistently motivate and nurture a pool of minority (African American) and women students in STEM fields through effective hands-on activities. To this end, we have provided excellent mentoring, teaching, academic advisement, career counseling, and research guidance in biology, mathematics, and physics through vigorous efforts, which include: (i) early intervention (junior high school), (ii) high school mentoring, (iii) academic advisement to undergraduates, (iv) experimental training in STEM and its related fields, (v) career counseling and explorations, (vi) placement of students in summer research internship programs across the United States, and (vii) effective teaching and tutoring. Efforts have also been made to strengthen student's backgrounds at the middle/high school level and hold their interest in science disciplines. Activities focused on these students resulted in many of them successfully completing their undergraduate education (by securing scholarships and academic stipends), with a high percentage of the graduates going on to graduate schools.

STEM mentoring objectives

We identified two significant and measurable mentoring objectives: (1) to use research to build students' character, confidence levels, and skills, and (2) to maximize students' potential. It has been proven at Southern University at New Orleans (White House News Release, 2007; National Archives, 2015) that our mentoring efforts enabled students to appreciate science while providing opportunities to experience academic success, learn scientific research skills, and develop professional skills. We have provided our mentees with mentoring at different levels. The details of our mentoring program are described below:

In our experience, undergraduate research experience and exposure are important tools for motivating students to pursue higher (graduate/professional) education and research careers (Blacks in Undergraduate Science and Engineering Education, 1992; Hill 1992a & b; Women and Minorities in Science and Engineering, 1992; Task Force on Women, Minorities, and Handicapped in Science and Technology, 1989; Rosser & Davidson, 1996). For over 20 years, we have mentored minority and women students in undergraduate research. We found this to be a highly effective activity for developing students. All our mentees were supported by stipends/scholarships/summer internships through funded grants. Each mentee is assigned a STEM mentor (faculty member or a scientist at a research institution or a national laboratory) and has an opportunity to conduct research and participate in research conferences. The externally funded programs have enabled us (in collaboration with our colleagues as PIs and co-PIs on different grants) to improve the research infrastructure on our campus. These infrastructure enhancements benefitted students and faculty immensely. It resulted in enhancing the participation of STEM majors in conducting quality STEM research projects. Furthermore, these efforts have positively impacted and expanded collaborations with academic institutions and research facilities supported by our peers and funding agencies.

Funded grants and plan to sustain mentoring activity

It is a known fact that minorities and women are under-represented in science and technology (Women and Minorities in Science and Engineering, 1992; Rosser & Davidson, 1996). We have successfully implemented mentoring activities in both teaching and research to under-represented minority students with support from the university administration and external funding (including housing for FaST and SULI research interns and faculty). Searching for appropriate grant solicitations, writing grant proposals in response to proposal guidelines, and securing funded grants is a very long, laborious, and competitive process. Once we get the grants funded, we implement the proposed activities and evaluate the outcomes of all the measurable objectives in a timely manner. These activities require strong leadership and time management skills and commitment to successful completion. Above all, we have dedicated teams of project personnel for various grants and administrative support to manage our grants successfully. The funds we received through state and federal agencies such as LA BoR, NSF, NIH, USEd, NOAA, and DoE provided opportunities to STEM majors and faculty at SUNO for research and professional development. Funded grants at SUNO have improved the recruitment and retention of minority and women students in STEM disciplines until post-Hurricane Katrina and pre-COVID-19 periods. These grants enabled us to serve as preceptors for students' undergraduate research. Recruitment and mentoring have attracted students and teachers to participate in Summer Enrichment Programs sponsored by HBCU-UP, S-STEM, MSEIP, and DOE for the past several years (Tantillo, 2018; Brookhaven National Laboratory Workforce Development and Education, 2023). This model is easily replicable at other academic and research institutions.

Mentoring methods and procedure

Enhance undergraduate education through mentoring and research

Methodology

The mentoring programs supported by external grants were initiated to increase student recruitment and retention in STEM programs. Incoming freshmen and sophomores with a G.P.A. of at least 2.7 and students with a strong interest in STEM are eligible to apply for consideration to be awarded these stipends. These programs were designed and enhanced to improve the educational experience of minority and women students in STEM, from high school through college.

Outcomes

These mentoring programs provided scholarships/stipends, travel support and mentoring for several hundreds of STEM undergraduates (pre-Katrina STEM departments in the College of Sciences - Biology, Mathematics, Chemistry, Computer Information Systems, and Physics; post-Katrina Department of Natural Sciences – Biology and Mathematics majors in the College of Arts and Sciences, Biology & Forensic science double majors; Biology and Education majors or Mathematics and Education majors, Mathematics and Biology or Mathematics and Computer Information Systems or Mathematics and Business Administration majors). For over 25 years, funding was secured through the NSF-HBCU-UP, S-STEM, LS-LAMP, S-STEM, and US Ed MSEIP, by the authors. The programs focused on undergraduate education and research experience. Nurturing these young researchers is a primary concern; the highest priority is given to providing mentees guidance and skills to ensure their success in undergraduate education and provide a pathway to entrance and success in graduate schools. This one-on-one faculty-student team interaction with *Scholars* has been a key aspect of effective mentoring. Specifically, from freshman to senior year, we mentored scholars through several activities such as:

- Recruiting students and advising them in course selection to assist in the successful completion of their undergraduate program in less than the normal institutional average of six years;

- Participating in enrichment opportunities such as guest speaker seminars, literature searches, test-taking skills and library skills workshops;

- Providing undergraduate research experiences (presentation and publication of research abstracts and papers with co-authorship with their mentors) by encouraging scholars to participate in summer research programs at research-intensive institutions, providing funds for students to travel and present their research findings at conferences and networking with the STEM professionals and community;

- Participating in GRE review workshops: Students are supplied with review materials (books, software etc.). Additionally, students are encouraged to participate in evening tutorial sessions in STEM disciplines;

- Providing graduate school information and applications for the best STEM programs: We assist students in obtaining financial support from federal or private agencies or university fellowships.

Impact

It is noteworthy that around 90% of our mentees obtained their bachelor's degree in STEM fields (some of them earned dual degrees) in significantly less time than the normal campus average of 6 years. This is very impressive when compared to the average graduation rate of 10-15% at Southern University at New Orleans (SUNO) over the years. For instance, the 2013 cohort at SUNO graduated 6% in 4 years, 23% in 6 years, and 25% in 8 years. The 2015 cohort graduated 18% women and 21% men, with an overall graduation rate of 19%. Based on ethnicity, 19% of Black or African Americans and 67% of White undergraduates of the 2015 cohort graduated in 2021 (National Center for Education Statistics, n.d. b). Based on these data points, mentoring in STEM disciplines is highly needed because it is a proven effective method for retention, graduation, and reduction in number of years to graduate.

Some of our former mentees, who are supported by funded STEM grants, are currently serving as professors/administrators at academic institutions of higher education (an Associate Professor of Mathematics at Southern University A&M College, Baton Rouge; an Associate Dean for Research, Graduate Programs, and Natural Sciences and Professor of Physics in the College of Arts and Sciences at Howard University; a Professor of Physics and Associate Dean for Faculty Success at University Texas, San Antonio; an Associate Professor of Biostatistics at Indiana University; an Associate Executive Director for the American Mathematical Society, a Data Analyst at Tulane University School of Medicine, a Regulatory Analyst at Entergy, to name a few), a Section Head at NSF); teachers in high school systems (several teachers in Orleans Parish Public Schools System, Jefferson Parish Public Schools, and out of state), professionals such as pharmacists, medical doctors, scientists, etc. These STEM ambassadors for SUNO have been positively impacting hundreds of thousands of STEM majors across the nation.

Increasing undergraduate participation in research during academic year and summer

Methodology

Our mentoring program is designed for undergraduates to provide research methodology through hands-on projects. At the sophomore and junior levels, students who have taken basic and gatekeeper STEM courses such as General Biology I and II with labs for Biology majors and pre-calculus for Mathematics majors will have the opportunity to work in the labs for 4-6 hrs. per week. They are allowed to conduct independent undergraduate research projects and attend monthly lab meetings. In addition, these students are required to attend and make scientific presentations at local, regional, and national meetings and conferences. In order to encourage students to continue to focus on their academics, they receive stipends based on their financial needs. Students who are chosen for our Summer Undergraduate Research Experience (SURE), work full-time for ten weeks during the summer alongside a faculty and or a research scientist (in teams) at a national lab or on campus. National lab summer interns receive research stipends and one round-trip travel ticket. Lodging expenses, for students and faculty, are incurred by the host institution or SUNO through funded grants. To be eligible for these programs an applicant must be enrolled full-time at SUNO with a declared STEM major, at sophomore or junior level, with a grade point average of at least 2.7/4.0.

Outcomes

Collectively, under this program, we have mentored hundreds of students during their undergraduate research. We believe, very strongly, that mentoring is a highly effective activity for preparing students for graduate and professional schools (Crisp et al., 2017; White House News Release, 2007; National Archives, 2015). We assisted students in publishing papers in peer-reviewed refereed national and international journals. We also publish students' research abstracts in local, regional, national, and international conference proceedings. In over 25 years, these students (100% STEM mentees) have presented hundreds of oral and/or poster presentations at local, state, and national scientific conferences/symposia. These accomplishments and exposures to the scientific community and their peers enabled many students to receive (a) travel awards to attend scientific meetings, (b) summer internships, (c) invitations to visit and/or apply to graduate schools, and (d) full financial aid (assistantships and/or tuition waiver) to attend graduate schools. In addition, our efforts in mentoring and student achievements highlight the importance of undergraduate mentoring (White House News Release, 2007; National Archives, 2015). These efforts serve as a major catalyst in attracting other faculty members and mentees to become mentors. Notably, over the years, the number of STEM faculty mentors has approximately increased from 4 in 2000 to 16 in 2023 (400% increase).

In addition, our mentees have participated in many exciting scholarly, cultural, and social activities. They met and interacted with research scientists (networking), served as judges in Science Fairs, participated in research seminars, attended Summer Sunday STEM Workshops/Exhibits, took part in brown bag lunches covering research topics of interest, and toured major research facilities at Brookhaven National Laboratory, Upton, NY. At the end of the summer programs, students delivered scientific presentations at the "Closing Ceremonies - Summer Symposia."

Building faculty/student relationships

Every academic semester, each of us advises 20-30 STEM majors (as an academic advisor) and teaches one freshman/sophomore course and two junior/senior courses. These interactions enable us to establish and maintain a close relationship with students. This acquaintanceship has been a key aspect of effective mentoring for us. Specifically, as advisers, beginning in the freshman year, we assist students with course selections for their undergraduate program and encourage them to participate in enrichment opportunities such as seminars, literature searches, test-taking skills, and scientific writing skills workshops. We conduct weekly meetings with students, during which we check on students' welfare and review their academic progress in order to determine if there is a need for intervention. We provide students with undergraduate research experience and encourage them to participate in summer research programs at major research institutions.

Quantitative and qualitative assessment

When we started our careers at SUNO, the lack of infrastructure was a major constraint for students to conduct biology/mathematics research projects. Consequently, the number of students attending graduate schools during that period was very minimal. During 1995-2023, we submitted several grant applications to LA-BoR-SF, the US Department of Education, NSF, and NIH and received many grant awards and subawards with collaborative institutions. The infusion of external funds and dedicated STEM faculty members and their unwavering efforts in mentoring over the span of 25 years enabled the department to provide an excellent atmosphere/environment for undergraduate students and faculty to conduct research. Additionally, we leveraged our funding and collaborations synergistically to increase the number of undergraduate student researchers. As a result of the availability of funds, leveraging, and improved research infrastructure, several students were able to participate in undergraduate research during the academic year and summer. The number of students attending and presenting their research outcomes at conferences almost tripled, and the students gaining admission to graduate schools steadily increased over the years until prior to COVID-19 pandemic. Some of our mentees have sought and earned graduate or professional degrees.

Collectively, the authors of this paper have over 70 years of experience as faculty and STEM mentors. The list of their extensive achievements includes two presidential awards (PAESMEM – Presidential Awards for Excellence in Science, Mathematics and Engineering Mentoring) in mentoring and contributions to human development, whereby they have turned dreams into reality and continued to commit to increasing the number of minorities and women in STEM careers.

Overall measurable impact

In summary, for over two decades, about 90% of STEM students who received academic stipends and summer research internships through funded grants, were retained. Those who were retained in the program graduated with a Bachelor of Science degree either in Mathematics or Biology, Physics, Chemistry, or double majored and earned dual degrees in Biology/Mathematics or Biology/Forensic Science or Mathematics/Computer Information Systems or Mathematics/Education programs successfully. The authors were involved in curriculum redesign, which streamlined double major requirements in Biology, Education, and Mathematics, which increased the number of students earning dual degrees. Compared to the national graduation rate of 64% and 36% for STEM majors among men and women, respectively, a higher percentage of bachelor's degrees were awarded to females (58%) than to males (42%) in 2015-16 (National Center for Education Statistics, n.d. a). The majority of the students who graduated and were supported by funded grants participated in at least one or two summer research internships either at Southern University in New Orleans or at collaborative institutions. In addition, these students had opportunities to participate in STEM and or guest speaker seminars, which expanded their knowledge base. Research interns were able to be exposed to a wider audience at local, regional, and national conferences, where they presented their project results. Consequently, they published their research abstracts in conference proceedings and peer-reviewed journals along with their mentors and contributed their findings to scientific literature. Finally, students with undergraduate research experiences are self-confident with enhanced self-esteem, have improved communication skills, possess excellent team spirit, have better listening and learning abilities, and have acquired better time management and multitasking skills, to name a few.

It is noteworthy that about 90% of our STEM mentees at SUNO obtained their bachelor's degree. This is in contrast to the national graduation rates among Black Women – the majority of SUNO STEM graduates are Black Women. This is very impressive on two important indicators of mentoring: (a) percentage of graduates among STEM mentees is 90% compared to the average graduation rate of 12-18% at SUNO over the years, and (b) percentage of Women graduates is >90% in STEM fields. Overall, the efforts of effective mentoring at SUNO have served as a major catalyst in improving the graduation and retention rate of STEM majors, enriching the undergraduate experience, expanding opportunities for students, improving students' oral and written communication skills, increasing the number of students attaining dual undergraduate and advanced degrees, attracting mentees and other faculty members to become mentors.

Conclusion

Mentoring at Southern University in New Orleans provides the opportunity for students to learn about the many aspects of STEM fields through academic engagement and hands-on-research projects. It also provides a springboard for science, mathematics, and engineering mentors to teach the importance of these fields in building and rebuilding a city and the society at large, especially after hurricane Katrina, the COVID-19 pandemic, and hurricane Ida. After these catastrophic events, the inspiring mentoring work of resolute mentors becomes even more important in the minority communities in this area. STEM education and research mentoring at Southern University at New Orleans and Southern University at Baton Rouge have contributed (a) to alleviating the shortage of minority and women students in STEM and (b) to increase the diversity and inclusion of minority and women STEM graduates and (c) to increasing minority and women mentors in STEM workforce, academia and business. To the best of our ability, we addressed these issues through mentoring programs, despite the challenges of low enrollment, shortage of manpower, lack of optimum quality and reliability of infrastructure and facilities, etc. We have a lot more work to do to sustain our efforts in mentoring in order to improve the number of competitive students who graduate with STEM degrees, pursue advanced degrees, and join STEM and its related workforce in order to continue to contribute their skillsets to improve the quality of life for future generations. Our work will continue to serve as a catalyst for aspiring minority scientists and as a model for a new generation of faculty members and mentors within our physical orbit of interactions and through dissemination.

These programs have a proven positive impact on the SUNO campus and could be transferred to or implemented at other institutions of higher education (academia), research institutions, research facilities, private and public institutions, business entrepreneurship, etc., as role model programs.

Acknowledgments

We express our deep sense of gratitude to the Louisiana Board of Regents, National Science Foundation, US Department of Education, US Department of Energy, National Institutes of Health, Louisiana Department of Health, and Centers for Disease Control and Prevention for financial support through funded grants and sub-contracts with collaborators. We thank Southern University at New Orleans and our collaborators for the facilities and support to work successfully on funded projects. Finally, we are very grateful to our former and current students, who have responded positively to our mentoring efforts and methods over the years, and especially to those who have become mentors.

References

American Institutes for Research. (2005). *Creating and maintaining excellence: The model institutions for excellence program.* Washington, DC.

Blacks in Undergraduate Science and Engineering Education, Special Report. (1992). Division of Human Resources. *National Science Foundation (No. NSF 92-305).*

Brookhaven National Laboratory, Workforce Development and Education, US Department of Energy. (2023). *Visiting Faculty Program.* Retrieved July 6, 2023, from https://www.bnl.gov/education/

Crisp, G., Baker, V. I., Griffin, K. A., Lunsford, L.G., & Pifer, M.J. (2017). Mentoring undergraduate students. In K. Ward & L. E. Wolf-Wendel (Eds.), *ASHE Higher Education Report. 43*(1). Wiley.

Guyton, P. (February 17, 2023). *9 best school districts in Louisiana.* Retrieved July 6, 2023, from ezhomesearch.com

Hill, S. (1992a.). Selected data on science and engineering doctorate awards: 1991. *NSF Division of Human Resources Studies (No. NSF 92-309).*

Hill, S. (1992b.). Undergraduate origins of recent science and engineering doctorate recipients, *Special Report (No. NSF 92-332).*

Hill, T. S. (2000). NSF Division of Science Resources studies, science and engineering degrees, by Race/Ethnicity of Recipients: 1991–2000. *NSF 02–329, table Arlington, VA: National Science Foundation.*

Institute for Higher Education Policy. (February, 2004). Serving the Nation: Opportunities and challenges in the use of information technology at minority-serving colleges and universities. https://www.ihep.org/publication/serving-the-nation-opportunities-and-challenges-in-the-use-of-information-technology-at-minority-serving-colleges-and-universities/

National Archives. (2015). The White House, President Barack Obama. Retrieved July 23, 2023, from https://obamawhitehouse.archives.gov/the-press-office/2015/03/27/president-obama-honors-outstanding-science-mathematics-and-engineering-m

National Center for Education Statistics. *(n.d. a). Indicator 26: STEM Degrees (ed.gov).* (retrieved July 6, 2023).

National Center for Education Statistics. (n.d. b). *IPEDS Data Center.* Retrieved July 6, 2023.

National Science Foundation, Committee on Equal Opportunities in Science and Engineering. (2005). *Broadening Participation in America's Science and Engineering Workforce. Washington, DC.*

Nkrumah, T & Scott, K. A. (2022). Mentoring in STEM higher education: a synthesis of the literature to (re)present the excluded women of color. *International Journal of Education, 9*(50), 1-23. https://doi.org/10.1186/s405 94-022-00367-7

NOLA Teacher Fest. (2023). *New Orleans Public School Statistics | New Schools for New Orleans.* Retrieved July 6, 2023.

Rosser, J. M. & Davidson, K. (1996). National Science Foundation, The EHR Advisory Committee Report "Shaping the Future." *Review of Undergraduate Education, Report NSF 96-139.*

Scott, M. (2007). Morgan Quitno Press: State and city ranking publications. Retrieved July 6, 2023, from http://www.morganquitno.com/index.htm

Skinner, V. (July 25, 2022). *Study ranks Louisiana public schools near the bottom nationally in both quality and safety.* Retrieved July 6, 2023, from The Center Square.

Southern University of New Orleans (SUNO). (n.d.), Retrieved July 6, 2023, from http://www.suno.edu

Tantillo, A. (August 9, 2018). *From Hurricane Katrina victim to presidential awardee: A SUNO professor's award-winning mentoring efforts Brookhaven National Laboratory.* Retrieved July 6, 2023, from BNL Newsroom, US Department of Energy.

Task Force on Women, Minorities, and the Handicapped in Science and Technology. (December, 1989). *Changing America: The New Face of Science and Engineering Education, Final Report.* Washington, D.C.

USAFacts (September 28, 2020, updated October 28, 2020) *How many women graduate with STEM degrees?* Retrieved July 6, 2023, from - USAFacts.

USAFacts (n.d.) *College graduation rate at four-year institutions, within six years of start.* Retrieved July 6, 2023, from USAFacts.

White House News Release 07-172. (November 19, 2007). *President Honors Mentors of Scientists and Engineers.* Retrieved July 6, 2023, from https://nsf.gov

Women and Minorities in Science and Engineering. (1990). *National Science Foundation.* NSF 90-301.

SECTION.
Mentoring Professional Women in STEM

The first two chapters in this next section move to mentor professional STEM women in academia, first with an informal peer mentoring group and then examining the differences between sponsoring and mentoring, bringing connections to the introductory model for the book with layers and axes of supportive relationships. The final two chapters share outcomes for pre-service STEM teachers both through an identity lens connecting to the second book section on gender identities and their nuances and importance.

Academia programs

Chapter 7: Found Poetry – Highlighting reciprocal mentor relationships and role shifting within an informal peer mentoring group

- Amber Simpson, PhD, Signe E. Kastberg, PhD, and Caro Williams-Pierce, PhD

Chapter 8: Leveraging mentoring and sponsoring relationships to get promoted in academia

- Carole Sox and Sheryl Kline

STEM teacher professional education

Chapter 9: Cultivating expressions of black womanhood in science education through culturally responsible mentorship

- Darrin Collins and Erica Dixon

Chapter 10: DUETS: Developing urban education teachers in STEM

- Deborah A. Harmon and Ph.D., Cheryl L. Price, Ph. D.

Chapter 7

Found Poetry: Highlighting Reciprocal Mentor Relationships and Role Shifting within an Informal Peer Mentoring Group

Amber Simpson
Binghamton University, USA

Signe E. Kastberg
Purdue University, USA

Caro Williams-Pierce
University of Maryland – College Park, USA

Abstract: Women in academia often experience institutional and systemic barriers that prevent them from advancing from one position to the next (e.g., assistant professor to associate professor) at the same rate as their male counterparts. Mentoring has been identified and utilized as one solution to support women in moving through what has been described as the clogged pipeline. The aim of this study was to examine our reciprocal mentor relationships and role shifting as we discussed and questioned academic needs, tensions, and desires within an informal peer mentoring group as three women academics who span the *clogged pipeline*. Utilizing social STEM identity as a lens to understand this phenomenon, we share our experiences and struggles in academia through found poetry but also share how our informal mentoring relationships created a safe space to be our authentic selves, to be seen and heard as people and as women in academia. Our mentorship was grounded in trust, mutual caring, and shared activities that supported and fostered our sense of belonging and social acceptance within our community(ies). We consider the significance of this chapter to lie in the power of centering people in our work, institutional structures, and mentorship models as a way to meet the demands and expectations of being a woman in academia.

Keywords*: Academia, Found poetry, Informal peer mentorship, Intimate methodology, Sense of belonging, Social acceptance

***

Poetic prologue

I feel known and seen
You care and I am cared for
We are becoming
I care and you are cared for
Becoming a better us

Found poetry – highlighting reciprocal mentor relationships and role shifting within an informal peer mentoring group

Women's career advancement within academia has been described as a "clogged pipeline" as fewer women are advancing from one position to the next (e.g., mid-career to full professor; American Association of University Professors, 2022; Miegroet et al., 2019). Prior research has documented institutional and systemic barriers that prevent women from advancing at the same rate as their male counterparts. Barriers include lower job satisfaction (Bilimoria et al., 2008), taking on more service roles (Macfarlane & Burg, 2019), unwelcoming academic climates (Cassad et al., 2021; McCutcheon & Morrison, 2018), feeling positioned as outsiders (Gibson, 2006; Holmes et al., 2007), and lacking understanding of institutional norms and required faculty expectations (Agosto et al., 2016). Women in academia have described career impacts resulting in attempts to attain work-life balance (Toffoletti & Starr, 2016). Additionally, women's productivity during COVID 19 decreased professional-emotional mentor support, increased planning for classes, decreased research/writing time, limited access to institutional facilities, and increased domestic duties (Dunn et al., 2022; Lambrechts et al., 2021; Paul et al., 2022).

Mentoring is one support for women moving through the clogged pipeline (e.g., Block & Tietjen-Smith, 2016; Gardiner et al., 2007; Schmidt & Faber, 2016). Researchers consistently highlight mentoring program benefits for women in academia. Benefits enable women to navigate institutional expectations by procuring grants, planning career trajectories, developing journal publications, and gaining research visibility (e.g., Quinn, 2012; Schmidt & Faber, 2016; Varkey et al., 2012). Yet, as Meschitti and Smith (2017) argued, additional mentorship research should consider how relational perspectives shape mentors and mentees. We contribute to this research by examining our reciprocal mentor relationships and role shifting as we discussed and questioned academic needs, tensions, and desires within an informal peer mentoring group of three women academics that span the *clogged pipeline*. Through found poetry, we document our experiences and struggles in academia through a lens of sense of belonging (or not) and social acceptance (or social nonacceptance) but also share how our mentoring relationships created a safe space to be our authentic selves, to be seen and heard as people and as women in academia. We argue that mentorship grounded in trust, mutual caring, and shared activities (i.e., academic friendship; Webster & Boyd, 2019) enables women to resist the individualistic, competitive nature of academia while fostering women's sense of belonging and social acceptance within a STEM community. The significance of this chapter lies in centering people in our work, institutional structures, and mentorship models to meet the demands and expectations of being women in academia, particularly women who identify as educators, researchers, and mentors within one or more STEM fields.

Theoretical grounding

In social identity theory, social identity is the extent to which a person views themself as part of a social category or group, such as nationality, religious affiliation, and gender (Hogg et al., 1995; Tajfel & Turner, 1985). A social category is one in which an individual feels a sense of belonging and acceptance in relation to members of the group (i.e., in-group; Tajfel & Turner, 1985). Social identities outline who belongs (or not) and what group membership means. For example, mathematicians have been defined through stereotypical and normative actions, behaviors, and/or assigned social categories (Hogg et al., 1995), such as male, exceptionally intelligent, unattractive, and socially awkward (Hall & Suurtamm, 2020; Piatek-Jimenez, 2008, 2015). This prototype of a mathematician defines the in-group. An individual without the body attributes, abilities, values, attitudes, and behaviors of mathematicians (Steele et al., 2002), such as women (Piatek-Jimenez, 2015; Steinke, 2013) and Black and Latin* students (Leyva et al., 2021; McGee & Martin, 2011), is positioned as part of the out-group. Additionally, an individual's organization, work group, and department may inform their social identity (Ashforth & Mael, 1989). In academia, there are distinctive characteristics and expectations that inform and define membership of the in-group, such as publishing peer-reviewed articles, pursuing and receiving grant funding, serving on university committees, and obtaining strong teaching evaluations. In this chapter, we draw upon Kim and colleagues' (2018) notion that STEM identity is a social identity. A STEM identity is the extent to which an individual perceives themselves as a member of a STEM discipline (i.e., a sense of belonging) and is accepted as a member by the STEM community. As women in academia, we ground our perceptions of self within an academia STEM identity, a social identity in the intersection of a STEM discipline, academia, institutional norms and expectations.

Relevant literature

Mentorship

There are multiple approaches and definitions that encompass mentorship. Traditional mentorship is the institutional pairing of a mentee (i.e., junior faculty) with a mentor or "knowledgeable" other (i.e., senior faculty) (Gardiner et al., 2007; Marino, 2021; Schmidt & Faber, 2016). This is often grounded in a hierarchical structure where the power position of the mentor dominates the relationship and may not support the career goals of the mentee but the objectives and expectations set forth by the institution (Wanberg et al., 2003). While such mentoring supports women in academia to advance in their careers by meeting the demands and expectations for tenure and promotion (e.g., Gardiner et al., 2007), challenges and limitations have also been identified. Women mentees expressed hesitancy in asking for help from a mentor within the same institution for fear of being unprofessional (e.g., Cohen et al., 2012; Corwin et al., 2012) and developing low self-esteem (Wasburn, 2007). They may be paired with a male mentor (Lewis & Olshansky, 2016) or an individual outside their disciplinary focus (Angelique et al., 2002). There are also few formal mentoring programs designed for mid-career women faculty.

Informal peer mentorship, or a community of practice mentoring approach (Bottoms et al., 2013), is developed "naturally and spontaneously without outside assistance" (Searby et al., 2015, p. 104). The mentorship is grounded in non-hierarchical structures focused on building a community among women in academia through reciprocity, flexibility, empowerment, and trust (e.g., Agosto et al., 2016; Dajani et al., 2021; Gibson, 2006; Wu et al., 2016). While benefits are similar to those highlighted above in formal mentoring approaches (e.g., career development), additional benefits include emotional support

(Agosto et al., 2016), collaboratively engaging in research- and writing-related practices (Bottoms et al., 2013), reduce feelings of isolation and increase one's well-being and self-worth (Angelique et al., 2002; Bottoms et al., 2013; Gibson, 2004; Wu et al., 2016), and opportunities for sharing personal and professional challenges and needs (Thomas et al., 2015). Yet, as acknowledged by Thomas et al. (2015) and Wu et al. (2016), building relationships and trust among peers in an informal mentorship is not immediate or easy as tensions may develop (e.g., too much socializing, little structure) and grow as individuals remain silent and abstain from collaborative opportunities.

Sense of belonging

Mentorship has also been associated with supporting women's sense of belonging (Wright-Mair, 2020; Wu et al., 2016). Sense of belonging in this study is defined as "the extent to which a person believes that they are accepted and included as a legitimate member of an academic community and that their presence and contributions to that community are valued" (Stachl & Baranger, 2020, para. 1). Post-secondary students' sense of belonging in a STEM community, as well as faculty from marginalized groups, are well represented in scholarship. This research provides a foundation to explore how a sense of belongingness supports the institutional affiliation and promotion of faculty (O'Connell & McKinnon, 2021; Ong et al., 2018), and similarly, student persistence and retention (Museus et al., 2017; Tinto, 2017). Collectively, researchers point to the importance of community and mentorship in developing and fostering an individual's sense of belonging toward advancement. For example, Wright-Muir (2020) discussed the significance of mentors supporting their colleagues as whole human beings (e.g., sexual orientation, ethnic identity, caregiver, abilities, hobbies, etc.). Such individuals experienced a sense of belongingness in an environment many expressed as unwelcoming and lonely. As another example, Ong et al. (2018) highlighted how safe social spaces and a supportive community helped to diminish women's negative experiences (e.g., microaggressions) and feelings of isolation in academia while also supporting their sense of belonging in STEM. Women of color were able to voice their struggles, frustrations, and experiences in a space where their voice was validated and their identities valued. As scholars argued, institutions should foster counterspaces and a supportive community among scholars, as the alternative - low sense of belonging and social exclusion - is often associated with negative and debilitating social and psychological factors (e.g., Arslan et al., 2020; Sargent et al., 2002).

Methods

As a dialogic community, we utilized intimate methodology (Hamilton & Pinnegar, 2014) to gain perspective and improve our informal mentoring practices. Intimate methodology allows the researcher to focus on the particular (Hamilton et al., 2016), namely experiences of informal mentorship. Characteristics of intimate methodologies (Hamilton & Pinnegar, 2015) are ways of knowing that involve (a) openness, (b) vulnerability, and (c) dialogue (Guilfoyle et al., 2004). Openness "examines and makes public what the researcher learned from experience" (Hamilton & Pinnegar, 2015, p. 135). Being vulnerable with others involves embracing "the possibility of embarrassment, loss, or emotional pain" (Lasky, 2005, p. 901) for the possibility of personal growth of self or others. Dialogue involves the "interchange of thought or talk" (Placier et al., 2005, p. 57) to consider ideas through analysis and alternative interpretations. While the dialogue is often viewed as interactive, our assertion is residue of the dialogue creates an intra-active space after the interaction. We used self-study (LaBoskey, 2004) as an intimate methodology to build from our experience of informal mentorship toward awareness of our practice. We unearthed meanings embedded in our dialogues through poetic writing (Edge & Olan, 2021).

Context

Our journey began three years ago when we met once a week for an hour as a research team interested in exploring math play in non-formal learning environments. As our relationships with one another intersected and shifted over time, our focus on research shifted over time as we began discussing and questioning academic needs, tensions, and desires as three women academics that span the clogged pipeline. Our discussions were often situationally and historically grounded (e.g., pandemic, shift in government power in the United States, the death of George Floyd) but also grounded in our multiple identities and multiplicities within our academic and personal lives. Therefore, our "mentoring relationships formed by chance" and took shape "without any rearranged schedule or agenda" (Bynum, 2015, p. 70). There was no clear boundary between mentor-mentee (NIH, 2012) as our mentoring relationship to one another was fluid. We were "just being and that was enough" (Signe, March 10, 2023).

Yet, we were more than colleagues having a conversation; we served as critical and academic friends (Klein & Taylor, 2022; Webster & Boyd, 2019). As stated by Signe, as she joined the October 20, 2020, meeting, "Hello my critical friends.

Not critical in the sense of your criticizing but critical in the sense of a lifeline." As an informal peer mentoring group, we provided alternative perspectives to a situation, encouraged each other to find their voice, and made statements of resonance to a "sticky situation" based on our own reverberating experiences.

As an informal peer mentoring group, we are three unique individuals. Amber self-identifies as a white, cis-gender woman, a mathematics teacher educator, and a researcher in STEM education. Over the span of three years, she received tenure and promotion as her title (and title alone) changed from an assistant professor to an associate professor. Signe self-identifies as a white woman nearing retirement age due to health challenges. The primary goal in Signe's work is learning through interactions with others. Caro self-identifies as a white, cis-gender, heterosexual woman from a working-class background who obsesses about design and mathematical learning through play. Over the span of three years, she changed states, institutions, and fields (moving from Education to Information Studies). Figure 7.1 is a visual representation of each author based on the data visualization work of Lupi and Posavec (2016), yet grounded in our academic discussions as an informal peer mentoring group. We invite readers to partake in this visual representation and reflect upon their STEM identity as individuals in academia by visiting the following link: https://bit.ly/3WcjZPl.

Figure 7.1. Author Self-visualizations Over Time

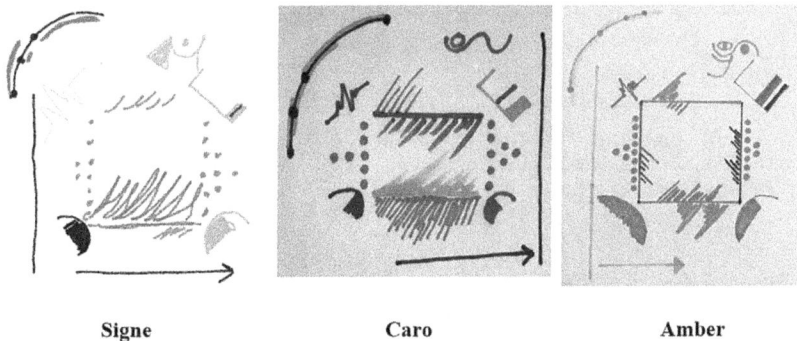

| Signe | Caro | Amber |

Data process

The data for this self-study was from our weekly meetings between September 2019 to December 2022. Each one-hour virtual meeting was video recorded and transcribed through an online artificial intelligence transcription program. Our data analysis process began with each author creating a content log of mentoring moments for one year. See Figure 7.2 as an example.

Figure 7.2. Content Log of Mentoring Moments

Date	Mentorship #1	Mentorship #2
Feb. 10, 2020	48-39-54:02: "I can see my own knowledge structures, developing over time, just by virtue of working in this group."; growth/mentorship within our discussion on research	~56:45-1:00:00: feeling like an outsider at conference
Feb. 17, 2020	4:12- 9:37: Writing process and working with editor	53:12-53:59: surveillance and rules of the ICLS community
Feb. 24, 2020	1:15:35-1:17:21: growing together in our understanding of CHAT theory	
March 2, 2020	0:00-20:10: tenure and promotion and telling other faculty to step up; saying yes/no to things	
March 23, 2020	3:48-11:11 & 17:59-30:45 & 48:13-59:17 & 1:07:42-1:12:38: impacts of COVID shutdown (e.g., CV, conferences, access to buildings, tenure)	39:25-45:45: how to respond to a weird email
March 30, 2020	6:53-13:11: impact of COVID (e.g., Faculty Senate, writing)	23:58-31:04: PMENA reviews, appropriate use of language, and comments on mentorship (e.g., "You guys mentor me every single week.")
April 13, 2020	5:21-6:46: how we are uplifting to one another	9:54-16:33: impact factor and tenure/ promotion during COVID and publication "game"

Note. CHAT = Cultural Historical Activity Theory. CV = Curriculum Vitae. ICLS -= International Conference of Learning Sciences. PMENA = Psychology of Mathematics Education – North America.

Next, we looked across content logs to develop larger themes: (a) Knowledge sharing and understanding through our research, (b) Feeling like an outsider and playing by the rules (e.g., conference, responding to weird email) or not, (c) Tenure and promotion, (d) Impacts of COVID shutdown (e.g., conferences, CV, teaching, tenure), and (e) Approach to writing and attending to reviewer comments, struggles working with co-authors. For this chapter, our focus was (b) as it aligned well with our objective, namely, to examine and understand our reciprocal mentor relationships and role shifting as an informal peer mentoring group through a social identity lens. We transcribed 16 moments verbatim.

The next step of our process was developing found poetry from our transcriptions (Edge & Olan, 2021; Pithouse-Morgan, 2016). Found poetry is an arts-based approach of borrowing verbatim words and phrases from existing texts, such as interview transcriptions and emails, and arranging those words and phrases to produce a poem (Butler-Kisber, 2002; Prendergast, 2006). We followed the analysis process as outlined by Pithouse-Morgan (2016) but took different approaches as a way to make sense of our own psychological sense of belonging and social acceptance within academia (i.e., social STEM identity). We conceptualize this as individually engaging in dialogic communication *around* and *through* the transcripts of our dialogic community. The different analytic approaches that led to our poetry were similar to us sitting in a room together, sharing our different perspectives. Klein and Taylor described this process as co-writing in which the meaning of our found poems came "from re-writing each other's stories" (p. 49). We each share our analytical approach with the first author providing specific examples to highlight her process.

Amber began her analysis by adding analytical memos that were reflective of her past experiences in the dialogic community while also reflecting upon her current experiences or insights that were spurred by the transcripts (Birks et al., 2008). This was intentional, as Amber was more reticent in the weekly meetings. These memos became integrated into the body of the transcript, purposefully placed at the point in which the dialogic interaction with the transcript occurred within her reflections (see brackets in Figure 7.3). Next, Amber color-coded phrases and words that highlighted different academic emotions, needs, tensions, and desires, as well as phrases and words that expressed experiences as an individual within the informal peer mentoring group (see Figure 7.3). Orange indicated "strength from being with each other and learnings from other's experiences" (e.g., "I find our three-person community to be a safe dialogic space where we do not squeeze out but create a space of belonging."); blue indicated "lack sense of belonging, an outsider, pseudo-" (e.g., "...communities that are not accepting, where your sense of belonging is low."); and magenta indicated "surveillance/obligated/bounded" (e.g., "...the need to be productive in ways that are about word counts and publication counts"). Additionally, the words and phrases highlighted were not always Amber's own but those of Signe and/or Caro. This speaks to the nature of our peer mentoring group in that when Amber "hears" Signe and/or Caro within the living transcripts, "it belongs to us, and I feel it as me" (Signe, February 24, 2023 meeting).

Figure 7.3. Analysis of Analytical Memos

But in terms of the academic space, I, the idea of the racialized space that we operate in, in academia, and the notion…of the need to be productive in ways that are about word counts and publication counts, squeeze out dialogue. [I find our three-person community to be a safe dialogic space where we do not squeeze one another out but create a space of belonging. However, this does not extend to ourselves within the larger community in which we are bounded and silenced by a community, particularly communities that are not accepting, where your sense of belonging is low. I am feeling this more and more in my research and feeling myself being closed in on as "not important."] actually because we're peer reviewing each other. So nothing really extreme is going to get into our journals. And that's kind of part of the checks and balances of our way of operating right now. While we have this really robust online community of so called free speech, and new journal opportunities that are, that are identified as…less because they're not in the Canon type of setup. They're not the gold standard, so they're less. But these are still ways of speaking in the academic world.

These color-coded phrases and words became the basis for creating four found poems, particularly using the format of a three-stanza pantoum poem as an organizational device (Pithouse-Morgan, 2016). Using this format limits the poet to six lines as the second and third stanzas repeat lines (Furman et al., 2006). This forced Amber to select phrases that were salient and/or emotionally reminiscent. Figure 7.4 demonstrates this process, from copying phrases from the transcript to the creation of a found poetry as aligned with the pantoum format.

Figure 7.4. Selection of Salient Phrases

Phrases from transcript	Pantoum format	Found poem
I felt really guilty	Stanza 1:	***Bounded and Committed***
Speaks to what is privileged	Line 1	
Things that count	Line 2	Word counts and publication
You need to do this	Line 3	counts
You need to do more of that	Line 4	You need to do this
You're not doing enough		Not the gold standard…less
No transparency	Stanza 2:	You need to do more
Checks and balances in place	Line 5 (repeat of line 2)	
Learn to say no	Line 6	You need to do this
Protect yourself	Line 7 (repeat of line 4)	Things that count
I often feel bounded and committed	Line 8	You need to do more
Being judged/evaluated		Judged…evaluated
Externally imposed vulnerability	Stanza 3:	
Certain things you have to	Line 9 (repeat of line 6)	Things that count
accomplish to be a "success"	Line 10 (repeat of line 3)	Not the gold standard…less
Put you in a box	Line 11 (repeat of line 8)	Judged…evaluated
See us in a way that makes us	Line 12 (repeat of line 1)	Word counts and publication
superhuman		counts
Word counts and publication counts		
Squeeze out dialogue		
Bounded and silenced		
Not the gold standards. They're less.		

Caro began much like Amber, memoing the transcript. In doing so, Caro saw pictures of strength and power within our community. She then crafted two sets of poems. In the first set, she selected lines only from the transcripts, using her and Amber's memos to guide her attention. She focused on compiling lines related to the main themes, using lines that strongly resonated, and crafted Pantoum poems from those lines. These poems focused on the ongoing tensions within which we lived, as we navigated institutions that often felt uncaring but asked us to constantly care about them. Consequently, in seeking strength, Caro started a second set of poetry that included Amber's memos in the poetry-seeking process. The first poem in this set was crafted solely from Amber's memos, while the second was crafted from both her memos and transcripts. Bringing in the first author's voice more strongly balanced the poetry, revealing more of our strength and fortune, but still not as positive as Caro had originally felt when reading the transcript.

Signe began by memoing on the transcripts. These memos were then included as part of the transcript. Each document was loaded into MaxQDA, and open coding of excerpts containing evidence of a sense of belonging and social acceptance in this informal mentoring group and STEM community were identified. Codes were grouped under three themes, each reflecting Signe's experiences within the mentorship group: (a) growth (interpretation of others, support, valuing, probing, alternative descriptions, and alternative interpretations); (b) STEM communities (values/actions in community, descriptions of community); and (c) making sense of self (self-interpretations, feelings). Excerpts within each code were then revisited, looking for "emotionally evocative" (Pithouse-Morgan, 2016, p. 5) phrases that represented memories of the mentorship experience. Because the poems only use six phrases, Signe selected the "most illuminating and evocative words and phrases" (p. 6), placing them in the poem in different positions to best represent her memories.

The last step was to reflect upon our individual poems, and past and present selves, to collectively create the tanka poem presented at the beginning of the chapter. Following the guidance of Pithouse-Morgan (2016), the poem has five lines with a 5/7/5/7/7 syllable count in the lines. Through this process, the tanka poem transformed into a function of us coming together in a dialogic space of academic and personal friendship.

Our Experiences

We each presented our found poems, our dialogic and critical engagement in our reciprocal peer-mentor relationships as we discussed and questioned academic needs, tensions, and desires. Utilizing social STEM identity theory, we focused our experiences in academia through a lens of a sense of belonging (or not) and social acceptance (or social nonacceptance). Similar to Agosto et al. (2016), we share our experiences and reflections in first-person narrative. We also found ourselves writing in the present and the past tense as we reflected upon our present selves and our past selves as individuals and collective informal peer mentoring group. This back-and-forth nature of our writing highlights the dialogic space in which we discussed and questioned our being and becoming as women in academia and our STEM identity.

Amber

My first poem, *Am I Enough?*, is a question I ask myself as a researcher, teacher educator, colleague, and mentor, particularly within a community I feel I should belong - mathematics education. My response is often NO! This is "not the field for me." I wear a mask that hides my vulnerabilities, my uncertainties, and my low sense of belonging as if I am superhuman, yet "fighting to be seen" and recognized. An example of this highlighted in my poem is the line "be seen and understood as a scholar." As someone whose research is within STEM education (e.g., engineering education with families) and in non-formal learning environments (e.g., museums, homes), I do not feel socially accepted as a mathematics education scholar. Where do I fit? Am I accepted? *Am I enough?*

Am I Enough?

Fighting to be seen
Be seen and understood as a scholar
Quintessentially me not accepted?
Not the field for me

Be seen and understood as a scholar
Pseudo-educator
Not the field for me
Fake…Inadequate

Pseudo-educator
Quintessentially me not accepted?
Fake…Inadequate
Fighting to be seen

These feelings of *Am I Enough?*, and "fighting to be seen," have pushed me as an academic to work harder to be seen within a community that I perceive as not accepting me. This is highlighted in my second poem, *Who am I if not a workaholic?*

Who am I if not a workaholic?

Work hard
Push forward
Keep my head down
Dig in

Push forward
Super human
Dig in
Lay low

Super human
Push forward
Lay low
Work hard

Being a workaholic has become a part of my identity as a scholar. On days I have off (e.g., fall break), I fight the urge not to analyze video data or devote a few hours to writing a manuscript. I am not able to turn myself "off." I "push forward," "dig in," and "work hard" for others to see me as "super human." Further, being a workaholic was also to fight the stigma that, as a woman, I am less productive than my counterparts.

Alternatively, as highlighted in my poem, *Safe Dialogic Space*, the mentoring relationships and critical friendships formed among Caro, Signe, and myself was a safe space where "I feel known and seen." I felt "comfortable in being me."

Safe Dialogic Space

I appreciate
I feel known and seen
I value
I feel comfortable in being me

I feel known and seen
I am thankful
I feel comfortable in being me
I am empowered

I am thankful
I value
I am empowered
I appreciate

As I read this poem, I relive the dialogic spaces and am able to shift my gaze from *Am I Enough?* to a gaze where my whole self feels (and felt) like I belong and am accepted. I am able to continuously draw strength from our informal mentoring relationships even when we are not physically or virtually together.

Caro

As a pre-tenured faculty member who changed institutions *and* fields at the four-year mark and then experienced a global pandemic, I have been pre-tenure for far longer than usual. My first poem reflects my tangled feelings about this.

The Door Itself

The tenure and promotion door
(Taking care of people is of the utmost importance)
What's going on on the other side of that door?
The way you get ahead is by sucking it up and doing work

(Taking care of people is of the utmost importance)
You're a junior person, be seen as a helpful scholar
The way you get ahead is by sucking it up and doing work
(But honestly, we have enough hands)

You're a junior person, be seen as a helpful scholar
What's going on on the other side of that door?
(But honestly, we have enough hands)
The tenure and promotion door

First, tenure is messy and scary - never have strangers had so much power over my life! Saying yes to requests, agreeing with powerful people, and "sucking it up" seemed the safest path. But there were two problems: (a) I burnt out during the pandemic and could no longer deliver on all the yesses, and (b) I have never been good at toeing the often invisible lines. Second, as a pre-tenured faculty member, the post-tenure life was opaque - much like the post-doctorate life was unimaginable when I was dissertating! I cannot see my future beyond the door of tenure, and I imagine that once I become tenured, I will quickly forget what pre-tenure life was like.

As someone who is a better 'fit' at her current position than at her last, and someone who is regularly encouraged to think about and plan for tenure, I struggle (and struggled) with what it means to be *me* - the authentic, happy, engaged, nerdy *me* - in academia. My second poem reflects this struggle.

Use Your Actual Voice

You benefit from laying low and doing your work
People who have spoken up and how they're treated
Learn how to say no until we become full professors
Then relearn how to say yes

People who have spoken up and how they're treated
Protect yourself and your emotional energy
Then relearn how to say yes
Use your actual voice

Protect yourself and your emotional energy
Learn how to say no until we become full professors
Use your actual voice
You benefit from laying low and doing your work

The next poem was crafted solely from Amber's memos on the transcripts, and thus reflects her and my perspective about her more than myself. Amber is a productive powerhouse, and was throughout a time when I was no longer able to be similarly productive. She has numerous grants, a long list of publications, and a life that often revolves around work above all else. I often worry about her! I am - at the same time - jealous of her ability to focus, worried about her prioritizing her own health and happiness, and grateful to have her in my life.

Who am I if I am not a workaholic?

Who am I if I am not a workaholic - just being?
We give up so much of our time for other things, when is it me time?
My workaholism is taken advantage of - if not me, then who?
Maybe I am trying to portray myself as super human

We give up so much of our time for other things, when is it me time?
(I must) be known, be seen, be heard
Maybe I am trying to portray myself as super human
I feel like an outsider, someone who does not belong

(I must) be known, be seen, be heard
My workaholism is taken advantage of - if not me, then who?
I feel like an outsider, someone who does not belong
Who am I if I am not a workaholic - just being?

My final poem comes from the transcripts and Amber's memos. It summarizes how we can be supported by our informal peer mentoring group that is simultaneously nested within communities that may not be supportive.

Community is Layered

We are bounded and silenced by a community
Keep my head and dig in
Being able to be who you really are, that is something
I feel known and seen with you two

Keep my head and dig in
Having a viewpoint is a very dangerous thing
I feel known and seen with you two
a sense of belonging and a sense of appreciation

Having a viewpoint is a very dangerous thing
Being able to be who you really are, that is something
A sense of belonging and a sense of appreciation
We are bounded and silenced by a community

Signe

I meet with different author groups each month. This group energizes me because it brings me a sense of becoming, growing in ways unanticipated. The experience of engaging with scholars whose academic journey is unlike my own seemed to produce personal growth in being an academic and a colleague. The wanting of others, the need to be accepted, and the necessity to accept rather than evaluate others is at the center of my poem, *Growth*.

Growth

What do you want to do?
Accept me
It could be a bad fit.
The self I so desperately want to portray

Accept me
Hate that no longer needs to be kept
The self I so desperately want to portray
I was scared and so were they.

Hate that no longer needs to be kept
It could be a bad fit
I was scared and so were they.
What do you want to do?

My next poem, *Working in Evaluation Culture,* highlights the development and representation of new knowledge that has always felt joyful to me. Yet, there is always a giveaway moment when you submit your work, and it is no longer yours. Turning my thoughts and ideas over to others for review shifted my view of my work. I became an object for others' assessment. Although I know that the critiques of my writing are meant to support its development, reviews that assert that I am a poor writer take me back to my school days when my work was scored. I learned to improve the scores on my papers that I knew were less than perfect. Amber and Caro are in different parts of the evaluation machinery. Still subject to review each year, and for promotion, their position is like and unlike my own. Like because they, too, create representations of ideas they have developed, unlike because they exist in different institutional structures with supports and challenges that I have not experienced. Yet, when I describe reviewing and being reviewed, I am reminded that our stories reveal different perspectives on the evaluation culture.

Working in Evaluation Culture

Evaluation culture
They don't know your life
It isn't a lie if I tell you I can't
I belong

They don't know your life
Just keep pushing through
I belong
They want to see competence

Just keep pushing through
It isn't a lie if I tell you I can't
They want to see competence
Evaluation culture

Growth was written to communicate how Amber and Caro support me as a scholar in transition. *Making Sense of Me* describes how I see myself in our group, the institutional climate, and the broader STEM academic community. I strive for a self that is authentic. Yet, I often see ways I position others with my words or my silence in meetings and discussions. I share advice as though Amber and Caro can learn from my words. I am a senior scholar whose experience lives in past events. Yet my past experience also lives in my present mind as I use that experience to decide what to do and say.

Making Sense of Me

Free advice....was I asked for it or did I just give it?
I feel I can, but should I?
I position myself.
I positioned her.

I feel I can, but should I?
I can stand up.
I positioned her.
Should I retire?

I can stand up.
I position myself.
Should I retire?
Free advice....was I asked for it or did I just give it?

Discussion

In this chapter, we examined and highlighted how our informal peer mentorship group has shifted and grown from one grounded in research to one grounded in supporting our academic needs, tensions, and desires as three women academics that span the *clogged pipeline* to one simultaneously supported by our personal friendship. As captured in the tanka poem at the beginning of the chapter, this is reflected in the movement of *me* to *we* to *us*, as we are continually becoming women in academia and evolving as an informal mentoring group. Through found poetry, we documented our experiences and struggles in academia through a lens of a sense of belonging (or not) and social acceptance (or social nonacceptance). As expressed by our individual poems, we often felt like an outsider (e.g., Hogg et al., 1995; Holmes et al., 2007), as not belonging and being accepted in a community in which our teaching, research, and/or service "lived."

Alternatively, we highlighted how our reciprocal mentoring relationship created a safe space to be our authentic selves - to be seen, cared for, and heard as people and as women in academia. Our weekly meetings served as a counterspace (Ong et al., 2018) for each of us to find our authentic academic STEM identities in which we were socially accepted and felt a sense of belonging with one another (Tajfel & Turner, 1985). Our experience counters typical institutional mentorship models, which prioritizes a hierarchical structure where a mentor is deemed more knowledgeable and able to support the mentee's career goals as defined by institutional norms and expectations (e.g., Schmidt & Faber, 2016; Wanberg et al., 2003). The relationship is built around a product-oriented environment (e.g., publications) as opposed to a collaborative and relational-oriented environment where "it feels like being, but the best version of being" (Signe, May 31, 2023). Therefore, we argue for the formation of spaces and mentorship grounded in trust, mutual caring, and shared activities (i.e., academic friendship; Webster & Boyd, 2019) as a way to resist the individualistic, competitive nature of academia and foster women's sense of belonging and social acceptance within the STEM community. As we negotiated our relationships and roles, we found strength in one another as we negotiated the institutional and systemic barriers at play, particularly within the pandemic and other moments of social and political unrest which exacerbated women's inability to be productive as researchers and effective as educators (e.g., Dunn et al., 2022; Paul et al., 2022).

We encourage individuals and mentoring groups in academia to utilize found poetry and visual representations as a way to authentically see themselves (i.e., self-based exploration; Edge & Olan, 2021). Our poems brought to the forefront ongoing tensions (e.g., evaluation culture) that are not yet resolved, and will likely not be resolved. Yet, it provided each of us with an outlet to express our struggles, tensions and emotions associated with our academic STEM identity. The creation of found poetry was a transformative and relational process as the words of another became our own. As stated by Black et al. (2019), found poetry not only became a "spilling over of multiple voices, multiple storylines, and multiple connections" (p. 534) but afforded us to see the development of ourselves.

To conclude, the significance of our work is multifold. First, we revealed a view of mentorship that contrasts sharply with the more traditional hierarchical model (e.g., Marino, 2021). Second, we illustrated the centrality of ourselves as whole human beings rather than merely work-centric individuals. We debunked the idea that workplace mentoring can ignore the complex life contexts that work is taking place within. Lastly, we believe that STEM fields benefit from welcoming diverse voices and contributions, and that we cannot - as scientists, as a field, and as individuals - expect our work to progress without embracing the changes that come with shifting roles and demographics.

References

Agosto, V., Karanxha, Z., Unterreiner, A., Cobb-Roberts, D., Esnard, T., Wu, K., & Beck, M. (2016). Running bamboo: A mentoring network of women intending to thrive in academia. *NASPA Journal About Women in Higher Education, 9*(1), 74-89. http://dx.doi.org/10.1080/19407882.2015.1124785

American Association of University Professors. (2022). *The Annual Report on the Economic Status of the Profession, 2021–22.* Retrieved from https://www.aaup.org/reports-publications/aaup-policies-reports

Angelique, H., Kyle, K., & Taylor, E. (2002). Mentors and muses: New strategies for academic success. *Innovative Higher Education, 26*, 195–209. https://doi.org/10.1023/A:1017968906264

Arslan, G., Allen, K. A., & Ryan, T. (2020). Exploring the impacts of school belonging on youth wellbeing and mental health among Turkish adolescents. *Child Indicators Research, 13*, 1619-1635. https://doi.org/10.1007/s12187-020-09721-z

Ashforth, B. E., & Mael, F. (1989). Social identity theory and the organization. *Academy of Management Review, 14*(1), 20-39.

Bilimoria, D., Joy, S., & Liang, X. (2008). Breaking barriers and creating inclusiveness: Lessons of organizational transformation to advance women faculty in academic science and engineering. *Human Resource Management, 47*(3), 423–441. https://doi.org/10.1002/hrm.20225

Birks, M., Chapman, Y., & Francis, K. (2008). Memoing in qualitative research: Probing data and processes. *Journal of Research in Nursing, 13*(1), 68-75. https://doi.org/10.1177/1744987107081254

Black, A. L., Crimmins, G., & Henderson, L. (2019). Positioning ourselves in our academic lives: Exploring personal/professional identities, voice and agency. *Discourse: Studies in the Cultural Politics of Education, 40*(4), 530-544. https://doi.org/10.1080/01596306.2017.1398135

Block, B. A., & Tietjen-Smith, T. (2016). The case for women mentoring women. *Quest, 68*(3), 306-315. http://dx.doi.org/10.1080/00336297.2016.1190285

Bottoms, S., Pegg, J., Adams, A., Wu, K., Smith Risser, H., & Kern, A. L. (2013). Mentoring from the outside: The role of a peer mentoring community in the development of early career education faculty. *Mentoring & Tutoring: Partnership in Learning, 21*(2), 195-218. https://doi.org/10.1080/13611267.2013.813730

Butler-Kisber, L. (2002). Artful portrayals in qualitative research: The road to found poetry and beyond. *The Alberta Journal of Educational Research, 48*, 229-239.

Bynum, Y. P. (2015). The power of informal mentoring. *Education, 136*(1), 69–73.

Cohen, L. M., Cowin, K., Ciechanowski, K., & Orozco, R. (2012). Portraits of our mentoring experiences in learning to craft journal articles. *Mentoring & Tutoring: Partnership in Learning, 20*, 75–97. https://doi.org/10.1080/13611267.2012.645601

Corwin, K. M., Cohen, L. M., Ciechanowski, K. M., & Orozco, R. A. (2012). Portraits of mentor-junior faculty relationships: From power dynamics to collaboration. *Journal of Education, 192*(1), 37-47.

Dajani, R., Tabbaa, Z., Al-Rawashdeh, A., Gretzel, U., & Bowser, G. (2021). Peer mentoring women in STEM: an explanatory case study on reflections from a program in Jordan, *Mentoring & Tutoring: Partnership in Learning, 29*(3), 284-304. https://doi.org/10.1080/13611267.2021.1927429

Dunn, M., Gregor, M., Robinson, S., Ferrer, A., Campbell-Halfaker, D., & Martin-Fernandez, J. (2022). Academia during the time of COVID-19: Examining the voices of untenured female professors in STEM. *Journal of Career Assessment, 30*(3), 573-589. https://doi.org/10.1177/10690727211057441

Edge, C. U., & Olan, E. L. (2021). Learning to breathe again: Found poems and critical friendship as methodological tools in self-study of teaching practices. *Studying Teacher Education, 17*(2), 228-252. https://doi.org/10.1080/17425964.2021.1910807

Furman, R., Lietz, C., & Langer, C. L. (2006). The research poem in international social work: Innovations in qualitative methodology. *International Journal of Qualitative Methods, 5*(3), 24-34.

Gardiner, M., Tiggemann, M., Kearns, H., & Marshall, K. (2007). Show me the money! An empirical analysis of mentoring outcomes for women in academia. *Higher Education Research & Development, 26*(4), 425-442. https://doi.org/10.1080/07294360701658633

Gibson, S. K. (2006). Mentoring of women faculty: The role of organizational politics and culture. *Innovative Higher Education, 31*, 63-79. https://doi.org/10.1007/s10755-006-9007-7

Guilfoyle, K., Hamilton, M., Pinnegar, S., & Placier, P. (2004). The epistemological dimensions and dynamics of professional dialogue in self-study. In J. Loughran et al. (Eds). *International Handbook of Self-Study of Teaching and Teacher Education Practices* (pp. 1109-1167). Springer, Dordrecht.

Hall, J., & Suurtamm, C. (2020). Numbers and nerds: Exploring portrayals of mathematics and mathematicians in children's media. *International Electronic Journal of Mathematics Education, 15*(3), Article em0591. https://doi.org/10.29333/iejme/8260

Hamilton, M. L., & Pinnegar, S. (2014). Intimate scholarship in research: An example from self-study of teaching and teacher education practices methodology. *LEARNing Landscapes, 8*(1), 153-171. https://doi.org/10.36510/learnland.v8i1.680

Hamilton, M. L. & Pinnegar, S. (2015). *Knowing, becoming, doing as teacher educators: Identity, intimate scholarship, inquiry.* Emerald Group Publishing.

Hamilton, M. L., Pinnegar, S., & Davey, R. (2016). Intimate scholarship: An examination of identity and inquiry in the work of teacher educators. In J. Loughran & M. L. Hamilton (Eds.), *International Handbook of Teacher Education: Volume 2* (pp. 181-237). Springer.

Hogg, M. A., Terry, D. J., & White, K. M. (1995). A tale of two theories: A critical comparison of identity theory with social identity theory. *Social Psychology Quarterly, 58*(4), 255-269.

Holmes, S., Danley, L., & Hinton-Hudson, V. (2007). Race still matters: Considerations for mentoring Black women in academe. *Negro Educational Review, 58*, 105–129.

Kim, A. Y., Sinatra, G. M., & Seyranian, V. (2018). Developing a STEM identity among young women: A social identity perspective. *Review of Educational Research, 88*(4), 589-625. https://doi.org/10.3102/0034654318779957

Klein, E. J., & Taylor, M. (2022). *Our bodies tell the story: Using feminist research and friendship to reimagine education and our lives.* Myers Education Press.

LaBoskey, V. K. (2004). The methodology of self-study and its theoretical underpinnings. In J. Loughran, M. L. Hamilton, V. K. LaBoskey, & T. Russell (Eds.), *International handbook of self-study of teaching and teacher education practices* (pp. 817-869). Dordrecht, The Netherlands: Springer.

Lambrechts, A. A., Larasatie, P., Boutelier, S., Guta, H. A., Leonowicz-Bukała, I., & Prashad, S. (2021). Why research productivity among women in academia suffered during the early stages of COVID-19 crisis: A qualitative analysis. Advanced online publication. https://doi.org/10.35542/osf.io/3awdq

Lasky, S. (2005). A sociocultural approach to understanding teacher identity, agency and professional vulnerability in a context of secondary school reform. *Teaching and Teacher Education, 21*(8), 899-916. https://doi.org/10.1016/j.tate.2005.06.003

Lewis, C., & Olshansky, E. (2016). Relational-cultural theory as a framework for mentoring in academia: Toward diversity and growth-fostering collaborative scholarly relationships. *Mentoring and Tutoring: Partnership in Learning, 24*(5), 383–398. https://doi.org/10.1080/13611267.2016.1275390

Leyva, L. A., Quea, R., Weber, K., Battey, D., & López, D. (2021). Detailing racialized and gendered mechanisms of undergraduate precalculus and calculus classroom instruction. *Cognition and Instruction, 39*(1), 1-34. https://doi.org/10.1080/07370008.2020.1849218

Lupi, G., & Posavec, S. (2016). *Dear Data.* Princeton Architectural Press.

Macfarlane, B., & Burg, D. (2019). Women professors and the academic housework trap. *Journal of Higher Education Policy and Management, 41*(3), 262-274. https://doi.org/10.1080/1360080X.2019.1589682

Marino, F. E. (2021). Mentoring gone wrong: What is happening to mentorship in academia?. *Policy Futures in Education, 19*(7), 747-751. https://doi.org/10.1177/1478210320972199

McCutcheon, J. M., & Morrison, M. A. (2018). It's "like walking on broken glass": Pan-Canadian reflections on work–family conflict from psychology women faculty and graduate students. *Feminism & Psychology, 28*(2), 231-252. https://doi.org/10.1177/0959353517739641

McGee, E. O., & Martin, D. B. (2011). "You would not believe what I have to go through to prove my intellectual value!" Stereotype management among academically successful Black mathematics and engineering students. *American Educational Research Journal, 48*(6), 1347-1389. https://doi.org/10.3102/0002831211423972

Meschitti, V., & Lawton Smith, H. (2017). Does mentoring make a difference for women academics? Evidence from the literature and a guide for future research. *Journal of Research in Gender Studies, 7*(1), 166-199. https://doi.org/10.22381/JRGS7120176

Miegroet, H., Glass, C., Callister, R. R., & Sullivan, K. (2019). Unclogging the pipeline: Advancement to full professor in academic STEM. *Equality, Diversity and Inclusion: An International Journal, 38*(2), 246-264.

Museus, S. D., Yi, V., & Saelua, N. (2017). The impact of culturally engaging campus environments on sense of belonging. *The Review of Higher Education, 40*(2), 187-215. https://doi.org/10.1353/rhe.2017.0001

National Institutes of Health (NIH). (2012b). *Mentoring women in science-for mentors* (NIH Publication no. 12-7871). NIH Office of Research on Women's

Health. Retrieved from http://orwh.od.nih.gov/career/pdf/ORWH-Mentor-Factsheet.pdf

O'Connell, C., & McKinnon, M. (2021). Perceptions of barriers to career progression for academic women in STEM. *Societies, 11*(2), Article 27. https://doi.org/10.3390/soc11020027

Ong, M., Smith, J. M., & Ko, L. T. (2018). Counterspaces for women of color in STEM higher education: Marginal and central spaces for persistence and success. *Journal of Research in Science Teaching, 55*(2), 206-245. https://doi.org/10.1002/tea.21417

Paul, K., Kim, J., Diekman, A., Godwin, A., Katz, A., & Maltese, A. (2022, August). *Collateral damage: Investigating the impacts of COVID on STEM professionals with caregiving responsibilities.* In 2022 ASEE Annual Conference & Exposition: Minneapolis, MN.

Placier, P., Pinnegar, S., Hamilton, M. L., & Guilfoyle, K. (2005). Exploring the concept of dialogue in the self-study of teaching practices. In C. Kosnik, C. Beck, A. Freese, & A. Samaras (Eds.) *Making a difference in teacher education through self-study* (pp. 51-64). Springer, Dordrecht.

Prendergast, M. (2006). Found poetry as literature review: Research poems on audience and performance. *Qualitative Inquiry, 12*(2), 369–388. https://doi.org/10.1177/1077800405284601

Piatek-Jimenez, K. (2008). Images of mathematicians: A new perspective on the shortage of women in mathematical careers. *ZDM, 40*, 633-646. https://doi.org/10.1007/s11858-008-0126-8

Piatek-Jimenez, K. (2015). On the persistence and attrition of women in mathematics. *Journal of Humanistic Mathematics, 5*(1), 3-54. https://doi.org/10.5642/jhummath.201501.03

Pithouse-Morgan, K. (2016). Finding my self in a new place: Exploring professional learning through found poetry. *Teacher Learning and Professional Development, 1*(1), 1-18.

Quinn, J. (2012). *Mentoring: Progressing women's careers in higher education.* Equality Challenge Unit. Retrieved from http://www.ecu.ac.uk/wp-content/uploads/external/mentoring-progressing-womens-careers-in-higher-education.pdf

Sargent, J., Williams, R. A., Hagerty, B., Lynch-Sauer, J., & Hoyle, K. (2002). Sense of belonging as a buffer against depressive symptoms. *Journal of the American Psychiatric Nurses Association, 8*(4), 120-129.

Schmidt, E. K., & Faber, S. T. (2016). Benefits of peer mentoring to mentors, female mentees and higher education institutions. *Mentoring & Tutoring: Partnership in Learning, 24*(2), 137-157. https://doi.org/10.1080/13611267.2016.1170560

Searby, L., Ballenger, J., & Tripses, J. (2015). Climbing the ladder, holding the ladder: The mentoring experiences of higher education female leaders. *Advancing Women in Leadership, 35*, 98–107.

Stachl, C. N., & Baranger, A. M. (2020). Sense of belonging within the graduate community of a research-focused STEM department: Quantitative assessment using a visual narrative and item response theory. *PloS One, 15*(5), Article e0233431. https://doi.org/10.1371/journal.pone.0233431

Steele, C. M., Spencer, S. J., & Aronson, J. (2002). Contending with group image: The psychology of stereotype and social identity threat. In M. P. Zanna (Ed.), *Advances in Experimental Social Psychology* (Vol. 34, pp. 379-440). Academic Press.

Steinke, J. (2013). In her own voice: Identity centrality and perceptions of workplace climate in blogs by women scientists. *International Journal of Gender, Science and Technology, 5*(1), 25-51.

Tajfel, H., & Turner, J. C. (1985) The social identity theory of intergroup behavior. In S. Worchel & W. G. Austin (Eds.), *Psychology of Intergroup Relations* (2nd ed., pp. 7-24). Nelson-Hall.

Thomas, N., Bystydzienski, J., & Desai, A. (2015). Changing institutional culture through peer mentoring of women STEM faculty. *Innovative Higher Education, 40,* 143-157. https://doi.org/10.1007/s10755-014-9300-9

Tinto, V. (2017). Through the eyes of students. *Journal of College Student Retention: Research, Theory & Practice, 19*(3), 254-269. https://doi.org/10.117 7/1521025115621917

Toffoletti, K., & Starr, K. (2016). Women academics and work–life balance: Gendered discourses of work and care. *Gender, Work & Organization, 23*(5), 489-504. https://doi.org/doi:10.1111/gwao.12133

Varkey, P., Jatoi, A., Williams, A., Mayer, A., Ko, M., Files, J., ... & Hayes, S. (2012). The positive impact of a facilitated peer mentoring program on academic skills of women faculty. *BMC Medical Education, 12*(1), Article 14. Retrieved from http://www.biomedcentral.com/1472-6920/12/14

Wanberg, C. R., Welsh, E. T., & Hezlett, S. (2003). Mentoring research: A review and dynamic process model. In G. R. Ferris (Ed.), *Research in Personnel and Human Resource Management* (Vol. 22, pp. 39–124). Elsevier.

Wasburn, M. H. (2007). Mentoring women faculty: An instrumental case study of strategic collaboration. *Mentoring & Tutoring: Partnership in Learning, 15,* 57–72. https://doi.org/10.1080/13611260601037389

Webster, N., & Boyd, M. (2019). Exploring the importance of inter-departmental women's friendship in geography as resistance in the neoliberal academy. *Geografiska Annaler: Series B, Human Geography, 101*(1), 44-55. https://doi. org/10.1080/04353684.2018.1507612

Wright-Mair, R. (2020). Longing to belong: Mentoring relationships as a pathway to fostering a sense of belonging for racially minoritized faculty at predominantly white institutions. *Journal Committed to Social Change on Race and Ethnicity (JCSCORE), 6*(2), 2-31.

Wu, K., Thorsos, N., & Kern, A. L. (2016). Dynamics of tensions and a sense of belonging in an informal peer mentoring community of women faculty. In B.

166 *Chapter 7*

G. G. Johannessen (Ed.), *Global Co-Mentoring Networks in Higher Education: Politics, Policies, and Practices* (pp. 95-111). Springer International.

Chapter 8

Leveraging Mentoring and Sponsoring Relationships to Get Promoted in Academia

Carole Sox
Columbia College, USA

Sheryl Kline
University of Delaware, USA

Abstract: This chapter will explore the differences between mentoring and sponsoring relationships and how they relate to academic career promotion, particularly highlighting opportunities within STEM fields. The differences between how men and women perceive these relationships will also be addressed. A call to action for equitable and proactive strategies to assist with career advancement will be extended, focusing on employing formal mentorship and sponsorship relationship programs in higher learning institutions.

Keywords: Mentorship, sponsorship, higher learning, advancement

***

Leveraging mentoring and sponsoring relationships to get promoted in academia

Healthy professional relationships positively impact career growth and career success. Therefore, developing and maintaining these relationships is essential at all levels of one's career. Building a solid network has also been linked to identifying job opportunities and expanding one's industry knowledge. Since initiating, creating, and sustaining these relationships have a positive and significant impact and can sometimes be crucial to one's career success, investing in them is key (Madden, 2023). While various opportunities for building relationships within academia (and the workforce) exist, mentorship and sponsorship programs offer ways for individuals to build these relationships within their work environment.

Research overwhelmingly indicates that mentoring relationships can assist with career advancement. Pertaining specifically to career advancement within academia, women have received the majority of PhDs, while men still hold the majority of high-level positions within higher education (Silbert et al., 2022). In addition to a call for action, research focuses on adopting intentional, proactive, and equitable strategies and procedures for elevating and promoting future generations of academic leaders. Strategies focus on including a much more diverse pool than currently exists (Silbert et al., 2022). While mentoring continues to support career advancement, sponsorship is an emerging strategy (Omadeke, 2021). Academics can leverage these two strategies to move more confidently and efficiently toward promotion and career next steps.

This chapter will explore mentoring practices toward promotion and introduce sponsorship as a critical component and facilitator of academic advancement. Background information and current research will be shared to illustrate the benefits of mentorship and sponsorship. The chapter will conclude with successful strategies employed within higher learning institutions to assist with mentoring and sponsoring relationships that work toward career development and progression.

Background

Developing and sustaining a successful career is not always a smooth or easy path. Undertaking this journey alone can make it much harder for individuals working toward success. Fortunately, mentoring and sponsoring opportunities can assist with the journey and produce positive outcomes. These strategies and or programs (if presented in such a format) offer the benefit of connecting with people who can offer assistance, guidance, and opportunities throughout one's career. These opportunities can also assist with promoting diversity at higher levels of administration within the organization. Mentorship and sponsorship programs can develop current talent into top talent and prepare junior colleagues to fulfill organizational leadership roles (Wooll, 2021).

While mentoring and sponsoring in higher education may take a formal or informal route, these strategies and/or programs are created through relationships. The benefits of these relationships are positive for mentees and mentors (Bell & Treleaven, 2020) as well as for sponsors and sponsorees. Some of the favorable outcomes of these relationships include networking opportunities, professional development, support, collegiality, and, for mentees, increased rates of promotion and advancement (Gardiner et al., 2007). For example, Ferman (2002) states that mentoring within higher learning institutions has been traditionally informal, unrecognized, and underutilized. To create a mentoring culture, however, more formal programs may be necessary (Bell & Treleaven, 2010). This is also true for sponsor programs (Huston et al., 2019).

Definitions, practices, and relevant theories

Mentor

While definitions of mentoring and sponsoring relationships vary, for this chapter, a mentor is trusted and considered wise within the industry in which they work (Friday et al., 2004). Mentors offer counsel and advice. They assist with problem-solving and share their wisdom from their previous experiences (Hewlett, 2013). Mentors usually have experience in the same area as their mentee, have similar goals, and serve as role models to the mentee (Wooll, 2021). A mentoring relationship is "a developmental relationship embedded within the career context" (Ragins & Kram, 2007, p. 5). A mentoring relationship may be formal or informal. It may be sponsored by an organization or occur organically (Bozionelos, 2002).

Traditionally, mentoring in academia consists of a professional relationship between two people, one of whom supports the other toward the next step in their career. This professional relationship is typically asymmetric, with information flowing from the mentor to the mentee (Hewlett, 2013). The two central mentoring functions provided by the mentor to the mentee are psychosocial and technical support (Haverty & Brown, 2021; Ragins & Kram, 2007; Sands et al., 1991; Zellers et al., 2008). Psychosocial support includes counseling, advising, friendship, social, and professional development (Behar-Horenstein et al., 2012; Chesney-Lind et al., 2006). Technical support may include coaching, advising, offering feedback, and providing measures for success (Behar-Horenstein et al., 2012; Cowin et al., 2012; Davis et al., 2011).

Faculty members and administration must know the mentoring opportunities and possibilities within each department. Faculty need to know when to partake in these opportunities and where they can be found. Mentoring opportunities can occur as early as the doctoral program and throughout an academic career. Early career mentor programs create opportunities for faculty to develop successful research agendas and grant proposals. The administration needs to create and facilitate these programs for success. Department chairs, for example, need to establish formal mentoring systems and assign junior faculty mentors (Committee on Effective Mentoring in STEMM, 2019). Mentoring opportunities and initiatives can include:

1. The creation of department and college-wide mentoring committees (engaging new faculty and providing feedback in their early stages).

2. Collaborations (partnering opportunities that include aspects of mentoring).

3. Opportunities to build networks and communities.

4. Nominating colleagues for awards (Spangle et al., 2021).

5. It has been suggested even to engage multiple mentors, particularly early in one's academic career. This approach suggests identifying specific roles for each engaged mentor (such as coach, connector, and associate) (Spangle et al., 2021).

Sponsor

A sponsor is "a person who nominates or supports another person's (protégés) promotion; sponsoring is the process of a sponsor nominating or supporting a protégé's promotion; and a sponsorship is a sponsoring relationship between a sponsor and a protégé" (Friday et al., 2004, p. 638). According to Hewlett et al. (2010), a sponsor introduces and advocates for the sponsoree about viable positions within the organization. A sponsor must be someone highly placed in an organization and can give highly visible assignments to their protégé or nominate them for awards and promotions. They must be in a position of power within the organization to be an effective sponsor.

Hewlett (2013) introduced sponsoring as separate and distinctive from mentoring. She found that sponsoring relationships contribute to career advancement more than mentoring relationships. Hewlett (2013) showed that 70% of sponsored men and women felt they were being promoted at a reasonable rate as compared to only 57% of their unsponsored peers.

For those considering building a sponsorship program among current faculty, it is necessary to consider a few factors. Sponsorship involves cultivating strategic relationships and alliances with key people in leadership positions who can drive the sponsor into leadership positions within their areas of expertise. This relationship is a mutual investment between the two parties, committed to assisting each other throughout their careers. A sponsor, therefore, considers advancing the career of their sponsoree as an investment in their own careers (Hewlett, 2013).

Numerous activities have been identified that are associated with sponsorship opportunities in academia:

1. Encourage or facilitate the sponsoree to engage in positive development training and opportunities.

2. Showcase a particular faculty who has been highly effective in a specific role or has negotiated or realigned their role according to their strengths.

3. Actively name and identify sponsorees, ensuring proper recognition is noted.

4. Protect sponsorees from less supportive faculty or administration.

5. Nominate the sponsoree for worthwhile speaking engagements.

6. Ensure the sponsoree is included on institutional panels and seminar opportunities.

7. Introduce the sponsoree to industry leaders and highlight their strengths (Huston et al., 2019).

Other activities will be discussed further within the chapter, but this information should highlight the advanced level of involvement and investment the sponsor makes to the sponsoree.

Mentor versus sponsor

There is a difference between mentoring and sponsoring. Many leaders think they are sponsoring individuals when they are only mentoring them. Understanding the difference between the two is imperative so leaders can fully support their protégés and enable their fullest potential (Chow, 2021). While mentoring and sponsoring opportunities may be available, all parties should identify their involvement and engagement in each perspective role at the forefront of the relationship to set expectations for all parties.

In a mentor relationship, the protégé's role is to listen to the mentor. However, in a sponsor relationship, the protégé works with his or her sponsor to complement their expertise and build their brand and vision (Hewlett, 2013). The mentor role can be filled by anyone willing, such as a peer, senior leader, or even a junior employee, really anyone with the requisite experience offered to their mentee. Typically, this person has experience in an area where the mentee is looking for guidance. A mentor can be viewed as an advisor who provides understanding and support (DiStasio, 2023).

Mentorship and sponsorship programs assist in making employees feel that their career development is supported. Mentors and sponsors can offer feedback, assist with developing networks, make introductions, and provide relationship guidance and support components. Both programs assist in decreasing inequities within the workplace. Both enhance employee engagement and have been proven to increase employee retention (DiSatios, 2023).

A mentor serves the mentee by listening, providing empathy, making recommendations, and providing support. A sponsor, however, has more of a role in driving the career vision of the protégé and serves as a visible champion for that individual when opportunities arise (Haverly & Brown, 2022). A sponsor is a senior person of influence in the organization who encourages risk-taking and has the back of their protégé. A sponsor believes in their protégé but has very high expectations of them since they consider them an investment (Hewlett, 2013). Table 8.1 may also help determine between the two:

Table 8.1. Mentor and sponsor comparison

	Mentor	Sponsor
Role	An experienced person who is skilled and knowledgeable.	A senior-level manager or administrator who influences decision-making in the organization.
Goal	Guides career choices and decisions. Provides psychological support and career support	Use influence and advocates for the sponsoree's advancement and or for highly visible assignments
Who drives the relationship?	Both the mentor and or the mentee. The mentee can drive the relationship.	The sponsor and this advocacy can be both public and private.
Actions	Listens, provides empathetic responses, and recommends ways to advance the mentee's career	Advocates for the sponsoree's advancement. Champions the sponsoree's potential and invests in their success.

A mentorship relationship can occur without a sponsoring component, and visa-versa, so while these relationships may work together, they are not interchangeable (Friday et al., 2004). While a mentoring relationship provides support, a sponsoring relationship is seen as more proactive and is considered to be instrumental in advancing one's career (Huston et al., 2019).

Mentorship focuses on a two-way relationship between the mentor and the mentee. Sponsorship, however, focuses on a three-way relationship between the sponsor, the sponsoree and the audience (those they are influencing and leveraging on behalf of the sponsoree) (Chow, 2021). Understanding a third component involved in the sponsor relationship may assist in clarifying the relationship between the two. A mentor speaks with you while a sponsor talks about you (Catalyst, 2022).

Mentorship can be more advantageous to those in the early stages of their careers, whereas sponsorship programs are more advantageous for growing talent for those at higher levels within their career. Both programs, therefore, have benefits and should be implemented and directed at the various career stages (DiStasio, 2023).

Gender differences

Research reports have identified barriers that women and other marginalized diverse groups face as they strive for promotion in STEM fields (Huston et al., 2019). Barriers can include vague promotion criteria, increased workloads, the unequal share of home and family responsibilities, lack of recognition, biases, and lack of sponsorship (Keating et al., 2022). While women hold 20% - 50% of full-time academic positions, more males reach upper levels of academic institutions than females in both rank and administrative positions (Huston et al., 2019). While goals for diversifying the pool of academics and academic leaders may include adopting fair and equitable strategies and procedures for promoting all academics, research reports show that men and women perceive and utilize mentoring and sponsoring relationships differently. Women tend to view these strategies from a relationship perspective. Their perspective reaches beyond career success (Noe, 1988; Smith, 2023). Males view these relationships from a more individualist perspective. In other words, men are likelier to seek how the relationship can benefit them (McKeen & Bujaki, 2007).

Understanding how to leverage mentoring and sponsoring relationships can be vital to advancing faculty careers. Research suggests men and women leverage mentoring and sponsorship relationships differently to improve career progression, with most companies traditionally supporting men's mentoring and sponsoring networks (Smith, 2023). Women and underrepresented minorities (and the organizations that support them) have the opportunity to learn from these strategies and use them to improve their career opportunities and progression. Developing and having robust networks and contacts is strategic capital that advances one's career (Wolff & Moser, 2010). An academic mentor provides more career success and socio-emotional support (Sorcinelli & Yun, 2007). In addition, having a sponsor is critically important to advancing one's career, especially in higher levels of administration (Hewlett, 2013; Kanter, 1977).

The advancement of women within STEM fields is often hindered by structural impediments and unwitting bias (Huston et al., 2019). These barriers within STEM fields, compounded by other obstacles (such as feelings of discomfort and harassment), lead to difficulty in recruiting, retaining, and promoting women within STEM fields into leadership positions (Metcalf et al., 2018). It has been noted that men have an invisible advantage over women, especially within the STEM fields, which are mainly male-dominated (O'Connor et al., 2019). In a recent study reviewing the opportunities of both men and women in academia, women reported a lack of access to senior positions. In addition, men were more likely to receive mentoring and sponsoring opportunities from male faculty (O'Connor et al., 2019). With senior positions held mainly by men and men receiving mentorship and sponsorship opportunities from men, we may have an explanation for why women lack opportunities in this area. Most people gravitate toward people who look like them, and women are at a disadvantage with men in the majority of higher-level positions (Anderson & Smith, 2019).

Recent research has highlighted that even when women are offered similar sponsorship opportunities to men, men overall have more competitive and aggressive approaches when leveraging these relationships when compared to women (Baldiga & Coffman, 2016). Regardless, research has also highlighted that sponsorship programs directed at women should increase the number of women in administrative positions and advanced ranks (Huston et al., 2019).

Self-efficacy and intervention

Self-efficacy theory has been defined as the belief people have in their ability to control and manage their performance and the events that impact their lives (Lopez-Garrido, 2023). Based on the work of Hackett and Betz (1981), it has been theorized that self-efficacy theory can explain why women are under-represented in many male-dominant careers (Betz & Hackett, 1997). As STEM careers are male-dominated, this theory applies.

Self-efficacy develops through the following factors: outcomes, vicarious experiences, persuasion, and feedback (Lopez-Garrido, 2023). The ability of a person to perform a task, for example, is influenced by previous positive and negative experiences, indicating the person's competence at the associated task. Through watching another perform a task, people can establish a high or low self-efficacy by comparing who they are watching with their competence level (Bandura, 1977). Another's encouragement (or discouragement) of a person's ability to perform a task can also be influential (Redmond, 2010). In addition, emotional arousal and body sensations experienced while performing a task can also factor into self-efficacy (Bandura, 1977).

Social Cognitive Theory suggests people will perform better with higher self-efficacy. Mentoring has been noted as an intervention to improve self-efficacy. In a 2022 study that explored the role faculty mentoring had on doctoral students, it was found that faculty mentoring (with mastery experience and consistent verbal support) improved leadership self-efficacy among the students participating (Orsina & Coers, 2022). This information suggests that mentorship and sponsorship approaches can be successful and well-applied in STEM academic career programs to achieve desired outcomes. Research within STEM fields has also provided empirical evidence supporting the Social Cognitive Theory as an acceptable model to explain factors impacting perseverance across gender, career stages, and ethnic groups from undergraduates to career faculty (Bakken et al., 2010; Byars-Winston et al., 2010; Gainor & Lent, 1998; Lent et al., 2005).

Improving self-efficacy, thus increasing performance, per the Social Cognitive Theory, can be directly addressed by mentoring and sponsoring programs within higher academia. By providing the tools for faculty and administration to be successful, learning institutions will be addressing and applying interventions to foster movement within this area.

Finding a mentor or sponsor

While these faculty relationships are positive and practical, they can also be difficult to initiate. Mentoring and sponsoring relationships are not passive support opportunities (Haverly & Brown, 2022); they are engaged and consistent with structure and support. Support comes from the leaders within the institution, and academic leaders should take the initiative to create and develop these programs for those seeking support.

Huston et al. (2019) identified a list of sponsorship initiatives that could prove relevant and valuable for academic leaders. As sponsorship is gaining more recognition within leadership and academia, it is essential to review approaches academics can take to initiate these successful relationships. Huston et al. (2019) suggest two main approaches to foster sponsorship. The first is promoting these relationships to senior leaders who are already engaging in these types of activities. This approach typically stems from a past professional relationship with the protégé (de Vries & Binns, 2018). Requesting nominations of proteges and sponsors within the institution may highlight some of these prior relationships (Huston et al., 2019). The second is to develop and initiate a more formal program with training, professional development, and institutional support. This approach would include additional engagement expectations for faculty. While both approaches to developing sponsorship programs can prove successful, the first step is to identify areas within the organization where diversity in leadership is necessary and target these areas for sponsorship programs.

Regardless of whether seeking a mentor or a sponsor individually or designing a program to foster these relationships, there are a few considerations when searching for a sponsor or mentor that should be considered. One example would be seeking someone with a different and/or diverse background. The Sponsor Dividend report stated that 71% of people who sponsor have the same gender or race as their sponsoree. It is no secret that people tend to gravitate toward similar people (Wooll, 2021), so reaching beyond that comfort area can provide different perspectives and helpful views. Encouraging and promoting diverse relationships while educating faculty on the benefits may also assist in creating a more equitable representation of high-level leaders within the work environment.

Another consideration for faculty members would be seeking people to assist with visibility within the workforce. Ideally, those sought out should take faculty to places they may not have access to showcase their abilities. Also, faculty should share their experiences beyond the workplace when seeking a sponsor or mentor. Often, what people have experienced beyond the workplace brings tremendous value to the position and the relationship (Khanna, 2022).

Best practices and strategies for mentoring and sponsoring

From the perspective of one successful female STEM professional, Taylor (2018) offers five ways to advance women in STEM professions. With over 30 years of professional experience, she strives for diversity, equality, and success within the technology industry. The five suggestions include:

Table 8.2. Suggestions for advancing women in STEM

Suggestions	Explanation
Pursue Mentorship in Atypical areas.	Step outside your professional focus while remaining in the same field to uncover fresh perspectives and new ideas.
Seek to recognize and improve your unconscious predisposition or bias	Recognize your bias and be more self-aware of your decisions and statements within your interactions.
Make Continued Progress	Perfection is not always possible or realistic, so learn the value of trial and error to keep moving forward. Use failure as an opportunity to improve.
You are here because You are Valued.	Share your perspective and insight. Ask questions. Seek clarification. Be heard.
Engage in Sponsoring and Mentoring Relationships	Foster the minds of younger STEM colleagues. Lead the change.

Taylor's suggestions include references to the importance of mentoring and/or sponsoring relationships. The importance of these relationships is held in high esteem by this seasoned professional and compliments the information shared previously about mentorship and sponsorship. Learning from those in the field working in STEM daily is imperative and supports academic research to date.

Huston et al. (2019) also encourage sponsorship activities and opportunities employed within academia. Activities such as providing opportunities for proteges to apply for development opportunities, identifying specific proteges to engage, and actively advocating for the protégé (Workplace Equity Agency & A. G., 2016) could all offer engagement opportunities for sponsorship relationships.

Hewlett (2013), one of the pioneers of the sponsorship concept, suggests that sponsors also advocate for the protégé outside of the institution for further growth and development. In addition, sponsors may advocate for protégé salary increases and allowances. The sponsor's engagement on behalf of the protégé can also include ensuring the protégé has adequate professional development opportunities such as serving on strategic institutional boards, building relationships with scholar leaders, engaging them in more senior roles, and engaging them in professional development opportunities. Overall, the sponsor is a vocal advocate of the protégé, continuously promoting exposure and development strategies and opportunities (Huston et al., 2019).

Chow (2019) identifies Amplifying, Boosting, Connecting, and Defending as the ABCDs of sponsorship. Amplifying involves sharing and communicating the protégé's work and accomplishments to enhance their reputation and impression. Boosting involves the sponsor underwriting the sponsoree or staking their reputation on the sponsorees' success. Connecting identifies the relevance of connecting the protégé with others so the positive feelings for one relationship are transferred to the other. Defending is working to persuasively transform a negative opinion of the sponsoree into a positive one. The ABCDs work together on behalf of the sponsoree to ensure intentional opportunities are identified for them as they progress within their careers.

Murrell and Fucci (2019) offer several tips for being a valuable and applicable sponsor:

1. Even if different from yours, be receptive to the needs of your sponsoree.

2. Work with the sponsoree to clarify career aspirations and identify opportunities.

3. Be honest, show mutual respect, and maintain confidentiality.

4. Engage in active listening and thoughtful questioning.

5. Promote the sponsoree by leveraging opportunities aligned with their career aspirations.

6. Acknowledge any unconscious bias to move beyond it for a successful relationship.

7. Regardless of the (sponsorship or mentorship) program chosen, it is necessary for the program's success for involved parties to meet monthly, create backup strategies for success, and share the realities each faces due to identification, race, or gender. The latter is significant as mentorship and sponsorship programs have been linked to creating a diverse workplace and inclusive culture (Khanna, 2023).

While mentoring and sponsoring programs sound promising, potential mentors and sponsors are faculty with many time constraints. This is important to consider when launching or managing the program. For example, faculty can have additional family care responsibilities, making family-friendly opportunities necessary when planning for sponsorship program success (Jamison-McClung, 2021).

Benefits to all

While the apparent beneficiary within these relationships is the protégé, others within the relationship and/or program process also benefit. Reviewing these relationships from other vantage points may assist in promoting their necessity and initiating the process. Both mentorship and sponsorship programs encourage engagement, skill development, belonging, and networking while promoting a more inclusive workplace (Ferguson, 2022).

In a sponsorship relationship, for example, while the sponsoree benefits through the many ways mentioned, the sponsors or executives can also benefit. Sponsorships offer a purposeful relationship and a chance to create a legacy within the organization. There may even be a performance measure linked to successful sponsorship. In addition, the sponsor may take this opportunity to make progress in diversity and change within the organization (Murrell & Fucci, 2019). Engaging in sponsorship relationships may assist sponsors in achieving their professional goals and help elevate their status as well (Hampel, 2021). In one study, sponsors showed increased levels of job satisfaction about job advancement, indicating the sponsor relationship proved effective (Coqual, 2023). In the same study, sponsors indicated increased capability and capacity to complete tasks. Sponsors were more satisfied with their timely delivery of quality work (Coqual, 2023).

Both mentorship and sponsorship programs can be used effectively to mitigate burnout and disengagement in the workforce. Human connection positively affects employees' productivity, health, and long-term success. The organization also benefits through these programs as they improve corporate culture, which is seen as best practices in Diversity, Equity, and Inclusion (DEI) (Ferguson, 2022). Overall, offering these programs is seen as a win for all involved. Implementing such programs can produce gains for all parties, including fast-track organizational and individual potential, performance, and growth (Hampel, 2021).

If not addressed within academia

Women are disproportionately represented in academia within the non-tenure track STEM fields. These non-tenure track positions can include adjunct, lab, management, and staff positions. While some of those positions allow individuals to contribute to research and student success, many of these positions lack stability. In addition, non-tenure track positions earn lower salaries than those in tenure track positions (Rannane et al., 2022).

It has been established that men and women are prepared similarly for these positions, such as achieving graduate school, securing funding, and gaining research experience; in addition, they share common family structures and job options after graduation (Rannane et al., 2022). Rannane et al.'s (2022) research has indicated that causes leading to the disproportionate situation remain outside these factors. Could mentoring and sponsoring help to improve this situation? Other research indicates that this could certainly assist.

The National Research Council (2006), on behalf of the National Academies of Sciences, Engineering, and Medicine (2006), suggests mentoring programs for female students and faculty as one initiative for retention and advancement in the STEM fields. Without initiatives to improve this situation, gender disparities in salary and workloads will remain for women within STEM fields. Women will continue to advance more slowly within academia, and a higher proportion will leave academic employment (The National Research Council, 2006).

Future trends and conclusions

Bäker et al. (2020) concluded that mentees who have their mentors serve in a sponsor role are more likely to reach higher-level positions in academia.

Mentors seen as sponsors, in this instance, had an even more significant impact when they helped to broker relationships between the mentee and the STEM community. We are moving this research further and clearly distinguishing between mentor and sponsor.

Opportunities for advancement increase through participation in mentorship and sponsorship relationships. By providing education on mentoring and sponsorship strategies and promoting and encouraging formal programs focused on these strategies, all leadership candidates within academia can gain further access to opportunities for promotions and high-level positions. While women face additional organizational, individual, and interpersonal barriers to advancement (Dashper, 2020), it is imperative to implement programs that address the needs of all candidates and potential leaders.

One study indicated a significant demand for more formal sponsorship programs. In addition, it was acknowledged that there is a need for clarification and training on being an effective sponsor (Murrell & Fucci, 2019). Those in higher-level faculty positions also reported less sponsorship experience than mentoring (Seehusen, 2021). Providing mentoring and sponsoring opportunities within academia and the workforce would support the development of a more prepared and diverse senior leadership pool.

Some important considerations before starting either of these programs would be to ensure that the organization can support either or both programs. Review the focus of your organization's current career development plan. Would the organization gravitate to one program or the other, or would it be open to either program (Hampel, 2021)?

Institutional commitment is required for either of these programs to succeed within academia. In addition, the collaboration and support of both faculty and administrators is necessary (Jamison-McClung, 2021). While these programs can assist all faculty in STEM, they are most helpful for first-generation STEM professionals (and others underrepresented within STEM). They are necessary for a successful STEM career trajectory (Jamison-McClung, 2021).

Both mentoring and sponsoring programs have been linked to positive consequences where they are employed. As STEM programs look to recruit, retain, and develop a diverse top talent pool, mentorship and sponsorship programs offer an attractive option and can be leveraged for promotion and career advancement within academia. However, suppose one looks at sponsorship as the next level of mentorship. In that case, STEM programs may need more sponsorship programs to support innovation, boost talent and career development, and further promote and enhance a diverse workforce (Murrell & Fucci, 2017).

Call to action

Calls to action for mentors, such as the Million Women Mentors, highlight the importance of mentoring girls and young women focused on STEM fields (Landis, 2019). Calls to action for sponsorship of women in STEM fields are needed. A call to action for sponsorship programs is imperative to continue to develop and support women in STEM fields. In 2023, A call to action made by PwC, UNICEF, and Generation Unlimited stated that equal opportunities should be given to women pursuing STEM careers to reduce the pay gap and enhance their security (Machaba et al., 2023). This call to action encouraged the creation of a more inclusive and supportive learning and work environment for women in STEM, leading to a more innovative, inclusive, and diverse workforce within these fields. The US Department of Education (2023) initiated a "Raise the Bar: STEM Excellence for All Students" program, yet ongoing support for the sponsorship of women throughout their STEM careers is needed. Therefore, a call to action to further initiate, improve, and support women in sponsorship programs within STEM fields is being made through this opportunity. Intentional support and commitment should be given to address the needs of women in STEM. Thoughtful and productive mentoring and sponsorship programs should be implemented through formal and informal opportunities. Academia should highlight these programs and encourage women to participate as mentors, mentees, sponsors and sponsorees. These thoughtful and intentional programs should be championed within academic institutions and held accountable for progress. We can do better.

SIDEBAR Dr. Adrienne Oxley Shares Her Career Journey through the Lens of Mentorship and Sponsorship

Dr. Adrienne Oxley is a Professor of Chemistry and the Dean of the Department of Health, Mathematics, and Sciences. She is in her 16th year at Columbia College in Columbia, South Carolina. Dr. Oxley has experienced both mentor and sponsor relationships throughout her career and, in a recent interview, discussed the benefits of both. As an undergraduate student, Dr. Oxley saw herself as a quiet and insecure student in a large educational institution. After her first year of college, she transferred to a smaller university that offered her a better fit. It was there that she found her first two mentors.

Her Academic Advisor was a very supportive male professor. He listened, guided her through the STEM curriculum, and proved helpful. In her junior year, a female chemistry professor joined the university and offered the opportunity for Adrienne to get involved in research. She mentored her, helped her overcome her insecurities, and encouraged her to attend graduate school. Adrienne said she pursued teaching due to this professor/mentor.

Dr. Oxley has also been sponsored during her career. When she joined Columbia College, two senior female faculty members provided career development opportunities and learning opportunities, stretched her comfort zone, and advocated for her to direct programs and take on leadership roles within the college. Additional female faculty members were key in her research development and collaboration initiatives. Her female sponsors advocated for her to get the Dean position when it became available, in addition to other leadership roles within the College.

When asked about the difference between the male and female mentor and sponsor experiences, she commented that while the male mentor was very supportive and made a definite positive impact on her life, the female mentor truly understood the challenges she was facing as a female and could provide more insightful guidance from that perspective. She stated that having a women mentor and numerous women sponsors assisted with guidance, helped her see her potential, and offered a glimpse into future career options.

Dr. Oxley believes in the power of mentorship and sponsorship relationships and stated that both have greatly assisted her throughout her career. She has benefitted and learned through these experiences and now has mentees and sponsorees of her own that she is working to assist and advance through their academic and industry careers. Dr. Adrienne Oxley is a true success story for mentoring and sponsoring relationships. She is now offering these opportunities to others to continue the pipeline of successful women in STEM careers.

References

Anderson, R. H., & Smith, D. G. (2019, August 7). What men can do to be better mentors and sponsors for women. *Harvard Business Review.* https://hbr.org/2019/08/what-men-can-do-to-be-better-mentors-and-sponsors-to-women

Bandura, A. (1977). *Social Learning Theory* (Vol. 1). Prentice-Hall.

Bäker, A., Muschallik, J., & Pull, K. (2020). Successful mentors in academia: Are they teachers, sponsors and/or collaborators? *Studies in Higher Education, 45*(4), 723–735. https://doi.org/10.1080/03075079.2018.1544235

Bakken, L. L., Byars-Winston, A., Gundermann, D. M., Ward, E. C., Slattery, A., King, A., Scott, D., & Taylor, R. E. (2010). Effects of an educational intervention on female biomedical scientists' research self-efficacy. *Advances in Health Sciences Education: Theory and Practice, 15*(2), 167–183.

Baldiga, N. R., & Coffman, K. B. (2016). Laboratory evidence on the effects of sponsorship on the competitive preferences of men and women. *Management Science, 64*(2), 888–901. https://doi.org/10.1287/mnsc.2016.2606

Behar-Horenstein, L., West-Olatunji, C., Moore, T., Houchen, D., & Roberts, K. (2012). Resilience post tenure: The experience of an African American woman in a PWI. Florida *Journal of Educational Administration & Policy, 5*(2), 58–67.

Bell, A., & Treleaven, L. (2011). Looking for Professor Right: Mentee selection of mentors in a formal mentoring program. *Higher Education, 61*(5), 545–561. https://doi.org/10.1007/s10734-010-9348-0

Bozionelos, N. (2004). Mentoring provided: Relation to mentor's career success, personality, and mentoring received. *Journal of Vocational Behavior, 64*, 24-46.

Byars-Winston, A., Estrada, Y., Howard, C., Davis, D., & Zalapa, J. (2010). Influence of social cognitive and ethnic variables on academic goals of underrepresented students in science and engineering: A multiple-groups analysis. *Journal of Counseling Psychology, 57*(2), 205–218.

Cao, J., & Yang, Y. (2013). *What are mentoring and sponsoring and how do they impact organizations?* Cornell University, ILR School. http://digitalcommons.ilr.cornell.edu/student/30/

Committee on Effective Mentoring in STEMM, Board on Higher Education and Workforce, Policy and Global Affairs, & National Academies of Sciences, Engineering, and Medicine. (2019). *The Science of Effective Mentorship in STEMM*. National Academies Press. https://doi.org/10.17226/25568

CoQual (2023). *The sponsor dividend.* https://coqual.org/reports/the-sponsor-dividend/

Cowin, K., Cohen, L., Ciechanowski, K., & Orozco, R. (2012). Portraits of mentor–junior faculty relationships: From power dynamics to collaboration. *Journal of Education, 192*(1), 37–47.

Catalyst (2022). *Sponsorship and mentoring: Ask Catalyst Express.* https://www.catalyst.org/research/sponsorship-and-mentoring-ask-catalyst-express/

Chesney-Lind, M., Okomoto, K. S., & Irwin, K. (2006). Thoughts on feminist mentoring: Experiences of faculty members from two generations in the academy. *Critical Criminology, 14*(1), 1–21.

Chow, R. (2021). Don't just mentor women and people of color. Sponsor them. *Harvard Business Review Digital Articles, 1–7.*

Dashper, K. (2020). Mentoring for gender equality: Supporting female leaders in the hospitality industry. *International Journal of Hospitality Management, 88*. https://doi-org.udel.idm.oclc.org/10.1016/j.ijhm.2019.102397

Davis, D. J., Reynolds, R., & Jones, T. B. (2011). Promoting the inclusion of tenure earning Black women in academe: Lessons for leaders in education. *Florida Journal of Educational Administration & Policy, 5*(1), 28–41.

de Vries, J., & Binns, J. (2018). Sponsorship: Creating career opportunities for women in higher education. *Universities Australia Executive Women* (UAEW).

DiStasio, C. (2023). *Sponsorship vs. mentorship: Which model is best for your organization?* SPARK. https://www.adp.com/spark/articles/2022/07/sponsorship-vs-mentorship-which-model-is-best-for-your-organization.aspx

Ferguson, J. (2022). Use sponsorship and mentorship to mitigate burnout, improve connection, and increase representation. Forbes. https://www.forbes.com/sites/forbesbusinesscouncil/2022/03/07/use-sponsorship-and-mentorship-to-mitigate-burnout-improve-connection-and-increase-representation/?sh=2ebf8f2e572f

Ferman, T. (2002). Academic professional development practice: What lecturers find valuable. *The International Journal for Academic Development, 7*(2), 146–158.

Friday, E., Friday, S. S., & Green, A. (2004). A reconceptualization of mentoring and sponsoring. *Management Decision, 42*(5), 628–644. https://doi.org/10.1108/00251740410538488

Gainor, K. A., & Lent, R. W. (1998). Social cognitive expectations and racial identity attitudes in predicting the math choice intentions of Black college students. *Journal of Counseling Psychology, 45*(4), 403–413.

Gardiner, M., Tiggemann, M., Kearns, H., & Marshall, K. (2007). Show me the money! An empirical analysis of mentoring outcomes for women in academia. *Higher Education Research & Development, 26*(4), 425–442.

Hampel, S. (2021). *Sponsorship vs mentoring: which is better?* Inkling Group. https://inkling.group/insights/sponsor-vs-mentor/

Haverly, C., & Brown, B. (2022). Mentoring across differences in science education: Applying a brokering framework. *Science Education.* https://doi.org/10.1002/sce.21720

Hewlett, S. A., Peraino, K., Sherbin, L., & Sumberg, K. (2010, December). The sponsor effect: Breaking through the last glass ceiling. *Center for Work-Life Policy.* https://30percentclub.org/wp-content/uploads/2014/08/The-Sponsor-Effect.pdf

Hewlett, S. A. (2013). Forget a mentor find a sponsor. *Harvard Business Review.*

Huston, W. M., Cranfield, C. G., Forbes, S. L., & Leigh, A. (2019). A sponsorship action plan for increasing diversity in STEMM. *Ecol Evol, 9,* 2340–2345. https://doi.org/10.1002/ece3.4962

Kanter, R. M. (1977). *Men and Women of the Corporation.* Basic Books.

Jamison-McClung, D. (2022). Mentorship, sponsorship, and professional Networking. In L. F. Bisson, L. Grindstaff, L. Brazil-Cruz, & S. J. Barbu (Eds.), *Uprooting Bias in the Academy.* Springer. https://doi.org/10.1007/978-3-030-85668-7_10

Khanna, D. (2022). Why mentorship and sponsorship are critical to women's success. *Professional & Continuing Education*. University of Washington. https://www.pce.uw.edu/news-features/articles/mentorship-sponsorship-critical-womens-success

Keating, J. A., Jasper, A., Musuuza, J., Templeton, K., & Safdar, N. (2022). Supporting Midcareer Women Faculty in Academic Medicine Through Mentorship and Sponsorship. *The Journal of Continuing Education in the Health Professions, 42*(3), 197–203. https://doi.org/10.1097/CEH.0000000000 000419

Landis, K. (2019). *Collaborative offers resources for STEM role models and mentoring*. INSIGHT to Diversity. https://www.insightintodiversity.com/ collaborative-offers-resources-for-stem-role-models-and-mentoring/

Lent, R. W., Brown, S. D., Sheu, H.-B., Schmidt, J. A., Brenner, B. R., Gloster, C., Wilkins, G., Schmidt, L., Lyons, H., & Treistman, D. (2005). Social cognitive predictors of academic interests and goals in engineering: Utility for women and students at historically black universities. *Journal of Counseling Psychology, 52*(1), 84–92.

Lopez-Garrido, G. (2023). *Bandura's self-efficacy theory of motivation in psychology*. SimplyPsychology. https://www.simplypsychology.org/self-efficacy.html

Machaba, S., Muhigana, C., Stihole, S., du Plessis, M., Mafico, M., & Greenland, C. (2023). *Igniting a path for women to thrive in STEM careers*. PWC Report. https://www.generationunlimited.org/media/7361/file/Igniting%20a%20pa th%20for%20women%20to%20thrive%20in%20STEM%20careers.pdf

Madden, T. (2023). *How to build and maintain professional relationships*. Forbes. https://www.forbes.com/sites/forbescoachescouncil/2023/02/02/how-to-build-and-maintain-professional-relationships/?sh=43b64fc669b0

Metcalf, H., Russell, D., & Hill, C. (2018). Broadening the science of broadening participation in STEM through critical mixed methodologies and intersectionality frameworks. *American Behavioral Scientist, 62*(5), 580–599.

Murrell, A., & Fucci, M. (2017). *Exploring the next evolution of mentorship*. PittBusiness: University of Pittsburgh. https://www.nationalacademies.org/ documents/embed/link/LF2255DA3DD1C41C0A42D3BEF0989ACAECE305 3A6A9B/file/D88EE752FA9F9A03C0ABC7519B756A9D7B8409F5B579.pdf

McKeen, C., & Bujaki, M. (2007). Gender and mentoring. In *The Handbook of Mentoring at Work: Theory, Research, and Practice* (pp. 197-222).

National Research Council. (2006). *To recruit and advance: Women students and faculty in science and engineering*. The National Academies Press. https://doi. org/10.17226/11624

Noe, R. A. (1988). Women and mentoring: A review and research agenda. *Academy of Management Review, 13*(1), 65–78.

O'Connor, P., O'Hagan, C., Myers, E. S., & Baisner, L. (2019). Mentoring and sponsoring in higher educational institutions: Men's invisible advantage in STEM? *HERD, 39*(4), 1-14. https://www.researchgate.net/publication/33699

0633_'Mentoring_and_sponsorship_in_Higher_Educational_institutions_M en's_invisible_advantage_in_STEM'_HERD_2019_39_4_1-14

Omadeke, J. (2021). *What's the difference between a mentor and a sponsor.* Ascend. https://hbr.org/2021/10/whats-the-difference-between-a-mentor-and-a-sponsor

Ragins, B. R. (2016). From the ordinary to the extraordinary: High-quality mentoring relationships at work. *Organizational Dynamics, 45*, 228–244.

Redmond, B. F. (2010). *Self-Efficacy theory: Do I think that I can succeed in my work? Work Attitudes and motivation.* The Pennsylvania State University, World Campus.

Sands, R. G., Parson, L. A., & Duane, J. (1991). Faculty mentoring faculty in a public university. *The Journal of Higher Education, 62*(2), 174–193.

Seehusen, D. A., Rogers, T. S., Al Achkar, M., & Chang, T. (2021). Coaching, mentoring, and sponsoring as career development tools. *Fam Med, 53*(3), 175-180. https://doi.org/10.22454/FamMed.2021.341047

Silbert, A., Punty, M., & Ghoniem, E. B. (2022). *The women's power gap at elite universities.* Eos Foundation. Womenspowergap.org

Smith, B. (2023). *Mentorship vs. sponsorship: How the difference impacts organizational advancement between genders.* Courtside Leadership. https://courtsideleadership.com/mentorship-vs-sponsorship-how-the-difference-impacts-organizational-advancement-between-genders/

Sorcinelli, M. D., & Yun, J. (2007). From mentor to mentoring networks: Mentoring in the new academy. *Change: The Magazine of Higher Learning, 39*(6), 58–61. https://doi.org/10.3200/CHNG.39.6.58-C4

Spangle, S. M., Ghalei, H., & Corbett, A. H. (2021). Practical advice for mentoring and supporting faculty colleagues in STEM fields: Views from mentor and mentee perspectives. *Journal of Biological Chemistry, 297*(3).

STEMM: Science & Gender Equity Australia (2018). Sage. https://sciencegenderequity.org.au/

Taylor, A. (2018). Advancing women in STEM begins with you: 5 ways to succeed as a female STEM graduate. *Leadership Excellence, 35*(7), 10–11.

US Department of Education. (2023). *Science, technology, engineering, and math, including computer science.* https://www.ed.gov/stem

Wolff, H. G., & Moser, K. (2010). Do specific types of networking predict specific mobility outcomes? A two-year prospective study. *Journal of Vocational Behavior, 77*(2), 238–245.

Workplace Gender Equity Agency. (2016). *Supporting careers: Mentoring or sponsorship?* Perspective Paper.

Wooll, M. (2021). *Mentor vs. sponsor: Why having both is key for your career.* BetterUp. https://www.betterup.com/blog/mentor-vs-sponsor

Zellers, D. F., Howard, V. M., & Barcic, M. A. (2008). Faculty mentoring programs: Reenvisioning rather than reinventing the wheel. *Review of Educational Research, 78*(3), 552–588. https://doi.org/10.3102/0034654308320966

Chapter 9

Cultivating Expressions of Black Womanhood in Science Education through Culturally Responsible Mentorship

Darrin Collins
University of Illinois, USA

Erica Dixon
Relay Graduate School of Education, USA

Abstract: Creating space for women and girls in STEM education has been a point of emphasis in research and educational policies for over a century (Bang et al., 2012; Condliffe-Lagemann, 2000). Women in general, and racially minoritized women in particular, have been historically marginalized in STEM academic spaces through cultural practices and educational policies (Gholson & Martin, 2014; Madden et al., 2020; Medin & Bang, 2014; Morales-Doyle, 2017). The othering of women in STEM spaces is evident in all levels of education and produces a lack of representation of women in science, technology, engineering and math-related professions (Gutstein, 2009; Madden et al., 2020). The purpose of this study is to explore the impact of culturally responsible mentorship (CRM) on the development and expression of a pre-service teacher's woman of science identity (Bishop et al., 2010; Tolbert, 2015). This case study (Yin, 1994) investigates the relationship between an experienced Black male mentor science teacher, Darrin, and a pre-service Black female science teacher, Erica. The primary question posed by the researchers is: *How does culturally responsible mentorship promote and foster expression of Black womanhood in science education?* Data collected consists of notes from weekly meetings, video recordings of instruction, survey responses, and interviews. The results of our study suggest that the cultural proximity of mentor and mentee, space offered for reflection, intentionality of collaboration, and quality of communication were components of the mentor-mentee relationship that impacted the expression of Erica's Black womanhood in the science classroom.

Keywords: Borderlands theory, communalism, Critical race feminism, cultural buffer, culturally responsible mentorship, decolonization, diverse learning instructor, justice-centered science, sociopolitical consciousness, Teachers of Color.

***

Cultivating expressions of black womanhood in science education through culturally responsible mentorship

Creating space for women and girls in STEM education has been a point of emphasis in research and educational policies for over a century (Bang et al., 2012; Condliffe-Lagemann, 2000). Women in general, and racially minoritized women in particular, have been historically marginalized in STEM academic spaces through exclusionary structures, cultural practices, systemic objectification, and educational policies (Gholson & Martin, 2014; Madden et al., 2020; Medin & Bang, 2014; Morales-Doyle, 2017). People of Color and women hold and pursue careers in science, technology, engineering, and math-related fields at significantly lower rates than White men (Lewis, 2003; National Science Foundation, 2023; Powell, 1990). "Women of Color are particularly underrepresented in science and engineering fields" (Wade-Jaimes & Schwartz, 2018, p. 680). In fact, Black women, who make up 6.7% of the adult population in the United States, account for 1.8% of science and engineering professionals (National Science Foundation, 2023). For Black women in science and engineering, success in these fields represents the traversing of a cultural boundary. This crossing of borderlands is a confrontation of identity and culture (Orozco-Mendoza, 2008). In the promotion of White hetero-patriarchal ways of knowing, Black women are often expected to perform in ways that support paradigms of dominant culture, and show manifestations of assimilation in order to be recognized as members of the science and engineering communities (Madden et al., 2020; Wade-Jaimes & Schwartz, 2018). These changes include, but are not limited to, changing appearance, mannerisms, the way Black women speak, and hiding their cultural ways of being (Madden et al., 2020; Orozco-Mendoza, 2008). This investigation explores the relationship between critical mentorship and resistance to these epistemological foreclosures and subsequent assimilation that participation in STEM spaces endorses regarding Black women.

The othering of women in STEM spaces is evident in all levels of education and produces a lack of representation of women in science, technology, engineering and math-related professions (Gutstein, 2009; Madden et al., 2020). We believe that equitable inclusion of Black women, Black ways of knowing, and Black ways of being in STEM fields is essential in establishing socially just medical, environmental, research, and educational practices within the discipline. Currently, the expectation for minoritized populations as we cross cultural boundaries is to abandon our cultural ways of knowing and seeing the world in order to adopt epistemologies of dominant White patriarchal culture that maintain our servitude (Orozco-Mendoza, 2008; Mutegi, 2020). Research supports a stereotypical narrative of Black Americans entering STEM-related fields. Much of the research suggests that Black Americans who find success in STEM show early interest in science and math (Mutegi, 2020; Thomas, 1984), hold membership in STEM-related extracurricular activities (Gilleylen, 1993; Mutegi, 2020) and participate in advanced math and science courses in secondary education (Griffin, 1990; Maple & Stage, 1991; Thomas, 1984). Very often in this experience, Black Americans' research interests, areas of study, and scientific practice are shaped by systemic white supremacy (Mutegi, 2020).

Through this case study (Baxter & Jack, 2008; Yin, 1994), we hope to add nuance to this stereotypical narrative and create avenues for a multitude of journeys into and through science and engineering disciplines for Black Americans. The purpose of this study is to explore the impact of culturally responsible mentorship (CRM) on the development and expression of a pre-service Black American teacher's woman of science identity (Bishop et al., 2010; Tolbert, 2015). This case study investigates the relationship between an experienced Black male mentor science teacher, Darrin, and a pre-service Black female diverse learning[1] science teacher, Erica. The primary question posed by the researchers is: *How does culturally responsible mentorship promote and foster expression of Black womanhood in science education?* Data collected consists of notes from weekly meetings, video recordings of

---

[1] Diverse Learning Department is also known as Special Education Department. Diverse learning teachers work with students who have physical, emotional, or cognitive limitations that impact their ability to learn.

instruction, survey responses, and interviews. The results of our study suggest that the cultural proximity of mentor and mentee, space offered for reflection, intentionality of collaboration, and quality of communication were components of the mentor-mentee relationship that impacted the expression of Erica's Black womanhood in the science classroom.

Theoretical framework

Teachers of Color are more likely to work in contentious urban school districts where they face challenges related to resource availability, racism, classism, xenophobia and a plethora of other social ills (Hilliard et al., 2003; Magaldi et al., 2018; Varelas et al., 2022). For Teachers of Color, mentorship that intentionally addresses the socio-political power dynamics of teaching Students of Color in low-resourced schools is essential in developing meaningful ways of resisting hegemonic white supremacy (Morales-Doyle 2017; Varelas et al., 2022). The theoretical framework supporting this investigation enlists several complementary theories centered around intersectional identities, particularly the intersection of marginalized identities. In Erica's case, these identities include being a Black economically disenfranchised woman single-mother Southside Chicagoan[2], among many other salient identities. Collins (2000) defines intersectionality as an "analysis claiming that systems of race, social class, gender, sexuality, ethnicity, nation, and age form mutually constructing features of social organizations, which shape Black women's experiences and, in turn, are shaped by Black women" (p. 299). Intersectionality contends that all identity categories are present and mutually contribute to the construction of who and how one is (Burning et al., 2015; Madden et al., 2020). This means that "a girl or woman is never just a gender type; she is simultaneously gendered, raced and classed" (Burning et al., 2015, p. 2).

In this investigation, we explore a Black woman's experience of entering a historically white male dominated space. The goal of this investigation is to explore how Erica navigates this space while cultivating her positionality as a Black woman science teacher. Within the research on Black women in STEM, we find that these confrontations with dominant hegemonic white supremacy

---

[2] These identities are in a constant state of negotiation. At different times and in different contexts some are more salient than others (Burning et al., 2015; Collins, 2000; Madden et al., 2020). This is the reason that the authors chose to organize them without hyphens or commas. Erica is all of her identities simultaneously; supporting the theory of border crossing.

are known as border crossings (Orozco-Mendoza, 2008). Border crossing represents "negotiations of the sociocultural values of different geographic locations, and the mandates to assimilate that each politicized space demands" (Madden et al., 2020, p. 75). This theory sets an agenda of understanding how colonized peoples interact with systems that encourage assimilation and maintain their servitude. Borderlands theory is "a project of resistance formulated as a set of processes aimed to guide the inner self of a colonized person in [her] struggle to achieve decolonization and liberation" (Orozco-Mendoza, 2008, p.3). Race-minoritized women perform acts of assimilation while holding fast to their minoritized identities, using their identities as a "passport back into native geographies" (Madden et al., 2020, p. 75). This investigation seeks to explore the impact that culturally responsible mentorship has on maintaining Black women's cultural identities as they cross into the historically White male dominated space of a science classroom.

The theories that form the foundation of this research center on decolonization as a way of reimagining the role of Black women in STEM education and related fields. In this study, we view hegemonic white supremacy as a predisposition in STEM-related spaces. This is because STEM fields espouse Eurocentric and patriarchal epistemologies that serve the purpose of foreclosing and othering cultural ways of knowing that do not align with White male-centered paradigms (Battey & Leyva, 2016; Malone & Barbarino, 2009; Martin, 2008, 2009, 2011; McGee & Martin, 2011; Mutegi, 2013). According to Madden, Pereira & Rezvi (2020), "these contexts can also be characterized as spaces that promote, valorize, and normalize the hegemonic masculinities that privilege heterosexual, White males" (p. 72). The primary purpose of this mentorship relationship, and this research, is to settle expectations that take white supremacy and the centering of White males as a given. Settled expectations are a "set of assumptions, privileges, and benefits that accompany the status of being white...that whites have come to expect and rely on across the many contexts of daily life" (Harris, 1995, p.277). In prioritizing decolonization, this mentor-mentee relationship is centered on critical race feminist paradigms and culturally responsible mentorship practices, which allow for the decentralizing of hegemonic white patriarchal epistemologies (Bang et al., 2013; Tolbert, 2015).

For the purpose of this study, decolonization represents a reimagining of the current Eurocentric knowledge power dynamics that maintain systems that marginalize and oppress non-Whites and create cultural hierarchies with whiteness as the standard (Fanon, 1963). Critical race feminism (CRF) is a theoretical framing that goes a step beyond critical race theory by promoting "theories and practices that simultaneously combat gender and racial oppression" (Madden et al., 2020, p.75). Critiques of critical race theory and feminist theories are that they overlook the dual experiences of race-minoritized women (Davis, 1981; Wing, 2003). Critical race theory has the potential to obscure the role of gender and promote theories and practices that only partially support the liberation and decolonization of Black women or other race-minoritized women (Cleaver, 2003; Crenshaw, 1991; Wing, 2003). CRT can obscure issues of race-minoritized women by ignoring the compounded nature of having two marginalized identities, being Black and a woman (Madden et al., 2020). Feminist theories and practices run the risk, as observed in the outcomes of civil rights legislation, of being co-opted by White women and reinforcing systemic white supremacy by funneling resources back to the White community (Madden et al., 2020). CRF embraces an anti-essentialist perspective of the experiences of Black women. It pushes an understanding that Black women have multiple identities and consciousnesses that shape their interactions within and outside of STEM spaces (Evans-Winter & Esposito, 2010). Literature on CRF has served the purpose of decentering White women's narratives as all women's narratives and contributing a nuanced and complex understanding of race-minoritized women's experiences that honors, among others, their gender, race, and class positions (Evans-Winter & Esposito, 2010; Madden et al., 2020).

Culturally responsible mentorship (CRM) is the theoretical frame that guides mentor and mentee interactions throughout the year-long residency. CRM is a method of mentorship that does not endorse a particular instructional practice, but rather, CRM focuses on the mentee teacher's development of critical and student-centered instructional practices and pedagogical paradigms that address issues of colonization and oppression. Culturally responsible mentorship focuses mentor-mentee discourse around five central themes: race, relationships, relevance, resources, and instructional complexity (Tolbert, 2015). These themes allow for the focus of mentee and mentor teacher instructional and pedagogical development to be anchored by power dynamics that impact their students inside and outside of the classroom. By addressing the systems of power that circumscribe the lives of oppressed peoples and viewing the students and their communities as bearers of scientific knowledge, teachers can begin the process of chipping away at the structures that maintain the international system of white supremacy (Morales-Doyle, 2017). For Teachers of Color, CRM also gives license to manifestations of their own race-minoritized and gendered identities within the boundaries of instruction. In the case of STEM education, CRM serves the purpose of expanding the boundaries of the discipline in order to include historically excluded epistemologies.

Culturally responsible mentorship is best understood as a co-construction of the mentor and mentee teachers' identities and practices. In this relationship, the mentor serves the role of "facilitator" for the growth of the mentee teacher's sociopolitical awareness. In this relationship, the mentor teacher's goal is to support and foster a "culturally responsive" positionality with the mentee teacher relative to the students and the community in which they serve (Tolbert, 2015, p. 1331). Zozakiewicz (2010) identifies this positioning of the mentor and mentee teacher as both an "obligation" and a "duty" to serve the diverse populations in which they teach (p. 140). In the CRM framework, by prioritizing teacher reflection on the themes of race, relevance, relationships, resources, and instructional complexity, particularly in the secondary science classroom, teachers are better able to combat the deficit-oriented thinking that has traditionally excluded minoritized students in science education. These themes help support a transition toward a decolonizing positionality within the teacher. As Frantz Fanon (1963) argues, decolonization is primarily a process of mental liberation. The colonized must take back ownership of their ways of being, ways of knowing, and understandings of nature in order to fully achieve a state of decolonization. Through situating teacher reflections in components that are directly linked to the work of decolonization, novice and veteran teachers alike are able to better position themselves, the students they teach, and the communities in which the students live and grow to deconstruct structural barriers to liberation (Morales-Doyle, 2017; Tolbert, 2015).

Methods

This investigation followed a qualitative case study design (Baxter & Jack, 2008; Yin, 1994). The qualitative case study is most appropriate because we are exploring the particular phenomenon of Darrin and Erica's mentor-mentee relationship. This investigation analyzes how the mentorship received facilitates Erica's border crossing experience while maintaining her cultural ways of being, knowing, and understanding. The context of the school, the authors, and the relationship that was developed are particular to the circumstances of Erica and Darrin's experience. Data sources include weekly mentee-mentor coaching meetings, open-ended surveys (performed quarterly), recordings of instruction, and two open-ended interviews (performed at the end of each semester). All mentor-mentee meetings were aligned to culturally responsible mentorship practices and centered conversations on issues of race, relevance, resources, and instructional complexity. The weekly meetings were audio-recorded with a running document where notes were kept by both Erica and Darrin. Notes from the previous week's note catcher were referenced at each coaching meeting to support reflection on practice and to measure progress. In accordance with CRM mentor-mentee coaching sessions were a collaboration rather than a dictation. The mentor, Darrin, facilitated Erica's pedagogical and instructional growth by encouraging reflection and promoting problem solving. Mentor-mentee coaching sessions addressed questions such as: What went well instructional this week? What are areas of growth from this week? How can planning and instruction be improved moving forward? What biases do we need to address in our practices that will promote student learning? These open-ended questions allowed Erica to ruminate on her practice as a teacher and to develop individualized strategies for continued growth.

Surveys were completed quarterly to support recalibrations in the mentorship experience. Semi-structured interviews were performed in the last week of each semester. The survey and interview protocols were informed by Spradley (1979). Survey and interview questions fell into two categories: 1. grand-tour questions and 2. open invitations to dialogue. Grand-tour questions are prompts that require general responses about the experience of the mentorship relationship. For example: What is something that has gone well this week? What is something that can be improved from this week? Open invitation-to-dialogue questions are prompts that elicit more detailed explanations about the mentorship experience. For example: How has the experience working with your cooperating teacher supported your expression of Black womanhood? How do your life experiences inform your identity as a teacher? In the surveys and interviews Erica was invited to share her k-12 STEM experiences, her journey to becoming a STEM teacher, and potential agreements and conflicts of her identity within her STEM experiences.

Analysis of interview data centered on crucial experiences during Erica's journey to and through STEM, Erica's perception of herself as a STEM instructor, and the impact that the mentor-mentee relationship had in fostering Erica's science teacher identity. Data was analyzed and compared to sort salient themes related to CRM. Coding was aligned to the principles of CRM. The goal of retelling Erica's journey is to contribute a new voice and story to the canon of Black women's experiences in STEM. Through contributing a new voice we hope to add nuance and diversity to the overarching narratives of Black women in STEM. In addition, we hope to identify tangible components of the mentor-mentee relationship that support expressions of Blackness and Black womanhood in the STEM classroom.

Author viewpoints

Erica's journey to and through science education

My experience in science has been very limited. Growing up, I viewed science as a foreign language. In elementary school, I had very positive experiences with school science. My grades were strong, and I enjoyed the experimentation. However, I struggled with test taking as an elementary student for a multitude of reasons. I would not find out the root cause of my testing issues until being diagnosed with attention deficit hyperactivity disorder (ADHD) at the age of 26. My high school experience with science was drastically different. In hindsight, this is when my ADHD began to manifest. I attended Dunbar Vocational High School in Chicago. I completed my first year of high school barely passing my courses. In my second year at Dunbar, I began to ditch classes. Often, I would skip my biology, algebra and other STEM classes. I spent my days in the lunchroom, avoiding STEM-related disciplines. I failed most of my classes during my sophomore year of high school. Staff informed me that I would not graduate on time and I was counseled into attending an alternative school. I was unsuccessful at my first alternative school and transferred to Benjamin Mays on the campus of Kennedy King Community College. I attended two semesters at Benjamin Mays before dropping out of high school altogether.

Shortly after dropping out, I gave birth to my first child at the age of 19. Two years later, I gave birth to my second child. Being a parent motivated me to go back to school. My children gave me a purpose. Fortunately for me Benjamin Mays closed a year after I unenrolled, and Kennedy King Community College was under reconstruction. All of the records for Benjamin Mays were lost after they closed, and when I went back to acquire my transcript, I was given an honorary diploma by Chicago Public Schools. With my honorary diploma and my new found motivation, I crossed the street and registered at Harold Washington Community College. My first semester did not go as anticipated. I was extremely underprepared. I had two young children, and my personal life was not in order. I failed the first semester. But this time I had to pay for it. It took me an entire year to pay off the debt. Once re-enrolled, I had a successful year and was able to transfer to the University of Phoenix, where I worked four years to complete a bachelor's in the art of business.

My interest in teaching came later. As mentioned, my children are and were my motivation to continue my education. At an early age, my first born was showing manifestations of a potential learning disability. At two years old, she began to receive speech-, occupational- and developmental- therapy through the University of Chicago's Friends and Family Connections. My daughter did not talk for the first five years of her life. I became extremely invested in her learning experiences, making sure that she was properly assessed and getting all of the support that she needed to mature and be a productive and functional member of society. At the age of six, she was diagnosed with oppositional defiant disorder (ODD). When she entered high school, I began to notice more distinctions between her and her peers. At the time I was working for Chicago Public Schools as a teacher's assistant in the department of diverse learners. I asked questions to my colleagues who had experience working with students with special needs and performed research on social disorders. Before she was assessed by mental health professionals, I diagnosed her with autism myself. It was during her second year of high school that she was officially diagnosed.

My daughter's trajectory through education has been one of my strongest motivators to become the special education teacher I wish she had. I could not help but blame myself. Both my child and I struggled with undiagnosed learning disorders that had extreme impacts on our educational experiences. My daughter's journey and the research that I performed on my own led me to believe that I could have a positive impact on the educational experiences of others, like myself and my daughter, who need an advocate.

So when my cousin told me about an opportunity to earn an alternative teacher certification and master's degree shortly after the COVID-19 pandemic, I seized it. I applied to the Relay Teacher Residency Program to become a diverse learning instructor. I had no intention of teaching a STEM-related course. However, teachers who work in special education can be called to teach any k-12 discipline. Upon acceptance into the teacher residency, I was placed in an elementary school. My initial cooperating teacher was a White woman in her early 20s who taught for less than five years. I believed that with her limited experience and lack of cultural fluency I would have been forced into the disciplinary role and learned very little to build my own teaching practice. After working as a teacher's assistant for more than a decade, I was wary of becoming a Black buffer for the White female teacher. I requested to be placed with a new cooperating teacher to fully have an opportunity to learn from an experienced cooperating teacher in a setting where I would be less likely to become a cultural buffer (Aikenhead, 2006).

However, I did not anticipate that this high school placement would be in a physics class. I was intimidated by the course of study. I openly communicated my anxieties about teaching high school science with Darrin over the summer. I missed out on a majority of my high school experience because of poor decisions and inadequate support. I did not take physics or the prerequisite math and science courses. I knew that I was at a deficit in terms of teaching high school physics. I was intimidated by the idea of teaching students a subject in which I had no experience. But I was determined to complete my degree and I was intentional about teaching and giving back to Black students. The journey to becoming a STEM educator started because of my biological Black children, and it has continued because of my desire to impact the Black children who I have adopted in my community.

Darrin's mentoring positionality

Mentorship plays a pivotal role in my teacher identity. I believe that nurturing the development of new teachers' practice and pedagogy simultaneously encourages me to grow and learn as a professional. Being a mentor also allows me to model anti-racist and justice-centered instructional practices. Pedagogically, I identify as a justice-centered science teacher. As a classroom teacher, I intentionally collaborate with community and non-profit organizations that promote equitable and transformative experiences for students. During my career, I have established collaborative relationships with the Friends of the Chicago River, EMBARC, the Joffrey Ballet, the Garfield Park Conservatory, Blacks in Green, Little Village Environmental Justice Organization, and Mobile Makers, among other organizations. Research supports that educational environments that "integrate students' racial identity, academic identity, and school pride"(Brown et al., 2017) and increased engagement in "out-of-school" learning spaces (Young & Young, 2018) have the potential to promote Black student success in STEM settings. Parsons and Morton (2022) argue that "out-of-school spaces can function as counter-spaces for Black students, providing physical and psychological space that allows them to determine who can and will excel in science" (p. 66). My goal in partnering with community organizations is to provide opportunities to extend the boundaries of the classroom and encourage students to think about the power dynamics that impact their lives. My research, instructional agenda, and mentorship practices address the intellectual starvation of Black youth resulting from pervasive white supremacy.

As a mentor, I am intentional about directly tackling issues of race and colonialism and fostering ways in which my mentees can actively resist the oppressive forces impacting their students. My journey as a teacher has been deeply influenced by mentoring relationships. In 2012, I chose to earn a Master's in the Art of Teaching through the Academy of Urban School Leadership (AUSL). During the 2012-13 school year, I worked at Orr Academy High School. As a component of the AUSL program I spent my preservice year as a resident teacher, working with a mentor who had a decade of science teaching experience. During this year, I experienced my first Chicago Teachers' Union strike, the closing of dozens of Black and Brown schools, the loss of students to violence, and the political landscape of Chicago as an institution. I saw firsthand the politics that surrounded the educational experiences of Black Chicago. Black families in Chicago have to fight redlining, redistricting, mayoral control of schools, and many other forces in order to achieve a fair education for their children (Ewing, 2018). The mentorship that I received during the 2012-13 school year was instrumental in supporting the development of my justice-centered science teacher identity. It also truly showed me the significance of a mentor in helping a novice educator establish their identity as a new teacher. The mentorship that I received helped me determine how I navigated some of the more challenging and unique components of being a teacher, such as comforting students after the loss of a classmate or maintaining relationships with the school community through a unionized labor strike.

These events and the mentorship that I received let me know that to have an impact on systemic forces of oppression, I needed more proximity to decision-making. I became a teacher, and later a doctoral student, because I want Black students to have opportunities to reimagine a future without the limiting factor of white supremacy. I intentionally chose a PhD program at the University of Illinois Chicago because of the College of Education's social justice orientation. During my doctoral studies, I discovered the culturally responsible mentorship framework, which aligned well with my justice-centered pedagogy and practices as a mentor. In my subsequent mentor-mentee relationships I have been intentional about foregrounding CRM practices and explaining the method of facilitating teacher learning. An essential element of my doctoral fellowship, Project Science Education for Excellence and Equity in Chicago (Project SEEEC), is mentoring pre-service and induction science teachers. As a part of my fellowship I have hosted multiple pre-service science teachers; I have also been responsible for mentoring a group of induction science teachers through a teacher inquiry group. In this position, I facilitated the induction science teachers' action research, in which they performed investigations of their own practices and classrooms. Throughout my career, I have mentored and been a cooperating teacher to 8 pre-service teachers and 23 induction teachers. In all of my mentor-mentee relationships, I have prioritized the principles of culturally responsible mentorship (race, relationships, relevance, resources and instructional complexity) with the goal of supporting my mentees in pushing back against systems of power that impact their students.

Findings and discussion

Culturally responsible mentorship fostering unapologetic manifestations of black womanhood in science teaching

In reflecting on the time that we have spent together, it is important to understand that the relationship we have constructed is very unique to our circumstances. This is in line with the case study methodology (Yin, 1994; Baxter & Jack, 2008). In analyzing our weekly meetings, daily discussions, recordings of Erica teaching, and survey data, we have genuinely tracked Erica's growth as a teacher, confidence in science, views of Darrin as a mentor, and relationships with students. Simultaneously we have tracked the development of a relationship between two Black professionals, a man and a woman, involved in the process of deconstructing their shared state of colonization. In this section, we hope to provide insight into ways that mentorship, in particular culturally responsible mentorship, can be used as an instrument to promote resistance to vestigial and modern structures of colonialism. Our goal in sharing our professional and personal experience is to contribute our voices to the chorus of liberation.

The results of our study suggest that the cultural proximity of mentor and mentee fostered confidence and trust between Erica and Darrin that supported Erica's genuine and unapologetic expression of her Black womanhood. Several attributes of Black educators that surfaced from the data were a sociopolitical consciousness (Coleman et al., 2016; Foster, 1990; Milner, 2006; Walker, 2009a, 2009b), emphasis on communalism (Ortiz & Morton, 2022; Parsons & Morton, 2022), assuming the position of a role model for Students of Color (Matthews et al., 2021; Ortiz & Morton, 2022), emphasizing the importance of emotion in learning (King & Schwartz, 2016; Parsons, 2008), and the use of storytelling in teaching and learning (Crenshaw, 1991; Mensah, 2019; Parson & Mensah, 2010). This mentor-mentee relationship catalyzed these expressions of Black womanhood by offering space for reflection, intentional collaboration, quality of discourse, and frequency of communication that contributed to Erica's resistance to white supremacy. In addressing the research question, we draw directly on the principles of culturally responsible mentorship. In this section, we will situate the findings within the reflections that Erica and Darrin shared about race, relevance, relationships, resources, and instructional complexity. Below, Table 9.1 shows the coding that we used and provides sample quotes aligned to each of the CRM principles.

Table 9.1. Culturally Responsible Mentorship Thematic Coding

CRM Principle	Code	Quote	Source of Quote
Race	R	Coming into this program, of course, I felt like this was going to be a piece of cake. Because of my past experiences as a substitute teacher and a SECA (teacher's assistant). I thought that, 'I am finna [sic] go up in here and kill this.' At my last school, I worked with mostly White women who did not relate to the students. So, I always became the teacher. The students respected me more than the actual teacher. I didn't want to be in that position again. That's why I wanted to be with a Black teacher who could show me how to work with Black students.	Quarter 1 Survey
Relevance	RE	Working through the problems like the students makes me more aware of the structure of the class. I do not want to be the teacher who just gives the students work that has no connection. Or giving them some remedial work that is super easy that they do not have to think about. I want to learn how to plan and backward map as well as you [Author 1]. It is really important that everything is connected.	Quarter 1 Survey
Relationships	REL	In one of our first conversations, do you remember Author 1? I told you about all of the anxiety I had about science. And me? Me being the one having to teach it. But I am truly glad that I was placed with you as my mentor. You broke down teaching and science so that even I could teach it.	Semester 2 Interview

Resources	RES	In this program, I made sure that I worked with a Black teacher and Black students. I wanted to be in a classroom where we were seen. Not a place where the teacher comes to work and then goes back to the northside, her own community. I wanted to be in a class where being Black was seen as a good thing, not just tolerated.	Week 5 Meeting
Instructional Complexity	IC	It feels good to have my first lesson behind me. This was the first lesson that I planned and taught. I felt like it got better as the day went on. The second period did not pull out the information from the scans that I wanted them to. But I am happy that throughout the day, I was able to improve and become a better teacher throughout the day.	Week 12 Meeting

The Salience of race and relationships

The tenets of race and relationships are the most salient influences on Erica's expression of Black womanhood in science. In Erica's teacher certification program, Relay Graduate School of Education, potential mentors and mentees interview one another in a mutual selection process. Erica and Darrin both interviewed other potential mentors and mentees prior to Erica's pre-service teaching experience. In the initial rounds of the process, Erica and Darrin did not interview with one another. Erica's goal was to stay in elementary education, therefore she chose to interview elementary teachers. Darrin, being a high school science teacher, was not an option initially. However, after being placed with a mentor, who was a White woman in her 20s, Erica requested to be transferred to another mentor. In a reflection early in our work together, Erica stated:

Coming into this program, of course I felt like this was going to be a piece of cake. Because of my past experiences as a substitute teacher and a SECA (teacher's assistant). I thought that 'I am finna go up in here and kill this.' At my last school I worked with mostly White women who did not relate to the students. So I always became the teacher. The students respected me more than the actual teacher. I didn't want to be in that position again. That's why I wanted to be with a Black teacher who could show me how to work with Black students. (Quarter 1 Survey)

Erica's decision to transfer to the program was based on her past experiences with White female teachers. Erica did not want to repeat her experiences of colonization and become another buffer between the worlds of the students who look like her and the privileging of whiteness (Aikenhead, 2006). Contributing to the subsequent alienation of Black students in their own education. The selection of mentor by mentee and mentee by mentor is vital to the buy-in of both participants in the relationship. This action also supports Erica's positionality. Erica wanted to be in a position where she could express herself and not be relegated to being a quasi-disciplinarian of young Black people, which is a common experience of Teachers of Color (Dixson, 2003; Royston et al., 2020).

Erica's eventual decision to be placed with Darrin is evidence of her self-advocating for her Black womanhood. Erica was expressing a need for communalism in her efforts to become a certified teacher. As the quote suggests, Erica felt like she would be most successful in a setting where her Blackness was viewed as an asset. From the beginning, the relationship was founded on the shared Black Chicagoan identity, with the added layer that the students we teach are predominately Black Chicagoans. Within the learning environment, there is a three-layered common experience with the physical, mental, and spiritual violence of localized white supremacy (Royston et al., 2020). Both Erica and Darrin, who had previously been Black children, and the students who they served know all too well the violence that Black children experience in and outside of school (Beauboeuf-Lafontant, 1999; Dixson, 2003; Royston et al., 2020; Walker, 1996). The lead teacher, pre-service teacher, and the students all share a mutual acquaintance with the dangers of white male heteropatriarchy.

In Erica's responses to questions about how the commonality of race, city of origin, and age played a part in her willingness to express her Black womanhood, several themes emerged. First, the shared experiences and common culture made Erica more comfortable and confident in the classroom, even though she struggled with the technical aspects of teaching physics. Second, aspects of Erica and Darrin's relationship were reproduced between Erica and the students. Third, the relationship formed between Erica and Darrin supported Erica through challenging periods in her teaching practice and graduate work.

In response to questions about how mentorship fostered expressions of Erica's unapologetic Black womanhood, she explains:

My Cooperating teacher has supported my expression of Black womanhood this year by understanding that I am new to this world of science and being patient with me as I learn, while also teaching different methods that I am going to need to be successful as I become a teacher of record. (Quarter 4 Survey)

I definitely feel like I am getting better. I don't feel as nervous when in front of the students. I don't feel as nervous about the science. You [Author 1] have helped me relax and be more confident. (Week 10 Meeting)

In one of our first conversations, you remember Author 1? I told you about all of the anxiety I had about science. And me? Me being the one having to teach it. But I am truly glad that I was placed with you as my mentor. You broke down teaching and science so that even I could teach it. (Semester 2 Interview)

As mentioned in Erica's positionality statement, she has very limited experience as a student in science. The experience of teaching science through her teacher certification program has been a palpable challenge. As she suggests in her responses, "this science world" was very foreign and intimidating for her. The idea of crossing the cultural border into the science classroom was filled with angst. It was the relationship that she forged with Darrin that gave her the confidence, comfort, and faith to believe that she was capable. The "affect," or the way that teachers/mentors make students/mentees feel, is vital in the education of Black learners. The emotions felt during the learning process are of equal importance to the content that is being learned (Parsons, 2008). One of the principles that Darrin enforced as the lead teacher is that the classroom is a learning environment and that "all stakeholders are in the classroom to create and share learning." This pedagogical approach, rooted in culturally responsible mentorship and justice-centered teaching, facilitated space for Erica's successes and mistakes. This pedagogical lens also supported the sense of Black American communalism expressed by both Erica and Darrin (King, 1994; Ortiz & Morton, 2022). Through establishing an environment where all stakeholders are learners and teachers, the mentor and mentee, while decentering their own positions of authority, created a space where students and teachers were 1. learning through Black collectivism and 2. consistently able to either show evidence of learning or fail forward[3].

---

[3] Failing forward is a growth mindset principle that suggests that failure only exists if one quits. This principle supports accepting failure and the lessons that it teaches in order to apply those lessons to future efforts (Maxwell, 2000).

Another takeaway from Erica's responses is the idea of "maintaining a calm demeanor" with students. This, too, emphasizes the importance of affect and emotion in educating Black students. In many ways, there was a dialogic relationship between the mentee-mentor dynamic and that of the mentee-student dynamic. The mentee-mentor relationship served as a model for the relationships that Erica formed with our students. Mentor-mentee reflections were focused on problem solving, not finger-pointing. In Erica's previous position, as a teacher's assistant, she often assumed a zero-tolerance positionality in the classroom as the quasi-disciplinarian. This required most of her interactions with students to be punitive. However, the structures of the mentor's classroom, including a well-established behavior management cycle[4], allowed Erica to focus on teaching and learning rather than student conduct. The educational relationship between Erica and Darrin served as an example of the mentor facilitating a pupil's learning experience. This model was reproduced between Erica and the students.

One of Erica's most notable takeaways was "not yelling." This was an action that had become normalized in her instructional practice as a teacher's assistant. In fact, she believed that because she could "control" a classroom, the residency program would be a "piece of cake." In response to questions about the instructional practices that Erica has learned throughout the school year, she states:

> The first thing I was taught is to never yell. Which is the best stuff ever. To learn to keep that straight face. Even the students said, "You are always happy." That's what you think. No matter what I'm going to give you the best me, so that I can get the best you. (Semester 2 Interview)

> When I think about what is going well so far. I think that my tone of voice and maintaining a calm demeanor are going well. Also, I think that my relationships with students are going well. (Week 24 Meeting)

For many, this revelation may seem minor. However, as a teacher, it is crucial that the students who are in front of you, and their learning, are prioritized. Not their obedience. From a justice-centered lens, it is key that Black students are not circumscribed. For Erica, changing this aspect of her instructional practice

---

[4] A behavior management cycle is a progressive set of classroom rules that is intended to maintain consistency and transparency in redirecting student (mis)behavior (Canter, 2009)

removes the punitive nature of her previous experiences, and it incorporates the emotion-driven learning found in Black American culture (Parsons & Morton, 2022).

In this example, we see a burgeoning justice-centered approach to teaching. Throughout the year, the appearance of control became less important in Erica's pedagogy. Instead, she prioritizes the students, their feelings, and their learning, which has far-reaching impacts on instruction and curricular choice (Brown et al., 2017). The goal, for a justice-centered teacher, is that the education be liberatory and deconstruct the systems that maintain the students' state of oppression, not to become agents of the oppression (Morales-Doyle, 2017). In these quotes, we see that the experience of CRM encouraged a shift in Erica's paradigm. No longer was Erica concerned with controlling students. Her goal was to establish positive relationships with students and begin to teach by prioritizing who she taught, not what she taught. The curriculum is only relevant if it has the potential to illuminate the power dynamics that circumscribe the lives of the students and encourage a liberatory response. She came to this understanding, through letting the students know her and through getting to know the students and the cultural assets that they brought to the class (Ladson-Billings, 2006; Tolbert, 2015). Simultaneously, in this process of unlearning, Erica noticed that controlling the students was less important when the teacher and the students shared ownership of their mutual learning.

Viewing the community as a resource: impacts on pedagogy and instructional complexity

In Erica's responses, her self-perceived growth was very much related to Darrin's example as lead teacher. It is also clear from her responses later in the year that she uses Darrin's example as a resource. As she gains confidence in her own teaching and becomes more grounded in her own pedagogy she learns ways to make routines, activities, and entire lessons that align with her teacher of science identity. Erica's confidence in her ability grows throughout the year. In Erica's responses from early in the school year, there is a heavy reliance on Darrin as a model of teaching. Erica states:

> There is so much that I want to work on. Because I am new to science, I want to work on everything. I really need to find my voice in the curriculum. I feel like I am mimicking you [Author 1]. I need to work on my transitions. Make them cleaner and also how I deliver information. (Week 6 Meeting)

In this response we see that Erica is searching for appropriate and legitimate ways to express herself and her Black womanhood in the classroom. At the beginning of the year, she "still felt like a SECA (student teacher)." She did not feel comfortable or confident giving instruction in a subject that she had never learned as a high schooler. As Erica states, she was attempting to "mimic" the gestures, tone of voice, mannerisms, and practices of Darrin to feel like and appear to be, the teacher. This was unnatural for her and felt disingenuous. Instead, Erica states that her goal is to "find her voice in the curriculum." In the early stages of the residency Erica was trying to make space for herself within the class.

Later in the year, once Erica had gained experience instructing, planning, and modifying lessons, her responses to similar questions changed. Erica begins to feel less anxiety around the content and she begins to find space for her own identity in the classroom. The first lesson that Erica planned and taught was in the second unit of the year on forces and collisions. Students investigated the impact of football collisions on the occurrence of concussions in the sport. In the lesson, students compared brain imaging from different athletes, looking for evidence of chronic traumatic encephalopathy (CTE). After this lesson, Erica stated:

> It feels good to have my first lesson behind me. This was the first lesson that I planned and taught. I felt like it got better as the day went on. Second period did not pull out the information from the scans that I wanted them to. But I am happy that throughout the day, I was able to improve and become a better teacher throughout the day. (Week 12 Meeting)

In this lesson, Erica shows a level of comfort in her practice. When viewing the video recording of the lesson, we also find that Erica shares personal anecdotes from her own life. While exploring the brain imaging with the students, Erica tells stories of her son, who at the time played college football. She explains, "I wish I had known about these injuries when my son started... I feel like I don't know if I would have let him play if I knew the types of brain trauma that football can cause." Erica also shares stories related to a recent knee injury that her son sustained. As Erica grows in her teacher of science identity, we see that she is more open about herself; we also find that Erica is openly renegotiating her teacher of science identity with other identities, like being a mother to a Black son (Morton & Parsons, 2018). Erica relies more on her own cultural background through the telling of stories to communicate learning (Crenshaw, 1991; Mensah, 2019; Parson & Mensah, 2010). This lesson coincided with the school football team winning the conference championship. Students were able to have pertinent and transparent conversations about themselves and their classmates engaging in a sport that can potentially cause long-term brain damage. This example supports the integration of both relevance and instructional complexity. Through this lesson, Erica and the students were able to have very real conversations about the science and ethics of high-impact sports for elementary and high school students. The lesson incorporated communal knowledge as a resource for the class. It was through this intentional connection that students offered their personal experiences and engaged one another as sources of knowledge.

This example also offers insight into the way that both mentee and mentor view teaching. Although Erica did not get the results she wanted the first time she taught the lesson, in the later periods of the day, she was able to show flexibility and make modifications to the lesson. The modifications that Erica made in consultation with Darrin were successful. In this way, she was able to move forward. The shortcomings from the previous period allowed her to grow. These in-the-moment audibles are indicative of Erica's growth and confidence that are directly related to the quality of communication and depth of reflection within the mentee-mentor relationship. These modifications support the asset-oriented lens of both mentee and mentor (Ladson-Billings, 2006); both teachers identified that there were ways to change the instruction so that students could access the intended learning objectives. Whereas a teacher with a deficit-oriented lens might suggest that the students need more "grit" or to "work harder." This example also shows Erica's use of Darrin's knowledge and experience as a resource for her own instructional practice.

In several of Erica's responses, we gain insight into the factors that she identifies are supporting her confidence as an instructor. In her responses about confidence and expression of her identity, the theme of repositioning emerges. Erica's repositioning relative to the students and the content that is taught provided the space for her to become more comfortable and manifest her Black woman of science identity. This repositioning had an iterative connection with Erica's perception of science education and her relationships with students. This repositioning also catalyzed Erica's growth mindset toward teaching. Because she did not have to be the sole person responsible for teaching and learning in the class, her science teacher identity was not deterred by making mistakes in her practice, miscalculations, or mispronunciations. Erica discusses this repositioning as follows:

I learned to stay on track. I always come back to classroom management. Because I feel like if the kids engaged then hell you won half of the battle. Then being able to teach a subject when you don't know what the hell you talking about. That right there. It's one thing learning to teach English. But physics. God set me up for something. (Semester 1 Interview)

Working through the problems like the students makes me more aware of the structure of the class. I do not want to be the teacher who just gives the students work that has no connection. Or giving them some remedial work that is super easy that they do not have to think about. I want to learn how to plan and to backwards map as well as you [Author 1]. It is really important that everything be connected. (Quarter 1 Survey)

I am getting better at understanding when the students do not understand. I am also able to take their criticism better. Like when third period corrects me. I tell them "This is an environment of learning. We are all learners here." (Week 28 Meeting)

There is a lot that is going well this week. First, B. and R. (students in the class), students who get it, believe in what I say. Even H. told me "you [Author 2] are the smart one and he [Author 1] is the mean one. I just feel like students and others in my graduate program seek me out for support. That is a really good feeling. (Week 33 Meeting)

In the above responses it is clear that as the year progressed Erica's feelings about teaching and understanding of her responsibility as a teacher shifted. At the beginning of the year, Erica thought that it was important to control students in the classroom. These quotes support the finding that as the year progressed, Erica found that classroom management was much more easily accomplished when she 1. had a stronger understanding of the curriculum and its interconnectedness and 2. students were engaged in the learning. These experiences encouraged Erica to plan lessons differently. As the above responses support, Erica was much more focused on the coherence and student-centeredness of lessons. As the year progressed backward mapping and building the instructional complexity naturally into lessons and units was more important than mastering specific physics concepts. There is a point toward the end of the first semester where this paradigm shift toward relevant and multifaceted scientific concepts becomes apparent. This repositioning is intimately related to the mentorship that she has received. As discussed previously, Erica chose to adopt Darrin's pedagogical frame that all of the classroom's stakeholders are learners. This shift in paradigm towards a communal learning space supported changes in instructional practice, planning, and student-teacher relationships. Subsequently, Erica's understanding of teaching science became more nuanced.

In short, culturally responsible mentorship practices facilitated the emergence of Erica's social-justice science teacher identity. Through building relationships, with Darrin and with the students who she taught, Erica's understanding of teaching and learning shifted. At the beginning of the residency experience, Erica believed that controlling a classroom meant instilling fear and respect in students. After experiencing a mentorship relationship situated in culturally responsible mentorship practices, her pedagogical lens became more student-centered. This shift in Erica's pedagogical lens promoted instructional practices that were relevant and complex. Through sharing the power of teaching and learning with the students, Erica became more confident in tackling complicated physics concepts with which she was previously unfamiliar. Finally, and most importantly, CRM helped Erica deconstruct her fear of teaching science and showed her how to create space for her Black womanhood within this foreign discipline.

Concluding thoughts

These two quotes from Marian Wright Edelman, founder of the Children's Defense Fund, fully capture the findings of this study:

1. "The challenge of social justice is to evoke a sense of community that we need to make our nation a better place, just as we make it a safer place" (Edington & Chin, 2008, p. 87);

2. "Those who came before us should've learned some things to help make the steps of those coming after us a little lighter" (Edelman, 2008, p. 26)

The state of social justice can only be achieved through collective action. Every actor in the community must take responsibility for the injustices that occur and recognize their agency in pushing back against systems and structures of oppression (Fanon, 1963; Mensah, 2019). The sense of community that Erica and Darrin established supported both of their growth as educators. The mentor-mentee relationship reinforced Erica's sociopolitical consciousness (Coleman et al., 2016; Foster, 1990; Milner, 2006; Walker, 2009a, 2009b) and helped her explore how to teach through a conscious lens. The experience of CRM exposed Erica to the intersections of science and racism. So, when Erica taught, addressing issues of race/racism was an organic progression. Not only were these principles of collectivism shared between mentee and mentor, but the emphasis on communalism and collectivism were pervasive throughout all aspects of teaching (Ortiz & Morton, 2022; Parsons & Morton, 2022). Erica and Darrin's collaboration toward a collective goal, founded in the Black American ontological principle of a shared destiny (Kane, 1972), was reproduced within the classroom with and between students. Through the establishment of relationships, that were in and of themselves resources, a hierarchical role modeling dynamic was established between mentor, mentee, and students. This, too, is supported by literature investigating relationships between Teachers of Color and Students of Color (Matthews et al., 2021; Ortiz & Morton, 2022). In this way, as Marian Edelman Wright suggests, the mentor is making the steps of the mentee lighter, and hopefully mentor and mentee are working to make the steps of the students lighter.

Creating space within STEM education for Black women is important, not only for representation and inclusion, but also because Black women's contribution to STEM is historically unmatched. Black women have contributed great ideas, new theories, and even their bodies to the development of STEM fields. The findings of our study highlight one method of reintroducing Black women to a discipline that we, as Black people, helped forge. This research supports the use of culturally responsible mentorship practices in fostering authentic expressions of Black womanhood in the field of science teaching.

This study highlights several ways in which Black teachers can be supported in teacher education programs. First, promoting Blackness as a legitimate way of being, knowing and seeing the world is essential for Black Americans generally, and Black women particularly, to feel successful in STEM professions, STEM classrooms, and as STEM educators. Research supports that although Teachers of Color bring a great deal of insight and sociopolitical awareness into the field, very little of their experiences and prior knowledge is used within teacher preparation (Gist, 2017; Montecinos, 2004). Numerous studies demonstrate that the focus and design of teacher education are for White teacher candidates, and the voices of Teachers of Color are either ignored or silenced within teacher preparation programs and classes (Amos, 2010; Parker & Hood, 1995; Sheets & Chew, 2002). One tangential finding from the research was that Erica and Darrin's relationship was unique in her teacher certification program. Throughout the year, Darrin and Erica had several discussions about mentors who did not share instructional materials with their residents, had unprofessional interactions in front of students, and were unsupportive of innovative teaching models. Several of the anecdotes truly support the need for culturally responsible mentorship practices for pre-service teachers. Erica states:

> My cousin was dealing with a mentor, an older Black woman. She was being combative with her. Yelling at her. Upset when she has resident meetings. Just being really aggressive and yelling at her. Until the point that my cousin dropped out of the program. She just quit. (Semester 1 Interview)

> I am truly thankful for having you as a mentor. When I am in class, I hear other people talking about the relationships that they have with their mentors. Mentors are yelling at adults and forcing people to quit. (Week 20 Meeting)

> Other residents I have heard some awful stories about the mentors yelling at them and not sharing information. Or not wanting to allow them to also be a teacher in the room. I would think that the mentor teacher's job, well responsibility, is to gradually put you in a place where you can learn to lead the class, help with lessons. Which has been my experience. Because I don't think that I could deal with someone yelling at me or mad when I don't get something. Because I myself have a lot of questions and I need a lot of confirmation before I do some things wrong. And the horror stories that I hear about mentors just not being helpful or just not wanting to be helpful. Not allowing the resident teacher to lead lessons. That's crazy. We have ten more weeks left. (Semester 2 Interview)

These examples support the importance of a reassuring and caring mentor-mentee relationship. They also suggest the importance of developing and nurturing relationships that are encouraging and respectful in order to genuinely build pre-service teacher confidence in their practice. One of the major differences between the relationships and their outcomes is the intentionality of reflection found in CRM practices. As Erica argues, in her experience with mentorship, she was able to "have a lot of questions" and receive the confirmation that she needed because Darrin gave space for questions, problem-solving, and uncertainty. From the examples in the quotes above, there appears to be little credence given to the human component of teaching. In these examples, preservice teachers are not given the room to learn and make mistakes as novice members of the profession.

Second, modeling is one of the more powerful tools in teacher education (Borko, 2008). Novice teachers benefit from seeing the theoretical components of their teacher education programs in practice. The quality of Erica's experience as a resident teacher is directly related to Darrin's CRM positionality. CRM posits that the mentor facilitates the mentee's learning. The mentor is not a sage with all of the answers, but rather, the mentor's job is to help the mentee identify areas of growth and promote their ability to problem solve. In assessing her experience with Darrin relative to those of her colleagues in the alternative certification program, Erica states:

> My mentor teacher has set me up for success by allowing me to grow at my own rate of understanding yet pushing me to my limits when I am having difficulties understanding. I am not really allowed to just not know I am pushed to higher understanding. My relationship with my cooperating teacher has been good. I believe he has helped me become an immersive educator which will prepare me to dominate as a special education teacher next school year. (Quarter 4 Survey)

> And with my experience I am definitely on track with one of the most important aspects which I have learned really great techniques. With my experience hell I've been taught physics. Which is probably the hardest. I still can't believe that, when I say 'I'm teaching physics.' And they say you're smart. No I'm not. Not really. But I am having a great experience in this program. I'm going to be crying when I have to leave in June and have to get my own class. The relationships are not going to be the same. I really love the relationship that I have with my mentor teacher. (Semester 2 Interview)

In these statements Erica suggests that the mentor-mentee relationship has provided her with a substantial and sustainable foundation for her teaching career. She also discusses a relationship that nurtured an environment for her learning. Through modeling, the mentor provides the cornerstone for the development of the pre-service teacher's pedagogical lens and instructional practice. The mentor has the ability to discourage or empower the mentee.

Third, providing space for reflection on principles of CRM, a particularly sociopolitical reflection, promoted Erica holistically. She did not have to abandon her Blackness, her womanhood, or any other aspect of who she was to teach science. In fact, all of her identities were celebrated, encouraged, and viewed as assets to her practice. However the work of reflecting on her identities and sharing them was Erica's responsibility. In the weekly reflections, Erica carried the onus of identifying and suggesting solutions to issues related to race, classroom dynamics, instructional strategies, resources, and pedagogical approaches. In her responses, this level of reflection and space to verbally process has been foundational in building her confidence in teaching her own classroom. We have found that situating the mentor-mentee relationship in culturally responsible mentorship practices promoted Erica's unapologetic expression of Black womanhood by allowing her to own her teacher journey. This is juxtaposed to the experience of her cousin, who was in a tenuous and combative relationship with a veteran Black female teacher. Suggesting that cultural and racial proximity are important in promoting a liberatory educational experience. However, they are not sufficient. Cultural sensitivity and an awareness of systems of oppression are the characteristics that support culturally responsible and justice-centered teaching.

In conclusion, we end this chapter by offering methods to build on our findings. The findings of this investigation center on the importance of relationships in establishing resources, cultural relevance, and instructional complexity. We recommend that future investigations explore CRM's -influence on the relevance of content taught, -instructional complexity of preservice and novice teachers, and -liberation of other marginalized group identities. This corpus of literature has the potential to move STEM education beyond inclusionary politics and toward a future where Black and other marginalized identities and epistemologies are celebrated as assets.

References

Aikenhead, G. (2006). *Science education for everyday life: evidence based science practice*. New York, NY: Teachers College Press.

Amos, Y. T. (2010). "They don't want to get it!" Interaction between minority and white pre-service teachers in a multicultural education class. *Multicultural Education, 17,* 31–37.

Bang, M., Warren, B., Rosebery, A. S., & Medin, D. (2012). Desettling expectations in science education. *Human Development, 55*(5-6), 302–318.

Battey, D., & Leyva, L.A. (2016). A framework for understanding whiteness in mathematics education. *Journal of Urban Mathematics Education, 9*(2), 49-80.

Baxter, P., & Jack, S. (2008). Qualitative case study methodology: Study design and implementation for novice researchers. *The Qualitative Report, 13*(4), 544-559.

Beauboeuf-Lafontant, T. (1999). A movement against and beyond boundaries. *Teachers College Record, 100*(4), 702–723.

Bishop, R., Berryman, M., Wearmouth, J., Peter, M., & Clapham, S. (2012). Professional development, changes in teacher practice and improvements in indigenous students' educational performance: A case study from New Zealand. *Teaching and Teacher Education, 28*(5), 694–705.

Borko, H. (2008). Professional development and teacher learning: mapping the terrain. *Educational Researcher, 22,* 3-14.

Brown, B. A., Mangram, C., Sun, K., Cross, K., & Raab, E. (2017). Representing racial identity: Identity, race, the construction of the African American STEM students. *Urban Education, 52*(2), 170–206.

Bruning, M.J., Bystydzienski, J., & Eisenhart, M. (2015). Intersectionality as a framework for understanding diverse young women's commitment to engineering. *Journal of Women and Minorities in Science and Engineering, 21*(1), 1-26.

Canter, L. (2009). *Assertive Discipline: Positive Behavior Management for Today's Classroom.* Atlanta, GA: Solution Tree Press.

Cleaver, K.N. (2003). Racism, civil rights and feminism. In W.A.K. (Ed.), *Critical Race Feminism* (48-56). New York: New York University Press.

Coleman, S. T., Bruce, A. W., White, L. J., Boykin, A. W., & Tyler, K. (2016). Communal and individual learning contexts as they relate to mathematics achievement under simulated classroom conditions. *Journal of Black Psychology, 43*(6), 543–564.

Collins, P. H. (2000). *Black Feminist Thought: Knowledge, consciousness, and the politics of empowerment* (2nd ed.). New York, NY: Routledge.

Condliffe-Lagemann, E. (2000). *An Elusive Science: The Troubling History of Education Research.* Chicago, IL: University of Chicago Press.

Crenshaw, K. W. (1991). Mapping the margins: Intersectionality, identity politics, and violence against women of color. *Stanford Law Review, 43,* 1241–1299. doi:10.2307/1229039

Davis, A.Y. (1981) *Women, Race & Class.* New York: Random House.

Dixson, A. D. (2003). "Let's do this!" Black women teachers' politics and pedagogy. *Urban Education, 38*(2), 217–235.

Edelman, M.W. (2008). *The sea is so wide but my boat is so small: Charting the Course for the Next Generation.* New York, NY: Hachette Books.

Evans-Winters, V.E., & Esposito, J. (2010). Other people's daughters: Critical race feminism and Black girl's education. *Journal of Educational Foundations, 24*(1/2), 11-24.

Ewing, E.L. (2018). *Ghosts in the Schoolyard: Racism and School Closings on Chicago's South Side.* Chicago: University of Chicago Press.

Fanon, F. (1963). *Wretched of the earth.* New York: Grove Press.

Foster, M. (1990). The politics of race: Through the eyes of African-American teachers. *Journal of Education, 172,* 123–141.

Gholson, M., & Martin, D. B. (2014). Smart girls, black girls, mean girls, and bullies: At the intersection of identities and the mediating role of young girls' social network in mathematical communities of practice. *Journal of Education, 194,* 19–33.

Gilleyen, C.E. (1993). *A comparative study of the science-related attitudes and the factors associated with persisting in science of African American college students in science majors and African American college students in non-science majors* (Unpublished doctoral dissertation). Indiana University of Pennsylvania.

Gist, C. D. (2017). Voices of aspiring teachers of color: Unraveling the double bind in teacher education. *Urban Education, 52,* 927–956.

Griffin, J.B. (1990). Developing more minority mathematicians and scientists: A new approach *Journal of Negro Education, 59,* 424-438.

Gutstein, E. (2009). The politics of mathematics education in the United States: Dominant and counter agendas. In B. Greer, S. Mukhopadhyay, A.B. Powell & S. Nelson-Barber (Eds.) *Culturally responsive mathematics education.* New York, NY: Routledge Group.

Harris, C.I. (1995). Whiteness as property. In K. Crenshaw, N. Gotanda, G. Peller, & K. Thomas (Eds.), *Critical race theory* (pp. 276–291). New York: New Press.

Hilliard, A., Perry, T., & Steele, C. (2003). *Young, gifted, and black: Promoting high achievement among African- American students.* Beacon.

Kane, C.H. (1972). *Ambiguous adventure.* Nairobi, KE: Heinemann International.

King, J. E. (1994). The purpose of schooling for African American children: Including cultural knowledge. In E. R. Hollins, J. E. King, & W. C. Hayman (Eds.), *Teaching diverse populations: Formulating a knowledge base* (pp. 25–56). State University of New York Press.

King, J. E., & Swartz, E. E. (2016). *The Afrocentric praxis of teaching for freedom.* New Jersey: Routledge.

Ladson-Billings, G. (2006). From the achievement gap to the education debt: Understanding achievement in U.S. schools. *Educational Researcher, 35*(7), 3–12.

Lewis, B.F. (2003). A critique of literature on the underrepresentation of African Americans in science: Directions for future research. *Journal of Women and Minorities in Science and Engineering, 9,* 361-373.

Madden, K., Pereira, O., & Rezvi, S. (2020). Cartographies of race, gender, and class in the white (male) settler spaces of science and mathematics: Navigation by black, afro-Brazilian, and Pakistani/American women. In E.O. McGee & W.H. Robinson (Eds). *Diversifying STEM: Multidisciplinary Perspectives on Race and Gender* (pp. 69-106). Newark, NJ: Rutgers University Press.

Magaldi, D., Conway, T., & Trub, L. (2018). "I am here for a reason": Minority teachers bridging many divides in urban education. *Race Ethnicity and Education, 21,* 306–318.

Malone, K.R., & Barabino, G. (2009). Narrations of race in STEM research settings: Identity formation and its discontents. *Science Education, 93*(3), 485-510.

Maple, S.A., & Stage, F.K. (1991). Influences on the choice of math/science major by gender and ethnicity. *American Educational Research Journal, 28,* 37-60.

Martin, D.B. (2008). Race, racial projects, and mathematics education. *Journal for Research in Mathematics Education.* 2013, *44*(1), 316-333.

Martin, D.B. (2009). Researching race in mathematics education. *Teachers College Record 111*(2), 295-338.

Martin, D.B. (2011). What does quality mean in the context of white institutional space? In *Mapping equity and quality in mathematics education* (pp. 437-450). Dordrecht: Springer.

Matthews, L. E., Jessup, N., & Sears, R. (2021). Looking for "us": Power reimagined in mathematics learning for Black communities in the pandemic. *Educational Studies in Mathematics, 108*(1–2), 333–350.

Maxwell, J.C. (2007). *Failing forward: Turning mistakes into stepping stones for success.* New York, NY. Harper Collins Publishing.

McGee, E.O., & Martin, D.B. (2011). "You would not believe what I have to go through to prove my intellectual value!" Stereotype management among academically successful Black mathematics and engineering students. *American Educational Research Journal, 48*(6), 1347-1389.

McKinney de Royston, M., Madkins, T.C., Givens, J.R. & Nasir, N.S. (2020). "I'm a teacher, I'm gonna always protect you": Understanding Black educators' protection of Black children. *Educational Research Journal, 20,* 1-39.

Medin, D., & Bang, M.(2014). The cultural side of science communication. *Proceedings of the National Academy of Science Journal, 10,* 1-6.

Mensah, F.M. (2019) Finding voice and passion: Critical race theory methodology in science teacher education. *American Educational Research Journal, 56*(4), 1412-1456.

Milner, H. R., IV. (2006). The promise of Black teachers' success with Black students. *Educational Foundations, 20,* 89–104.

Montecinos, C. (2004). Paradoxes in multicultural teacher education: Students of color positioned as objects while ignored as subjects. *International Journal of Qualitative Studies in Education, 27,* 167–181.

Morales-Doyle, D. (2017). Justice-centered science pedagogy: A catalyst for academic achievement and social transformation. *Science Education, 101,* 1034-1060.

Morton, T. R., & Parsons, E. C. (2018). BlackGirlMagic: The identity conceptualization of black women in undergraduate STEM education. *Science Education, 102*(6), 1363-1393.

Mutegi, J.W. (2013). "Life's first need is for us to be realistic" and other reasons for examining the sociocultural construction of race in the science performance of African American students. *Journal of Research in Science Teaching, 50*(1), 82-103.

National Science Foundation, National Center for Science and Engineering Statistics. (2023). *Women, Minorities, and Persons with Disabilities in Science and Engineering: 2023.* Special Report NSF 17-310. Arlington, VA.

Orozco-Mendoza, E.F. (2008). *Borderlands theory: Producing border epistemologies with Gloria Anzaldua* (Doctoral dissertation). Retrieved from http://hdl.handle.net/10919/32268

Ortiz, N.A. & Morton, T.R. (2022) Empowering Black mathematics students through a framework of communalism and collective Black identity. *Journal of Urban Mathematics Education, 15*(1), 54-77.

Parker, L., & Hood, S. (1995). Minority students vs. majority faculty and administrators in teacher education: Perspectives on the clash of cultures. *Urban Review, 27,* 159–174.

Parsons, E. R. C., & Mensah, F. M. (2010). Black feminist thought: The lived experiences of two black female science educators. In K. Scantlebury, J. B. Kahle, & S. N. Martin (Eds.), *Re-visioning Science Education from Feminist Perspectives: Challenges, choices and careers* (pp. 13–24). Rotterdam, The Netherlands: Sense.

Parsons, E. C., Tran, L., & Travis, C. (2008). An investigation from the perspective of race of student roles in small, racially mixed science groups. *International Journal of Science Education, 30*(11), 1464–1489.

Parsons, E.C., & Morton, T.R. (2022) My best science teacher: the views of Black students and implications for science education reform. *Cultural Studies of Science Education, 17,* 63-83.

Powell, L. (1990). Factors associated with the underrepresentation of African Americans in mathematics and science. *Journal of Negro Education, 59*(3), 292–298.

Sheets, R. H., & Chew, L. (2002). Absent from the research, present in our classrooms: Preparing culturally responsive Chinese American teachers. *Journal of Teacher Education, 53,* 127–141.

Spradley, J.P. (1979). *The ethnographic interview.* New York: Holt, Rinehart & Winston.

Thomas, G.E. (1984). *Black college students and factors influencings their major field of choice.* Baltimore: Johns Hopkins University, Center for Social Organization of Schools.

Tolbert, S (2015). "Because they want to teach you about their culture": analyzing effective mentoring conversations between culturally responsible mentors and secondary science teachers of indigenous students in mainstream schools. *Journal of Research in Science Teaching 52*(10), 1325-1361.

Varelas, M., Seguar, D., Bernal-Munera, M., & Mitchener, C. (2022). Embracing equity and excellence while constructing science teacher identities in urban schools: Voices of new teachers of color. *Journal of Research in Science Teaching,* 1-38.

Waide-James, K., & Schwartz, R. (2018). "I don't think its science" African American girls and the figured world of science. *Journal of Research in Science Teaching, 56*(1), 679-706.

Walker, V. S. (1996). *Their highest potential: An African American school community in the segregated south.* North Carolina: University of North Carolina Press.

Walker, V. S. (2009a). *Hello professor: A Black principal and professional leadership in the segregated South.* North Carolina: University of North Carolina Press.

Walker, V. S. (2009b). Second-class integration: A historical perspective for a contemporary agenda. *Harvard Educational Review, 79*(2), 269–284.

Wing, A.K. (Ed.). (2003). *Critical race feminism: A reader.* New York: New York University Press.

Yin, R.K. (1994). *Case study research: Design and method.* New York, NY: Sage.

Young, J., & Young, J. (2018). The structural relationship between out-of-school time enrichment and black student participation in advanced science. *Journal for the Education of the Gifted, 41*(1), 43–59.

Zozakiewicz, C. (2010). Culturally responsible mentoring: Exploring the impact of an alternative approach for preparing student teachers for diversity. *The Teacher Educator, 45*, 137–151.

Chapter 10

DUETS: Developing Urban Education Teachers in STEM

Deborah A. Harmon
Eastern Michigan University, USA

Cheryl L. Price
University of Massachusetts (UMASS), USA

Abstract: The DUETS Program, Developing Urban Education Teachers in Science, Technology, Engineering, and Math (STEM), was aimed at recruiting and retaining STEM preservice teachers and STEM teachers of color. The Creative Scientific Inquiry Experience (CSIE) Program, an NSF-funded STEP initiative and the Minority Achievement, Resiliency, and Success (MARS) Program combined to support the preparation of STEM teachers for urban schools. The merging of these two programs led to the creation of a comprehensive support system that follows DUETS scholars through preservice into five years of teaching. The result has been STEM teachers of color who are highly effective in urban schools who continue to receive support into their novice years of teaching.

Being an African American female in the STEM field requires an identity as a female and, even more importantly, an identity as an African American. It is this intersection or duality of these identities that will be addressed. To understand this phenomenon, this chapter begins with a discussion of the history and experiences of African American females in the United States. The contributions of African American females in the history of education will be examined as well. Next, research related to the inequities faced by African American STEM females in school settings is examined through the research findings from the Minority Achievement, Retention, and Success (MARS) Program and Developing Urban Education Teachers in STEM (DUETS). This will be followed by a discussion of how the MARS and DUETS programs mentored, prepared, and fostered the identities of African American female

STEM preservice teachers and STEM teachers. The final part of the chapter will discuss the impact of the MARS and DUETS mentoring programs and provide recommendations for mentoring programs to support African American females in STEM education.

Keywords: STEM, African American Female, retention, recruitment, self-efficacy, racial identity, microaggressions, stereotype management

***

DUETS: Developing urban education teachers in STEM

The challenge

The Minority Achievement, Retention, and Success (MARS) students were very excited about meeting Dr. Williams, a new African American math professor, at their monthly seminar. None of them had ever seen an African American math professor. As he asked questions about their experiences in math classes at the university, it became clear that most of the students had very negative experiences with math, except the math majors. One student remarked, "Math is like a 4-letter word to me!" What concerned me was that the majority of these students were preparing to become elementary teachers who would spend a third of their day teaching math. What kind of experiences would their students have with math considering their negative, defeatist feelings about math – especially the female students who seemed to feel that it was acceptable that females perform poorly in math.

Solution: The DUETS program

STEM education faces a great challenge with a high demand for effective STEM teachers in urban and high-need schools and the lack of culturally diverse STEM teachers who also act as role models. Many students of color do not find mathematics and science curriculum and instruction contextual or meaningful and do not see its value. They perceive math and science as subject areas that are for White students (Ford, Moore, Harmon, 2005; Meggan et al., 2020; Moody, 2004; Silva & Moses, 1990).

The Developing Urban Educators Teaching STEM (DUETS) Program was designed to address these issues by combining a focused, hands-on, integrated, interdisciplinary, academic service-learning, and entry-level science curriculum, Creative Scientific Inquiry Experience (CSIE) with a proven urban-education teacher preparation program, Minority Achievement, Retention and Success

(MARS). The merging of these two programs led to the creation of a comprehensive support system that followed DUETS scholars through their professional education curriculum and the teacher education program into five years of teaching. The anticipated outcomes of the program were to (1) increase the number of secondary education STEM majors who graduated and placed in high-need school districts; (2) increase the retention of new secondary STEM teachers in urban school districts; (3) increase secondary STEM teacher effectiveness in the classroom; and (4) positively impact both curricular and pedagogical approaches to secondary education.

Components of the DUETS Program were: (1) recruitment and financial support, (2) academic and career advising and mentoring, (3) specialized professional-development training, and (4) mentoring of newly placed teachers. The DUETS scholars were able to observe math and science classes in secondary schools in urban communities. They worked with science and math teachers, facilitating small group activities, assisting with laboratory experiments, as well as working with individual students. Students also participated in the MARS seminar to prepare students for the realities of being a STEM teacher of color and how to effectively teach students, and support their students.

The DUETS program proved to be very successful, with all participants graduating with teacher certification in STEM. The success of this program illuminated many issues that need to be considered when preparing African American students for teaching. According to students, the MARS seminar had the most significant impact on their success in completing the teacher education program and on their teaching. It was through the MARS seminar that female DUETS students learned about the intersection of race and gender and were able to foster a dual identity that provided them with the self-efficacy needed to be successful as teachers.

The MARS program: Minority, Achievement, Retention, and Success

The MARS program was designed to recruit, retain, and support students of color in the teacher preparation program through graduation and teacher induction or the first years of teaching. Between 2001 and 2017, it served close to four hundred students of color, largely African Americans. The MARS program expanded over the years, offering various kinds of support for students, graduate students, teachers, principals, and school administrators of color.

Development of the MARS program

The initial steps in the development of the MARS program involved interviewing current African American teacher education students in all phases of the teacher education program about their experiences in the program. A review of research literature focused on three areas: 1) the experiences of African American students in K-12 schools, African American students at predominantly white institutions (PWI); 2) experiences of African American K-12 teachers; and 3) best practices in the recruitment and retention of African American students at PWIs and HBCUs. Results led to a further review of the literature on the history of African American education. With the emphasis on teacher preparation for the effective teaching of African American students, research on culturally responsive teaching, cultural learning styles, and culturally responsive curriculum was included.

Upon completion of the literature review, the importance of the history of African American education became very apparent and proved pivotal in understanding the experiences of African American students in both K-12 and higher education today. MARS/DUETS students reported that one of the most significant motivators for them was learning and understanding their own part in history education (Price, 2021). In addition, the impact of culturally responsive teaching on learning led to the decision that the practices of culturally responsive teaching would be incorporated into the MARS program. What follows is a discussion about the history of African American education, experiences of African American females, experiences of African American students in teacher education programs, experiences of African American K-12 teachers, recruitment and retention programs for African American students, and culturally responsive teaching.

History of African Americans education

Ancient Mali

One of the oldest universities in the world was the University of Sankore in the city of Timbuktu in the ancient Kingdom of Mali during the twelfth century. It was founded by the chief judge of Timbuktu and financed by a wealthy Mandinka woman. Over 125,000 students attended from all corners of Africa. Students could obtain various degrees such as 1) a primary degree in Arabic or the Holy Qur'an; 2) a secondary degree in general studies, math, geography, history, physics, astronomy, chemistry, jurisprudence, or trade; 3) a superior degree which was highly specialized and focused on research; or 4) become a professor or scholar. Men were able to attend the university, while women were responsible for running the household, raising children, and farming. They also were diplomats, bureaucrats, and artists in the imperial court.

The university remained until 1591, when the Moroccan invasion removed most of its scholars.

Slavery

From 1501 to 1867, more than 12.5 million Africans were captured, sold, and brought to the Americas to work as enslaved people. Enslavers feared Black literacy, realizing that literacy made the sublimation and control of individuals and communities very difficult. The notion of educated African Americans went against beliefs of racial inferiority. Some Northern whites suggested African Americans had limited intellectual ability. Many white Southerners engaged in a host of strategies, including violence and death, to restrict African-American captives from access to reading and writing. Even with the threat of physical punishment or death, captives learned how to read and write and taught each other (Butchart, 2010; Williams, 2005).

Reconstruction

Northern states supported public education and provided segregated schools for African American students. A common curriculum was used, including reading, writing, and arithmetic, and teachers used a more traditional approach to teaching. Southern states did not have a public school system. In 1865, African Americans were freed, and states were required to build a public school system for everyone. Under the protection of the Union army, African American schools opened up in abundance, largely owned by female African American teachers and retired Union soldiers. African Americans' desire to learn to read and write was overwhelming. Literacy brought the assurance of emancipation, freedom to think for oneself, independence, and self-respect (Anderson,1988; Walker, 2001). Hundreds of students, from young to old, attended the newly formed African American schools (Butchart, 2010). While most schools were created by African American teachers, many White southerners established schools with the belief that there was a need to keep African Americans "in their place" (Butchart, 2010). Some missionary schools were constructed with the intent to recruit church members (Anderson, 1988; Williams, 2005).

African American teachers understood the culture and needs of their students and incorporated them into their instruction and curriculum. The curriculum included all traditional subject areas such as math, reading, writing, science, and history and was enhanced with the history and contributions of African Americans. Textbooks were created that reflected the curriculum and used authentic and accurate pictures that instilled African American pride in students (Anderson, 1989; Walker, 2001). Students were encouraged to question what they read and engage in problem solving. Teachers differentiated the curriculum to meet the needs of their multi-age students using small groups and cooperative learning.

There were many concerns about the curriculum used in African American schools. Many White Southerners did not believe that African Americans could be educated the same way that White children were educated. They did not believe that African Americans deserved or needed the same kind of curriculum that was available to White students (Butchart, 2010). In 1872, Samuel Chapman Armstrong had concerns with how and what African Americans were being taught and became active in a regional and national education association to critique the curriculum and instruction used in African-American-owned schools. He initiated a report stating that African Americans did not need math in their curriculum but, instead, needed practical life skills. He also asserted that there was no need for content areas that required abstract thinking because African Americans could not retain the information. A new curriculum was created that was "better suited" for African Americans and did not contain math and science or much of the literature of that time. The instructional strategies were basically traditional, relying solely on lectures. Textbooks were created that contained inaccurate and disparaging illustrations of African Americans and other minorities. The curriculum was totally free of charge and was marketed as the official state curriculum and distributed to all schools (Butchart, 2010).

In 1877, Union soldiers were withdrawn from the Southern states, leading to the decline and closure of many established African American schools. Without the protection of the soldiers, schools were vandalized and burned. Teachers were threatened and even lynched by the Ku Klux Klan. Many African American teachers migrated to the Northern states, often ending up in schools within segregated communities. Teachers were able to continue to practice culturally responsive teaching and develop meaningful relationships with their students, family and community. In the Southern states, schools were taken over by the state, and the curriculum and instruction were often changed to a vocational curriculum (Walker, 2001).

Segregation

Segregation of schools became legal in 1869 with the assurance that separate schools based on race would still receive equal allocations of funding. Amidst this change African American schools continued to do very well. Teachers and students were part of the same community, and teachers felt very responsible for them. They were very caring, described as warm-demanders, and developed a 'kinship' kind of relationship involving 'other-mothering' (Walker, 1996). Teachers held high expectations for their students and invested their time and resources to ensure they were successful. Critical life skills were taught, which enabled them to navigate the realities of being African American. Teachers understood how their students learned and engaged in culturally responsive instruction using a culturally responsive curriculum (Harmon, 2012).

The inequities that did result as a result of poor funding, inadequate infrastructure, and unfair policies were far-reaching and negatively affected African American schools. However, in many African American communities, members worked collectively to support and protect their schools. Principals were much more than instructional leaders and reached out to the community in many different roles to support the schools as well (Walker, 1996). Teachers did much more than deliver instruction and ensure their students were safe and had what they needed. Teachers and principals cared about their students, families, and community.

Desegregation

In 1954, the *Brown v. Topeka Board of Education* decision made the segregation of schools illegal and required the process of desegregation to begin. African American students were taken from their neighborhood schools and bussed to predominantly White schools. African American students were placed in classrooms with White teachers who were not given any professional development or training about African American culture or how to teach culturally diverse students. African American students were embedded in classrooms that were not designed for them, were often hostile, with teachers who could not provide the kind of care and concern they needed. African American students were sitting among White students who had very little knowledge or contact with students like themselves. What these students and teachers did have were stereotypical beliefs, deficit thinking, and low expectations for these new African American students. In addition, there was a lack of presence of teachers of color in the schools. This lack of preparation of the principals, teachers, staff, and students had a devastating and long-term effect on the performance and achievement of African American students (Harmon, 2002).

Bussing African American students to predominantly white schools resulted in the most destructive loss of qualified African American teachers and principals. Over 36,000 experienced, credentialed, and licensed African American teachers lost their jobs and were replaced with underqualified White teachers, some with no licensure. African American principals, who were instrumental in the building and operation of schools by working with families and communities, were demoted or fired (Tillman, 2004).

Resegregation

In 1971, students went back to their own neighborhood schools as court-ordered bussing to desegregate schools ended. African American students returned to find the same teachers and the same curriculum and instruction. They found themselves in classrooms with White teachers who were not culturally competent and did not understand their experiences or learning needs. They continued to deal with stereotypes, deficit thinking, low expectations and a classroom environment that was not designed for them to learn (Milner & Ford, 2005).

Examining the evolution of African American education reveals that race and racism are central factors in understanding African American's educational experiences. The questioning of African American's intellect began during slavery and survives today. Strategies and practices involving politics, inequitable policies, lies, and even violence have been used to block and restrict African American's access to education for fear of the loss of White power and control. History also reveals the importance, determination, and resilience of the African American community in accessing education. It identifies what African American students need to learn: 1) culturally competent teachers who are knowledgeable about the culture and experiences of African Americans; 2) culturally responsive instruction; 3) culturally inclusive curriculum; 4) teachers with high expectations who care about them and support their success.

African American experiences

K-12 experiences of African American females

The relationship African American females have with their teachers, staff, and administrators is one of the most critical factors in achieving success (Harmon and Ford, 2013). As teachers, their experiences in early elementary grades with teachers are limited and brief. They are often put in a maternal caregiver role, helping their classmates rather than being asked to help with academic skills. When confronted verbally or physically, African American girls are more likely to fight back or retaliate (Harmon & Ford, 2013). In upper elementary, students receive fewer positive responses and opportunities with their teachers than White female students. Over time, African American females begin to expect less interaction with their teachers (Harmon & Ford, 2013). In middle school, they begin to feel invisible, excluded, and socially isolated and often work alone.

African American girls who do achieve often find themselves in Advanced Placement (AP) or gifted education classes that are predominantly White, which increases their feelings of loneliness and isolation. They report that their White teachers and peers did not believe they were capable of completing the work in the AP class. Their White peers would avoid working with them in small group projects or would not include their contributions to the project (Milner, 2009). Among their African American peers, they were accused of "acting white" because of their high achievement, enrollment in AP, and use of Standard English. To gain acceptance from their own peers, they may actually choose to underachieve (Ford et al., 2005).

Experiences of African American women

African American women have always had to deal with the stereotypes and restrictions against African Americans and against women. Even though they share a similar history and oppression with African American males, they are socialized very differently. They have always struggled with their relationship with African American men to keep their families and their community together. During slavery, they took care of their own children in addition to others serving as nannies. They worked in the fields and cared for their owner's children. When their children were sold off, they engaged in "fictive kinship," which is adopting other children and creating a family (Richardson, 2002, p. 682). They had no choice but to find ways to protect themselves and their family. They were survivors because of their perseverance, assertiveness, innovation, and self-reliance, in addition to being exceptionally resilient (Harmon and Ford, 2013; Williams, 2005).

African American women's reality conflicts with societal ideas about women's femininity and motherhood. When compared to White women, they are often viewed as unfit, immoral, and the antithesis of White women. This incongruence in the definition and image of women resides in many African American women seeking to emulate the female image, body, language, behavior, and parenting styles of society (Harmon and Ford, 2013). The family plays a critical role in the development of the identity of African American females. Family and community are instrumental to the process of racial socialization - learning your culture, what it means to be African American, and what it means to be female.

Experiences of MARS students

Like other African American students attending a PWI, MARS students reported experiencing an overwhelming "sea of whiteness," leading to feelings of isolation as they were often the only or one of a few African Americans throughout the campus. They often struggled with maintaining their own identity as they were forced to negotiate two worlds, their own self-identity and the other, which often conflicted with their own values (Price, 2021).

Students complained about faculty and peers harboring negative stereotypes about them and felt they had to work hard to dispel them. All of the students believed they had to work harder for their grades and continuously prove they understood the content. In some cases, this stereotype threat led to students thinking they could not perform as well as their White peers.

Students reported that many of their professors engaged in deficit thinking resulting in having low expectations for them. The instructional methods that professors used did not align with the ways that students learned. Professors would use examples from their own experiences when describing concepts, which were often very different from the students' experiences. When they would seek out help, their professors were often unapproachable or could not understand what they were struggling with in their class.

By far, the most challenging for students were the constant microaggressions or subtle verbal or non-verbal insults based on racial stereotypes. Many of these came in the form of discrediting students' points of view, discounting their work, and questioning their knowledge. In total, students found the university a hostile environment where they endured stereotypes, microaggressions, and deficit thinking (Banks, 2016; Price, 2021). These experiences led some students to consider whether they should remain in the teacher education program.

Experiences of African American female DUETS students

Female DUETS students shared they had the same experiences as their male peers but spoke of additional challenges in their STEM classes. They frequently felt their White peers did not believe they were capable of completing work related to group projects. A DUETS student shared that she was not trusted to do her part in her small group projects and was constantly sent reminders and questioned about it. Within her group, she felt invisible, as no one wanted to hear her perspective or ideas. Another student felt she was undermined by her peers as they excluded her from meetings. Work that DUETS students completed for their groups was often reviewed, edited, or eliminated by someone in the group.

When working on individual research projects, many students were steered away from topics involving racial or gender issues. Research theories related to African American issues, such as stereotype threat or critical race theory, were not well received by White faculty. Students reported not receiving the same support from their professors as their White peers and African American male peers.

DUETS female students did report challenges that were common to other African American female students. As family was critically important to African American females, they were concerned that their relationship with their family would change after going to college.

They were careful not to use "educated" language around their family or their friends so they would not think they were better, showing off, or disrespecting them. They also expressed concerns about finding a partner who would not feel intimidated by their level of education.

Experiences of MARS/DUETS teachers

African American MARS teachers reported that their experiences teaching in predominantly White schools were very similar to their experiences attending a PWI. Due to the low percentage of African American teachers in the workforce, they found themselves in schools with predominantly White teachers and administrators and felt isolated and alienated from some of their White colleagues. Many of their White colleagues and administrators held negative stereotypes about African Americans, and they found themselves in the position of dispelling negative stereotypes and dealing with microaggressions and deficit thinking. Often, times White teachers were jealous of MARS teachers' relationships with students of color in the classrooms as they understood how to engage and manage students.

African American female DUET teachers found their White colleagues engaged in deficit thinking regarding them and students of color. They reported some of their White colleagues were dismissive of their concerns for students of color, were not using culturally responsive teaching, and were not increasing opportunities for STEM programs. They felt that some of their White colleagues undermined their efforts to support African American students and diminished their students' accomplishments. Overall, African American female STEM teachers felt very marginalized.

Recruitment and retention programs

Retention programs on university campuses focus on supporting students with the process of acclimating to the campus, navigating the system, and accessing resources, financial information, and advising. Tinto (1999) suggested that universities should provide students with:

1) Encouragement for high expectations;

2) Advising as well as an understanding of the curriculum;

3) Academic, social, and personal support;

4) An environment where they feel valued; and

5) Places that foster learning.

What is overlooked are the specific needs of culturally diverse students attending a PWI that has a safe place to deal with isolation, alienation, and negative stereotypes. When students are not able to acknowledge their cultural identities, their chances for success decrease (Museus, Nichols, & Lambert, 2008). Many African American students find or create their own social and cultural networks to remedy their exclusion from the White oriented university community (Allen, 1988, 1992).

Culturally responsive pedagogy

Culturally responsive teaching

Culturally responsive teaching is one of the most effective means of meeting the learning needs of culturally different students (Ford, 2010; Harmon, 2002; Ladson-Billings, 1994. It recognizes the importance of caring for learning and emphasizes the development of meaningful relationships with students and families. Within the classroom, teachers create a nurturing community of learners, much like an extended family where teachers engage in 'other mothering' or kinship toward their students (Ladson-Billings, 1997). Students are held to high expectations and are supported so they can achieve and experience success.

Culturally responsive curriculum

The culturally responsive curriculum includes multicultural content and materials. It provides opportunities for students to view issues from multiple lenses and engage in authentic problem-solving while addressing issues of social justice. Students are able to relate to and see themselves within the curriculum and learn about the contributions that people like themselves make to society (Gay, 2000; Ladson-Billings, 1997). Students become intrinsically motivated to learn because the curriculum is interesting to them, and they can relate to it. Students learn that they are not powerless and that their views are important (Ford et al., 2005; Harmon, 2005; Martin, 2000; Matthews, 2003).

Culturally responsive instruction

Culturally responsive teaching is student-centered and built upon knowledge about cultural learning styles and cultural assets. Boykin et al. (2005) developed the concept of asset-based instruction, which uses cultural assets as the foundation for instruction. Cultural assets refer to cultural behaviors African American students bring into the classroom that can often be problematic to teachers who are not culturally competent (Ford, 2010). Cultural assets include spirituality, harmony, expressive individualism, affective, oral communication, communalism, movement, verve, and social time perspective. Boykin et al. (2005) assert that the cultural behaviors of African American students must not be viewed as deficits but as assets.

Culturally responsive instruction creates opportunities for students to learn and understand concepts and use them in application, analysis, and evaluative thinking. Through authentic problem-solving, students are able to engage in creative thinking (Ford et al., 2005). The emphasis is on teaching through the use of differentiating what is taught, how it is taught, and how students demonstrate their understanding of concepts. Project-based learning is also encouraged as a way of evaluating students (Harmon, 2012; Irvine, 2002; Milner, 2009).

Protective factors

When individuals are facing oppressive environments, such as a hostile campus due to discrimination and prejudice, it is their resilience that helps them cope and survive. Two variables that impact resilience are risk factors and protective factors. Risk factors, such as negative stereotypes, can adversely affect the development of resilience. Protective factors are instrumental in providing a pathway for resilience to thrive by affirming an individual's abilities and determination to succeed. There are two kinds of protective factors: family units and external supports (Price, 2021; Werner, 1993).

There were several risk factors MARS students were facing in their education program, on campus, and in schools, such as isolation, alienation, negative stereotypes, stereotype threat, deficit thinking, low expectations, and microaggressions. In addition, students lacked academic, social, and emotional support, knowledge about navigating the university system, and professional skills. Needs that were identified by students' responses included: 1) a safe space with others like themselves; 2) stereotype management; 3) caring; 4) understanding of the systems and how to navigate them; and 5) cultural capital. The MARS program was designed to address many of these needs and risks.

MARS program

The MARS program goals were to (a) increase racial identity development; (b) foster the development of cultural competency through an exploration of self-awareness, cultural awareness, and acquiring more cultural and social capital; and (c) increase the knowledge and skills of culturally responsive pedagogy. These goals were accomplished primarily through the MARS seminar. Student outcomes were to complete the teacher preparation program, graduate, obtain their teaching certificate, and secure a teaching position.

The MARS program had four components: 1) mentoring, 2) resources, 3) support programs, and 4) a seminar. Mentors played a crucial role, especially in the DUETS program. Faculty experienced in urban education and MARS teachers acted as mentors and were present at the seminars. Students looked to their mentors for advice and support in dealing with a variety of challenges they faced in their courses and student teaching.

Students had access to numerous resources, including textbooks, computers, advising, tutors, faculty, MARS teachers and MARS student mentors. The MARS office was within the College of Education in a space where students could come to work or socialize with other students and faculty. Support programs for students included workshops on test taking, test anxiety, interviewing skills, resume writing, and study groups.

MARS seminar

The MARS seminar was designed to address students' needs and risks identified by MARS students. Guidelines were developed to serve as protective factors for students, including 1) developing cultural competency, 2) understanding and gaining cultural capital and cultural accouterments, 3) using culturally responsive teaching, 4) caring for students, and 5) facilitating stereotype management. All components of the MARS program supported these guidelines.

Students reported that the experiences and the content of the MARS seminar sessions had the greatest positive impact on their success as a student and a teacher. MARS seminar provided a safe space and a community of color with students, staff, and faculty like themselves who understood and shared their challenges. Over time, the seminar evolved into a family unit with students caring for and supporting each other. Each session began with a meal which allowed students to interact and share concerns. After the meal, there was a presentation given by the MARS Director, Assistant Director, MARS faculty, or special guests. At the end of each presentation, there were discussions where students could ask questions and share comments. The seminar ended with each student writing a brief entry into their MARS journal about the presentation and sharing two words to describe how they were feeling. Following is a list of seminar topics.

Cultural competency

To teach MARS students how to teach in their diverse classroom, they need to know who they are and who their students from a different cultural perspective are. Developing cultural competency involves learning your own history, the history of others, and, as a result gaining insight and understanding into how different cultures are interrelated and how to relate to diverse students. To begin this process, students learn about the multicultural history of our country in addition to the multicultural history of education (Gay, 2002; Harmon, 2012; Ladson-Billings, 1994;1997).

Racial identity

In order for students to understand the prejudice and discrimination they deal with on a daily basis, they need to understand the development of their own racial identity and the role it plays in managing their behavior (Cross & Vandiver, 2001). A high level of racial identity development is critical when one is in the minority. As students are able to acknowledge their cultural identities, their chances for graduation increase (Carter & Goodwin, 1994; Oyserman et al., 2001; Museus et al., 2008).

Stereotype management

Stereotype management provides students with a deeper understanding of various coping mechanisms that can be used in dealing with prejudice

(McGee & Marrin, 2011). Stereotype threat acts as a confirmation that negative stereotypes are indeed true and compromises the performance of African American students by adding additional fear and anxiety. Instead of allowing stressors to affect their performance, students used them as motivation to achieve and disprove the negative stereotypes. This process of resilience in the face of persistent racial stereotypes and stereotype threat is called stereotype management (McGee and Martin, 2011; Price, 2021). With stereotype management, students are constantly alert to the negative attitudes, beliefs and policies of people around them and use that knowledge as motivation to overcome their anxiety to prove them wrong. As students mature, the desire to learn or to become a role model for other students dealing with stereotype threat becomes their motivation to achieve. This movement is congruent with their movement through their racial identity. In fact, understanding the developmental process of racial identity, gender identity and mathematics identity facilitates stereotype management (Carter & Goodwin, 1994; Martin, 2000).

Culturally responsive teaching

Students learned about cultural learning styles, cultural assets, and how to engage in culturally responsive teaching. They were taught how to create culturally responsive lessons that included critical thinking, creative thinking, and differentiation. Students also learned how to include families and support staff in providing support for students.

Caring

Students learned that caring for their students allowed them to identify and meet their students' needs. They were able to observe and experience 'other mothering' and 'kinship through the MARS seminar (Roberts & Irvine, 2009). MARS faculty and staff engaged in the kind of caring strategies that increase students' efficacy. Students were held to high expectations, were given the support to experience success, and acknowledged and praised when they achieved their goals. Through their practicums and student teaching, students were able to interact with students' families, manage challenging behavior, and conduct meetings with parents.

Cultural capital

Cultural capital refers to the social and cultural knowledge of the mainstream culture that allows one to understand, participate, and successfully navigate within it. Students were exposed to the importance of standard English, mannerisms, posture, clothing, and how to handle oneself in a variety of situations. Understanding cultural capital will assist students in sharing this knowledge with their own students (Harmon, 2002; 2012; Irvine, 2002).

Professional skills such as developing a resume and cover letter, completing applications, and presentation skills were taught. Students were included in writing grants, articles, and presentation proposals with MARS faculty. They had opportunities to attend and present at educational conferences, thus exposing them to career opportunities.

Student teaching

There were no university supervisors of color to observe student teachers and assist MARS student teachers. MARS students continually complained about their difficulties with working with university supervisors and classroom teachers. The university supervisors often complained about the MARS student teachers not speaking standard English when conversing with students or getting too involved with students by attending their sports games and events. There was often tension on the part of the classroom teacher with the relationships MARS student teachers had with their students. MARS faculty would advocate for the MARS student teachers and ask to place students in classrooms with MARS/DUETS teachers who would mentor them and care for them. Female DUETS student teachers were placed with African American female STEM teachers to address the realities of being a female African American in STEM.

DUETS mentors

Mentors acted as guides and coaches for students as they deconstructed their own experiences within their classrooms, those of culturally diverse students, and the urban community. All mentors were experienced in urban education and had teaching experience in STEM classrooms. Both faculty and MARS teachers acted as mentors and were present at the seminars, at school visits, and in the classroom during student teaching. Once students were hired by schools, the mentors continued to provide support for DUETS students in and out of the classroom for the first 5 years of teaching. Mentors played a crucial role in the DUETS program. Students looked to their mentors for advice and support in dealing with a variety of challenges they faced in their courses, student teaching, and the first years of teaching.

Impact of DUETS program

The DUETS program proved to be successful, will all of its participating students graduating with a STEM teacher certification and securing teaching positions. Mentoring continued for five years, with some DUET students attending and presenting at MARS seminars. What follows are components of the DUETS program that students, now STEM educators, believe had the greatest impact on their teaching:

- It was through the support of the MARS seminar that participants were able to become part of a community of color and build much-needed relationships with peers and professors.

- Within the MARS seminar, students gained a better understanding of racism and became better enabled to deal with it through stereotype management.

- The immersion of DUETS students into urban classrooms and communities, along with the opportunity to hear the perspectives of teachers, administrators, students, and family members who gave DUETS students an authentic insight into the learning needs of students and the importance of developing relationships.

- Culturally responsive teaching was one of the most helpful skills that students learned through the MARS seminar. Knowing how students learn best, developing lessons that students can relate to and knowing how to ensure they are successful served DUETS students well when they became classroom teachers.

Recommendations

The lack of culturally diverse teachers is very evident in STEM education. Great efforts have been made to recruit culturally diverse students into STEM education, but much more effort is needed to retain those students and teachers. The success of the DUETS Program resulted in understanding and insights into how to improve the recruitment of African American STEM teachers, the preparation of all STEM teachers for urban classrooms, and the retention of African American STEM teachers in education. Important lessons learned are discussed below:

- Begin with identifying the needs and risks of the students throughout the entire teacher education program. For African American students, the needs of males are different from females, and both need to be acknowledged. Identify ways to address risks and needs and create protective factors to guide the structure of the program.

- Students' greatest need is a community of color for culturally diverse students. A sanctuary for students is necessary where they can feel safe, be with people like themselves, be validated, and have the opportunity to make sense of what they are experiencing.

- Mentors are critical support for students, but only if students can relate to them. It is important that mentors are culturally competent and have experience with STEM education. Mentors should be available to advise and counsel students in addition to observing them in their practicums, student teaching, and in their own classrooms.

- Student teachers must become more culturally competent to understand the realities of teaching, understand their students' needs, and build the kinds of caring relationships with their students that are crucial for learning. Traditional teacher preparation programs may include a course on multicultural education, but that is not sufficient for developing cultural competency. Fostering the development of cultural competency needs to be intentional and evident.

- Student teachers need to have significant experiences, practicums, and student teaching in high-needs urban schools and communities to foster their understanding of the urban context.

- More than just content and basic instructional strategies need to be learned as students in urban schools have difficulty relating to science and math, which historically does not have a context that is congruent with urban students and their communities. Student teachers need to learn culturally responsive teaching so they can teach to all of their students.

STEM teacher education faculty need to be culturally competent and proficient in culturally responsive teaching.

References

Allen, W. R. (1988). Improving Black student access and achievement in higher education. *The Review of Higher Education, 11*(4), 403-416.

Allen, W. (1992). The color of success: African-American college student outcomes at predominantly White and historically Black public colleges and universities. *Harvard Educational Review, 62*(1), 26-45.

Anderson, D. (1988). *The education of blacks in the south, 1860-1935.* University of North Carolina Press: Chapel Hill.

Banks, J. (2016). *An Exploration of the experiences of black high school students in the mathematics classroom: A Qualitative Study* [Unpublished doctoral dissertation]. Eastern Michigan University.

Boykin, A. W., Albury, A., Tyler, K. M., Hurley, E. A., Bailey, C. T., & Miller, O. A. (2005). Culture-based perceptions of academic achievement among low-income elementary students. *Cultural Diversity and Ethnic Minority Psychology, 11*(4), 339 - 350.

Boykin, A.W. & Noguera, P. A. (2011). *Creating the opportunity to learn: Moving from research to practice to close the achievement gap.* ASCD. *Brown v. Board of Education,* 347 U.S. 483 (1954).

Butchart, R. E. (2010). *Schooling the freed people: Teaching, learning and the struggle for black freedom, 1861-1876.* University of North Carolina Press: Chapel Hill.

Carter R.T. & Goodwin A.L. (1994). Racial Identity and Education. *Review of Research in Education. 20(1),*291-336.

Cross, W. E., Jr., & Vandiver, B. J. (2001). Nigrescence theory and measurement: Introducing the Cross Racial Identity Scale (CRIS). In J. G. Ponterotto, J. M. Casas, L. A. Suzuki, & C. M. Alexander (Eds.), *Handbook of multicultural counseling* (pp. 371–393). Sage Publications, Inc.

Ford, D. Y. (2010). Multicultural issues: Culturally responsive classrooms: Affirming culturally different gifted students. *Gifted Child Today, 33*(1), 50-53.

Ford, D.Y., Moore III, J.L., & Harmon, D.A. (2005). Integrating multicultural education and gifted education: A curricular framework. *Theory Into Practice,44*(2), 125-132.

Gay, G. (2002). Preparing for culturally responsive teaching. *Journal of teacher education, 53*(2), 106-116.

Harmon, D.A. (2002). They won't teach me: The voices of gifted African American gifted inner-city students. *Roeper Review, 24*(2), 68-75.

Harmon, D.A. (2012). Culturally responsive teaching through a historical lens: Will history repeat itself? *Interdisciplinary Journal of Teaching and Learning,1(2),* 1-22.

Harmon, D.A. and Ford, D. Y. (2013). The experiences of African American gifted females: "Damned if you are and damned if you aren't." In Zamani-Gallaher, E.M. and Polite, V.P. (2013). *African American Female: Addressing Challenges and Nurturing the Future* (pp. 45-76). Michigan State University Press: East Lansing.

Harmon, D.A. & Price, C. L. (2023) Uncovering a pathway towards equity in STEM education for African American males. In A.G. Robins, L. Knibbs, T. N. Ingram, M, N. Weaver, Jr., & A. A. Hilton (Eds.), *Unveiling the cloak of invisibility* (pp.5-20). Information Age Publishing, Inc.

Irvine, J. J. (2002). *In search of wholeness: African American teachers and their culturally specific classroom practices.* Palgrave.

Ladson-Billings, G. (1994). What we can learn from multicultural education research. *Educational Leadership, 51*(8), 22-26.

Ladson-Billings, G. (1997). It doesn't add up: American students' mathematics achievement. *Journal for Research in Mathematics Education, 28*, 697-708.

Martin, D.B. (2000). *Mathematics success and failure among African American youth: The role soft social-historical context, community forces, school influence, and individual agency.* Mahwah, NJ: Erlbaum.

Matthews, L.E. (2003). Babes overboard! The complexities of integrating culturally relevant teaching into mathematics instruction. *Educational Studies in Mathematics, 53* (1), 61-82.

Meggan, J., Lee, Jasmine D. Collins, Harwood, SA, Mendenhall, R., Hunt, M.B. (2020). 'If you aren't White, Asian or Indian, you aren't an engineer': Racial microaggressions in STEM education. *International Journal of STEM Education,* 7(1) doi: 10.1186/s.40594-020-00241-4

Milner, H.R. (2009). Preparing teachers of African American students in urban schools. In L. Tillman (Ed.), *The Sage Handbook of African American Education* (pp.123 - 139) Sage: Los Angeles.

Milner, H.R. & Ford, D.Y. (2005). Racial experiences influence us as teachers: Implications for gifted education curriculum development and implementation. *Roeper Review, 28*(1) 30-36.

Moody, V.R. (2004) Sociocultural orientations and the mathematical success of African American students. *The Journal of Educational Research, 97*(3), 135-146.

Moses, Y.T. (1989), *Black women in academe: Issues and strategies,* Washington, DC: Association of American colleges.

Museus, S. D., Nichols, A. H., & Lambert, A. D. (2008). Racial differences in the effects of campus racial climate on degree completion: A structural equation model. *Review of Higher Education: Journal of the Association for the Study of Higher Education, 32*(1),107–134. https://doi.org/10.1353/rhe.0.0030

Oyserman, D., Harrison, K., & Bybee, D. (2001). Can racial identity be promotive of academic efficacy? *International Journal of Behavioral Development, 25*(379), 379- 386.

Price, C.L. (2021). *Like a fly in buttermilk: The lived experiences of African American teacher education students at a predominantly White university* [Unpublished doctoral dissertation]. Eastern Michigan University.

Richardson, E. (2002). "To protect and serve": African American female literacies. *College Composition and Communication,* 675-704.

Roberts, M. A. & Irvine, J. J (2009). African American teachers' caring behavior: The difference makes a difference. In L. Tillman (Ed.), *The Sage Handbook of African American Education* (pp.141-152). Sage.

Silva, C., & Moses, R. P. (1990). The algebra project: Making middle school mathematics count. *Journal of Negro Education, 59*, 375-391.

Tillman, L.C. (2004). (Un)Intended consequences?: The impact of the Brown v. Board of education decision on the employment status of black educators. *Education and Society, 36*(3), 280–303.

Tinto, V. (1999). Taking retention seriously: Rethinking the first year of college. *NACADA Journal, 19,* 5-9. http://dx.doi.org/10.12930/0271-9517-19.2.5

Walker, V. S. (1996). *Their highest potential: An African American school community in the segregated south.* North Carolina Press: Chapel Hill.

Walker, V.S. (2001). African American teaching in the South: 1940-1960. *American Educational Research Journal, 38*(4), 751-779.

Williams, H. A. (2005). *Self-Taught: African American education in slavery and freedom.* University of North Carolina Press: Chapel Hill.

Werner, E. (1993). Risk, resilience, and recovery: Perspectives from the Kauai longitudinal study. *Development and Psychopathology,* 503-515.

Contributors

Introduction Author

Cecilia (Ceal) D. Craig, PhD, was a technology executive in high-tech and is now a researcher and Science, Engineering, Technology, and Mathematics (STEM) robotics education advocate. She is a Society of Women Engineers Fellow and, in 2018, was recognized with a Distinguished Alumni Award for Career Achievement by The Ohio State University.

Craig earned a Ph.D. in Education from Walden University, an M.S.E (mechanical engineering) from California State University at Fullerton, and a B.S.M.E. (mechanical engineering) from The Ohio State University. Dr. Craig held senior technical executive roles in manufacturing and program management for large and small companies, working in high-tech for over 35 years. At one point, she took a sabbatical from high-tech to teach high-school math and then worked with young people for several years before re-entering high-tech until retiring in 2011.

In 2002, a sixth-grade student in Dr. Craig's first Johns Hopkins University's Center for Talented Youth (CTY) science and engineering class asked if she would include robotics in the curriculum. Using student-made wall-hugging mouse robots for several CTY summers, her passion for STEM education and robotics was born. She and her engineer husband mentored a high-school robotics team for seven years, and she has continued to bring robotics education and competitions to young people in the Northern California Bay area since 2004. Craig's dissertation study explored how the For Inspiration and Recognition of Science and Technology (FIRST) Robotics Competition influenced young women's career decisions.

Along the way, Ceal has been a volunteer and oft times BOD member in many not-for-profit organizations, as an officer or committee chair for the Society of Women Engineers (at the local, regional, and national levels), Mission Chamber Orchestra, San Francisco Bay Wildlife Society, Western Region Robotics Forum, Silicon Valley Engineering Council, and the American Educational Research Association Mentoring and Mentorship Practices Special Interest Group.

Chapter 1 authors

Dr. Joe Omojola is a Professor of Mathematics and Physics and the James and Ruth Smith Endowed Professor of Science at Southern University at New Orleans (SUNO).

Dr. Omojola received several awards for his teaching, grants writing, and mentoring efforts, including a 2006 Presidential Awards for Excellence in Science, Mathematics and Engineering Mentoring (PAESMEM) for his exceptional mentoring efforts that increased the graduation of underrepresented student groups in STEM, a 2006 Faculty Role Model Mentoring Award from the Minority Access Inc, and a 2018 proclamation from the City Council of New Orleans in recognition of his mentoring and impact on STEM programs at SUNO for over twenty years.

Individually and collaboratively with others, Dr. Omojola has attracted over 12 million dollars in external funding to enhance mentoring, scholarship, faculty development and infrastructure. The broader impact of Dr. Omojola's work is evident in the number of his former students who are drawn into mentoring.

Dr. Murty S. Kambhampati (Dr. Kam), Professor of Biology at Southern University at New Orleans (SUNO), New Orleans, LA, USA, joined the Department of Biology as an Assistant Professor and moved up in the ranks. Over the years, he secured about $11M in state and federal grants. These grants impacted student stipends, mentoring activities, summer research internships, travel, outreach programs, departmental infrastructure and curriculum enhancement. He mentored about 90 undergraduate biology majors and three Doctoral STEM students in interdisciplinary research projects of biological and environmental sciences at SUNO and at collaborative research facilities such as Brookhaven National Laboratory (BNL), Louisiana Universities Marine Consortium (LUMCON), etc. More than 80% of his undergraduate mentees and 100% of his doctoral mentees were African American women.

Dr. Kam serves as an active member and a sponsor of the National Institute of Science, Beta Kappa Chi, and TriBeta National Biological Honor Society (NIS/BKX/BBB) Chapter at SUNO and recruited hundreds of minority and women student members. Several of these members were sponsored by funded grants to present at conferences and publish abstracts. Many of his mentees won awards at the conferences. He volunteers his time at the high school to serve as a judge and moderator at science fairs and conferences. Through the funded grants, collaboratively with his peers, he enhanced the biology and mathematics curricula.

Also, collaboratively with his colleagues, Dr. Kam has designed and developed a BS in Forensic Science and a BS in Nursing programs. During his tenure at SUNO, Dr. Kam received several awards, including the Presidential Award for Excellence in Science, Mathematics, and Engineering Mentoring (PAESMEM) from President Barack Obama in 2015 and a Proclamation from the City Council of New Orleans recognizing his Excellence in STEM Teaching, Mentoring, and Grants at SUNO.

Dr. Phyllis Okwan is an Associate Professor of Mathematics in the Mathematics and Physics Department at Southern University and A&M College, Baton Rouge (SUBR). She received her PhD in 2016 from SUBR. Before joining SUBR as a faculty, she worked at Southern University at New Orleans (SUNO) as a program coordinator for the NSF-funded Enhancement, Enrichment, and Excellence in Mathematics and Science (E^3MaS) from 2010 to 2014. She also worked as a mathematics instructor from 2014 to 2017. In these positions, she served as a mentor for both K-12 and undergraduate students.

While at SUNO, she served as a data analyst for the campus LS-LAMP (Louis Stokes Louisiana Alliance for Minority Participation) program. Currently, she is the departmental mentoring coordinator for LS-LAMP at SUBR, where she collaborates with STEM mentors and mentors undergraduate students.

Dr. Okwan is a 2015 recipient of the Minority Access, Inc.'s National Role Model Award and a 2019 recipient of the Gulf States Math Alliance's Outstanding Service Award. She is the current National Editor of the Beta Kappa Chi (BKX) Scientific Society and the Executive Secretary for the National Institute of Science (NIS). Dr. Okwan is an active member of the National Alliance for Doctoral Studies in the Mathematical Sciences (Math Alliance) and currently serves as the President of the Gulf States Math Alliance (GSMA).

Chapter 2 authors

Dr. Medha Dalal is an assistant research professor and associate director of scholarly initiatives, in the Fulton Schools of Engineering at Arizona State University. She holds a PhD in Learning, Literacies and Technologies with a focus on engineering education from Arizona State University, an M.S. in computer science from New York University, and a B.S. in electrical engineering from India. Dr. Dalal's research at the crossroads of engineering, education, and technology seeks to democratize engineering education by exploring ways of thinking, identifying effective professional development approaches, and uncovering pedagogical techniques to enhance students' engineering curiosity, engagement, and learning.

Tara Nkrumah, Ph.D., is an assistant professor in the Department of Teacher Preparation at Mary Lou Fulton Teachers College at Arizona State University. Nkrumah holds a B.S. in Environmental Science from Middle Tennessee State University, an M. Ed in Curriculum and Instruction from Tennessee State University, and a Ph.D. in Educational Leadership & Policy Studies from the University of South Florida, Tampa. Her research on equitable teaching practices for anti-oppressive discourse in education and science, technology, engineering, and mathematics (STEM) uses the theatre of the oppressed to explore culturally relevant/responsive leadership and pedagogy.

Dr. Jennifer Kouo is an Assistant Research Scientist at the Center for Technology in Education (CTE) at the Johns Hopkins School of Education. Dr. Kouo holds a B.S. in Integrated Elementary and Special Education from Towson University, an M.S. in Special Education from Johns Hopkins University, and a Ph.D. in Special Education with an emphasis in severe disabilities and autism spectrum disorders from the University of Maryland, College Park. She is engaged in multiple research projects that involve transdisciplinary collaborations in the fields of engineering, medicine, and technology, as well as research on teacher preparation and the conducting of evidence-based practices in multiple contexts.

Dr. Stacy Klein-Gardner is an Adjunct Professor of Biomedical Engineering at Vanderbilt University and the Executive Director of Engineering for US All (e4usa). Dr. Klein-Gardner holds a B.S.E. in biomedical and electrical engineering from Duke University, an M.S. in biomedical engineering from Drexel University, and a Ph.D. in biomedical engineering from Vanderbilt University. Her career in P-12 STEM education focuses on increasing interest in and participation by all students in engineering and teacher professional development. Dr. Klein-Gardner formerly served as the chair of the American Society for Engineering Education (ASEE) P12 Commission and the PCEE division. She is a Fellow of the Society.

Chapter 3 author

Zingiswa Jojo is a full professor in Mathematics Education in the Department of Secondary and post-school education at Rhodes University. She serves in the Commission for African Women in Mathematics (CAWM) committee (South

African Chapter) and leads the newly created organization on the role of mathematics education in women empowerment (RMEWE). She has led several projects focusing on mathematics's continuous professional development, the role of mathematics education in women's empowerment and the learning of mathematics. She has served as a visiting lecturer in international tertiary institutions, served as a keynote speaker at Conferences and is a member of professional bodies like AMESA, EASA, HELTASA, ISTE, SAARMSTE, OSSREA, SAERA, ISATT, AFRIMEC and serves as a board member for ATINER.

Chapter 4 authors

Dr. Phyllis Okwan. See Chapter 1 authors.

Dr. Joe Omojola. See Chapter 1 authors.

Dr. Murty S. Kambhampati. See Chapter 1 authors.

Chapter 5 authors

Dr. Jacqueline Genovesi (she/her) is the Executive Director of the Center for STEAM Equity. She is an informal science museum practitioner-researcher and developer of STEM curricula and programs for diverse public audiences, from early childhood to adults and teachers. She earned her PhD in Educational Leadership and Technology from the School of Education at Drexel University. Her early work in museum accessibility for families with children on the autism spectrum translated into a 35-year-long career dedication to stimulating STEM learning among families and youth from underserved and systemically disadvantaged backgrounds. Her work with Philadelphia's most at-risk public high school girls caps a 40+-year institutional commitment to young Women in Natural Science (WINS) at the Academy of Natural Sciences. In 2018, she was proud to accept the prestigious Presidential Award for Excellence in Science, Mathematics and Engineering Mentoring for the WINS program at the White House in Washington, DC. Genovesi earned her Master's degree in Education and Science from the University of Pennsylvania and her Bachelor's degree in Biology from Rider University.

    Dr. Ayana Allen-Handy is an Associate Professor of Urban Education and Interim Department Chair of the department of Policy, Organization, and Leadership (POL) in the School of Education at Drexel University. She received her Bachelor of Arts with Honors from the University of North Carolina at Chapel Hill, a Masters of Education from the University of St. Thomas in Houston, TX, a PhD in Urban Education from Texas A&M University in College

Station, TX, and she completed a Post-Doctoral Fellowship at *The Urban Education Collaborative* at the University of North Carolina at Charlotte. She is the founding director of *The Justice-oriented Youth Education Lab (The JoY Lab)*, a diverse, intergenerational collective of youth and community residents, faculty, and undergraduate and graduate research partners who center JoY through a humanizing, asset-forward, and critical-participatory action research approach… in pursuit of educational, racial, and social justice.

Dr. Kimberly Sterin has worked as an educator, researcher, and policy analyst within public school districts, higher education, and industry. Her research interrogates the ways power is leveraged across the K-12 school finance and resource landscape with a focus on educational justice for historically marginalized groups. With the Justice-Oriented Youth (JoY) Lab, she has contributed to several federally funded research projects related to supporting the advancement of underrepresented women of color in STEM and promoting civic engagement in anti-displacement strategies through arts-based community-driven participatory action research in West Philadelphia. Sterin earned a Master's degree from Johns Hopkins University and a Ph.D. in Education Policy and Leadership from Drexel University.

Dr. Katie Mathew holds a Ph.D. in Educational Leadership and Policy from Drexel University's School of Education. She has a Bachelor of Arts in Psychology and Linguistics from the University of British Columbia and a Master of Arts in Child Study and Education from the University of Toronto. Prior to embarking on doctoral studies, she was a teacher for seven years in a variety of school contexts both in Canada and the United States. Her primary research interests focus on families and children's beliefs about school. She has also been involved in various research projects related to supporting the advancement of underrepresented women of color in STEM and promoting equitable development through arts-based, community participatory action research strategies.

Tajma Cameron is a 4th year Ph.D. candidate in the School of Education at Drexel University pursuing her degree in Education Leadership and Policy and is a certified secondary education Biology teacher. Tajma's overall research focuses on how culturally affirming, sustaining, and creative instructional practices and curriculum can be utilized to cultivate and nurture Black girls' STEM identity in formal school settings and informal STEM environments.

Kimberly Godfrey, Manager of the Women In Natural Sciences Program, has been with WINS for 10 years. She was born and raised in Philadelphia but attended high school at Milton Hershey School. She received her bachelor's in marine biology from Eckerd College in St. Petersburg, FL. For 25 years, she has explored the natural sciences, including animal husbandry, marine mammal research, and environmental education. A proud resident with a strong love for ALL things Philadelphia, she developed a passion for urban ecology and enjoys spending time exposing others to the beauty that exists right in front of us. With the support of her colleagues, she gets to be this person for WINS every day! She tries her best to embrace her geek in all its forms, reminding her and others to hold on to the things that make us who we are.

Dominique Thomas is a second-year Executive Master in Public Health student at Drexel University's Dornsife School of Public Health. She is the Coordinator of Social Justice Programs at The Academy of Natural Sciences and works with young people participating in the Women in Natural Sciences (WINS) program. As a Philadelphia native and proud WINS alumna, Dominique believes mentorship to be a fundamental aspect of a young person's journey. She often seeks opportunities to utilize the trauma-informed sanctuary model to positively impact young people from her community. She hopes to encourage positive decision-making through the promotion of community building and youth advocacy.

Janai Keita is a creative storyteller, future social worker, mentor and a Women In Natural Sciences Alumna. Janai currently leads the WINS III Component of the WINS Program. Through this work, she is able to continue to pour back into a program that has watered her throughout the years.

Chapter 6 authors

Dr. Murty S. Kambhampati (Dr. Kam) See Chapter 1 authors

Dr. Joe Omojola See Chapter 1 authors.

Dr. Phyllis Okwan See Chapter 1 authors

Chapter 7 authors

Amber Simpson is an Associate Professor of Mathematics Education in the Teaching, Learning and Educational Leadership Department at Binghamton University. Her research interests include (1) examining individual's identity(ies) in one or more STEM disciplines; (2) investigating family engagement in and interactions around STEM-related activities, particularly in their home environments; and (3) understanding how mathematics is embedded within non-formal and cultural learning environments.

Caro Williams-Pierce is an Assistant Professor in the College of Information Studies at the University of Maryland. She received a bachelor's in mathematics from the University of Maine at Fort Kent, a joint master's in mathematics and education and a PhD in mathematics education from the University of Wisconsin. Dr. Williams-Pierce focuses on how to best design for mathematical play, particularly in informal environments such as video games.

As a scholar of teaching and learning, **Signe Kastberg** explores and contributes to public understanding of mathematics teaching and learning and mathematics teacher education. Dr. Kastberg's discovery, learning, and engagement activities are undertaken to develop and contribute to an understanding of the beauty and complexity of teaching, learning, and learning to teach mathematics learners.

Chapter 8 authors

Carole Burton Sox, PhD, CHE, is an Associate Professor and the Department Chair of the Undergraduate Business Program at Columbia College in South Carolina. Dr. Sox has developed, added, and enhanced numerous minor and concentration options for the program while in this position. She teaches courses in hospitality and business. She earned her BA in Language and Literature from St. Mary's College of Maryland, her MS in Management from Southern Wesleyan University, and her PhD in Hospitality Management from the University of South Carolina. Dr. Sox has almost 20 years of corporate experience and 17 years of academic experience at higher learning institutions, and she is the author and co-author of nationally and internationally presented research. Most recently, Dr. Sox was the recipient of the Faculty Excellence Award (Columbia College, 2023), Educator of the Year Award (South Carolina Restaurant and Lodging Association, 2020), and Rookie Innovative Educator Award (Columbia College, 2019).

Sheryl Fried Kline, Ph.D., is an accomplished leader with extensive experience in business and hospitality management and higher education. She is the Deputy Dean at the Lerner College of Business and Economics and Aramark Chaired Professor at the University of Delaware. Throughout her career, Dr. Kline has demonstrated exceptional leadership in both academic and professional settings. She has published numerous research papers in leading academic journals, and her work has been widely cited and recognized for its contributions to the field of hospitality management. In addition to her research, Dr. Kline has also played a critical role in developing and implementing various academic programs and advancement initiatives. She has served as the Interim Dean and Associate Dean of the University of South

Carolina, College of Hospitality, Retail, and Sport Management. Before joining academia, she had a successful career as a manager in the casino hotel industry. She holds a B.A. in Economics and English from Rutgers University, an MS in Hotel Administration from UNLV, and a Ph.D. in organizational psychology from Temple University.

Chapter 9 authors

Darrin Collins, a doctoral student in the Math and Science Education Program at the University of Illinois Chicago, has carved a remarkable path in the realm of science education. With a career spanning over 13 years as a science teacher on the vibrant southside of Chicago, Darrin brings a wealth of real-world experience and a profound commitment to his work in the field. Darrin's journey into the world of education has been one characterized by an unceasing dedication to fostering learning and growth in the minds of young learners. At the core of Darrin's research and teaching is his unwavering belief in the power of mentorship and its role in shaping the future of science education. With a research focus squarely centered on science teacher mentorship, he places a special emphasis on cultural responsiveness. Darrin understands that the key to nurturing the next generation of scientists lies in creating inclusive, culturally aware learning environments.

In addition to his contributions to the field of science education, Darrin is also an accomplished author. He has published several titles, including his debut novel, 'Native Invisibility.' Through his writing, Darrin explores nuanced themes that resonate with his commitment to a more inclusive and equitable society. Darrin's work embodies a profound vision—a decolonized reimagining of the world. His research, writing, and teaching all align with this overarching goal as he strives to dismantle barriers, challenge established norms, and foster a transformative educational experience for students and educators alike. In the anthology on Black women in science education, Darrin Collins co-authors a chapter that offers a unique perspective rooted in his extensive experience and research. His contribution is a testament to his unwavering dedication to the advancement of science education and his commitment to a more equitable, inclusive, and decolonized world.

Erica Dixon is a diverse learning teacher who advocates for inclusive education and is a beacon of inspiration in the Chicago Public School system. Born and raised in the vibrant city of Chicago, Erica's journey as an educator is deeply rooted in her own educational experiences.

A proud alumna of Chicago Public Schools, Erica understands the unique challenges that students face in this diverse and dynamic urban environment. Her passion for education led her to pursue a bachelor's degree in business administration from the University of Phoenix, where she honed her skills in management and leadership. Currently, Erica is a graduate student at the Relay Graduate School of Education, working to earn her Masters in the Art of Teaching. Erica's decade of experience has proven her to be a committed and compassionate educator. What sets her apart is her unwavering dedication to teaching through a social justice lens. She firmly believes that education is a powerful tool for breaking down barriers and addressing systemic inequalities. She prioritizes her students' needs and fosters a sense of communal learning and knowledge-sharing. Her teaching goes beyond textbooks; it's about empowering students to become critical thinkers and change-makers in their communities.

As a mother of a child with special needs, Erica brings a unique perspective to her role as an educator. Her personal experiences have not only deepened her empathy but have also informed her pedagogy and instructional practices. She understands the importance of creating an inclusive and supportive environment for all learners. Erica Dixon is more than just a teacher; she is a dedicated and hardworking advocate for her students and their communities. Her tireless commitment to education, coupled with her passion for social justice, makes her a true asset to the Chicago Public School system and an inspiration to educators everywhere.

Chapter 10 authors

Deborah A. Harmon is a retired Professor of Curriculum and Instruction in Teacher Education and the former Director of the Office of Urban Education and Educational Equity in the College of Education at Eastern Michigan University. Dr. Harmon earned her Doctor of Philosophy degree in Educational Leadership and Human Resource Development (1999) with a specialization in Multicultural Education, Urban Education and Gifted Education and a Bachelor of Science degree in Psychology and Child Development (1975) from Colorado State University. As Director of the Office of Urban Education and Educational Equity, Dr. Harmon acquired funding to recruit and retain culturally diverse undergraduate and graduate students in teacher education and STEM education. She is the creator of the Minority Achievement, Retention and Success (MARS) Program model, the Developing Resiliency and Education Achievement in Minority Students (DREAMS) program, and the Developing

Urban Educators Teaching STEM (DUETS) program. Dr. Harmon's research and consulting focuses on (1) recruiting and retaining culturally diverse students in urban, gifted, and STEM education; (2) culturally responsive teaching; and (3) teacher preparation for urban, gifted, and STEM education. Currently, Dr. Harmon is a consultant for Exploring Diversity LLC.

Cheryl L. Price is the Director of Student Leadership and Civic Engagement at the University of Massachusetts (UMASS), Boston, Massachusetts. She received her B.S. Degree in Speech and Language Pathology and M.S. and Ph.D. in Higher Education Administration and Community College Leadership from Eastern Michigan University. She was the Program Coordinator for the MARS, DREAMS and DUETS programs at Eastern Michigan University. Dr. Price's research and consulting focuses on 1) the experiences and challenges of students of color in higher education, 2) stereotype management in students of color in higher education, and 3) academic achievement as a protective factor for African American students in higher education.

Index

SUNO, 123, 124, 126, 128, 129, 130, 132, 133, 134, 136
support, 55
supportive community, 145
supportive relationships, xviii, xix, xx, xxiii
SURE, 130

T

Teachers of Color, 190
teamwork, 35, 38
Technology, 75, 77, 78, 86
tenure and promotion, 154
testimonies, 82
Trends in International Mathematics and Science Study, 78
trust, 145
trustworthiness, 33

U

undergraduate, 84, 85, 87, 124

underrepresented, 75, 77, 78, 90
USEd, 128

W

weaknesses, 88
Whistling Vivaldi, 31, 32, 42, 49
White House, 125, 126, 131, 135, 136
willingness to sacrifice, 5, 8
WINS, 53, 93, 94, 95, 96, 97, 98, 99, 100, 101, 102, 103, 104, 105, 106, 107, 108, 109, 110, 111, 112, 113, 114, 115, 116, 117, 119
Women, 56, 77, 123, 124, 125, 127, 133, 136
Women in Natural, 53
Women in Natural Sciences WINS, 93, 94, 95, 109, 120
women of color, xxii, 78, 98, 101, 246
workers, 75, 79
workforce, 125, 126, 134

www.ingramcontent.com/pod-product-compliance
Lightning Source LLC
Chambersburg PA
CBHW072057020426
42334CB00017B/1539